俄羅斯傳媒新戰略
——從普京到梅普共治的時代

Russian Media Strategy from Putin to Medvedev—— under the Power of Putin

本書為教育部獎勵大學教育卓越計畫贊助

胡逢瑛　著

圖一：2009 年 3 月 19 日，元智大學通識教學部舉辦了「2009 全球在地文化」
國際學術研討會。王立文主任（右一）邀請了俄羅斯外交部莫斯科國立
國際關係學院國際新聞系首席教授阿爾丘莫夫（右二）赴台為大會作主
題演講；胡逢瑛助理教授（左一）在阿爾丘莫夫教授訪問期間專門負責
接待與翻譯。元智大學彭宗平校長（左二）特地會晤了阿爾丘莫夫教授
並且向他介紹了本校的國際交流理念。

圖二：元智大學彭宗平校長（圖中）向阿爾丘莫夫教授回應了國際體系多極化
趨勢的看法，彭校長認為台灣應該努力參與國際事務，學習並且熟悉國
際環境的變化。

圖三：阿爾丘莫夫教授向本校一年級學生分享了遍遊七十多個國家的外交生涯
　　　經歷。學生均表示第一次在自己的教室裏聆聽外國教授暨外交官的演
　　　講，因此普遍感到歡欣鼓舞。

圖四：莫斯科駐台北辦事處第一副代表白富多（右二）與領事組組長謝妙賦（左
　　　一），熱忱接待阿爾丘莫夫教授（中），吳非副教授（右一）和胡逢瑛助
　　　理教授（左二）特地陪同阿爾丘莫夫教授前往交流。

元智大學通識教學部九十七學年度第二學期
全球化與全球在地文化系列專家座談會
中俄專家對談

FROM UNIPOLAR TO MULTI-POLAR WORLD:
RUSSIA, CHINA AND THEIR ROLE TO THE NEW WORLD ORDER

從單極到多極：
俄羅斯與中國對世界新秩序的建立與影響

Date: **March 17th, 2009** (星期二)PM1:10~2:10
Location: R5509
Host: **Prof. Lin-Wen Wang (王立文)**
Dean of the College of General Studies of Yuan Ze University
Commenter: **Feng-Yung Hu(胡逢瑛)**
Assistant Professor, College of General Studies of Yuan Ze University
Participant: **Wei-Shu Lin(林煒舒)**
Military Education Teacher, College of General Studies of Yuan Ze University

Speaker: V. L. Artemov,
Tenured Professor (Chief),
School of International Journalism of Moscow
State Institute of International Relations of the
Ministry of Foreign Affairs
of Russian Federation (MGIMO-University)
主講人：俄羅斯外交部莫斯科國立
國際關係學院國際新聞系名譽教授
阿爾丘莫夫教授

Speaker: Fei Wu, Ph.D of Moscow State University,
Associate Professor of JiNan University,
Columnist of HK Newspaper Takungpao.
主講人：莫斯科大學傳播社會學博士
廣州暨南大學新聞與傳播學副教授
香港《大公報》大公評論兩岸國際版
專欄作者
吳非教授

教育部獎勵大學教學卓越計畫 贊助

Timing財經網 － 充電、理財、股市、保險稅務、機械鋼鐵五金、地方服務整合平台

2009年7月6日

孫明明 心理測驗

首頁　充電網　理財網　股市網　保險稅務網　機械鋼鐵五金網　地方服務網

全文檢索

地方服務網 - 校園視野 - 校務推手

俄羅斯外交部莫斯科國立國際關係學院國際新聞系終身教授阿爾丘莫夫應元智大學邀請來台講學訪問，台俄學術交流展開新頁

【黃志方／中壢報導】2009/07/01 工商時報

2009年3月中旬，俄羅斯和平基金會顧問、俄羅斯外交部莫斯科國立國際關係學院國際新聞系教授阿爾丘莫夫應邀來台講學訪問，邀請者是元智大學通識教學部主任王立文教授，並且由彭宗平校長親自接待會晤。王立文主任認為，這是元智大學開啟與俄羅斯官方和學術單位多元交流的新頁，今後將持續加強雙邊多元的學術交流。

元智大學通識教學部助理教授胡逢瑛表示，阿爾丘莫夫教授是第一位來自於莫斯科國立國際關係學院的教授，他目前是俄羅斯和平基金會的顧問，這意味代表著俄羅斯政府與外交學術核心的人物首度進入了台灣。

莫斯科駐台北代表處第一經濟副代表白富多（右二）與領事組組長謝妙斌（左一），熱忱接待阿爾丘莫夫教授（中），廣州暨南大學吳非副教授（右一）和胡逢瑛助理教授（左二）特地陪同阿爾丘莫夫教授（中間者）前往交流。

俄羅斯和平基金會與文化外交：俄羅斯和平基金會成立於2007年6月21日，是俄羅斯現任總理普京，在擔任總統時的最後一年親自下達總統令成立的。普京與現任總統梅德韋杰夫所組成的共治政體被外界稱為雙核體制，梅德韋杰夫過去曾是普京政府掌管經濟事務的第一副總理，兩人在2008年建立的雙核組合，目的主要是讓俄羅斯過去執政八年的經濟成長和國家政策方向能夠延續下來，使俄羅斯國家整體還能享受過去俄羅斯經濟成長所帶來的成果。

為什麼俄羅斯和平基金會要在總統層級下設立？胡逢瑛表示，俄羅斯還是很有戰略眼光和前瞻性的！因為俄羅斯在經濟成長之後，普京希望能夠在他所倡議的國際多極體系目標下拓展俄羅斯的國際空間。然而在軍事、政治和經濟方面，俄羅斯並沒有比美國為首的西方國家更有利可圖，但是俄羅斯的文化、藝術、音樂、文學確是全世界有影響力的，俄羅斯高層認為，從文化方面交流著手外交，俄羅斯絕對有優勢的。俄羅斯和平基金會就從推廣俄羅斯新聞語言下手。俄羅斯認為，俄語是俄羅斯文化中最重要的組成要素，因此在全世界推廣學習俄語和俄羅斯和平基金會的首要任務。例如，今年我們看到在中國大陸方面，三月份開始了中國的俄語年，這就是繼中俄兩國官方互相進行了俄羅斯年和中國年之後，由俄羅斯和平基金會著手在中國推動的俄語年活動。

世界經貿合作繼合政軍緊張：胡逢瑛表示，俄羅斯和平基金會的宗旨很清楚，除了首要在全世界推廣學習俄語之外，還有它的國家戰略目的，就是要改善俄羅斯國際地位的困境和俄羅斯在國際間的國家民族形象，以及建立與俄羅斯友好的關係，培養與俄羅斯友好的組織和人才，幫助海外俄羅斯僑民的生活或協助其返國。為了使國際輿論有利於俄羅斯方面，胡逢瑛認為，俄羅斯和平基金會是落實俄羅斯外交政策很重要的組織。2008年8月，喬治亞向南奧塞梯自治區開砲，並將軍隊駛進其首府茨欣瓦利市，南奧塞梯向俄羅斯求援，俄羅斯以三天軍事打擊控制了茨欣瓦利的局勢，隨後在聯合國協調無效後，南奧塞梯與阿布茲官部獨立，俄羅斯立刻宣布承認，俄羅斯繼梅德韋杰夫與期國總統在克里姆林宮內舉杯慶祝三國正式建交，於是喬治亞當方與俄羅斯斷交，這是俄羅斯在獨聯國家內領導地位全面的關鍵性一位，證明北大西洋公約組織在美國引發全世界金融海嘯之後，將無法再吸納烏克蘭和喬治亞進入北約，北的東擴計劃確定受阻。

彭宗平校長認為，未來俄羅斯將會以文化和科技方面的交流，來緩和軍事或政治方面的衝突和挑釁作法，與世界各國強化經貿合作的關係。這是俄羅斯落實多元外交和多極國際體系目標的重點方向，展望台灣將在國際多極體系中扮演重要的角色。

http://www.yi123.com.tw/forum_47737.html

推薦序

　　元智大學通識教學部近年來致力於推動「全球在地文化」與「經典教育」的研究教學政策，為此我們出版了元智通識叢書全球化系列的學術研究著作，並且於 2007 年 10 月，發行了本部專門的研究刊物《元智全球在地文化報》雙月刊，作為闡述元智通識教學理念和教育政策的發表平台。過去以來，我們舉辦了「全球在地文化國際學術研討會」、全球化系列專家學者座談會、教師研習會等等學術活動，可以說，在全球化的洪流下，元智通識教學部察時審勢、因勢利導，在全球化的研究框架下，擬訂了因應時代潮流變化的教學方針，並且制定有效長遠的研究目標和發展政策。

　　外交與文化的關係又為何？中國近代史研究權威蔣廷黻在《近代中國外交史資料輯要中卷》自序中寫到一段話：「外交與文化有什麼關係？這不是一個難答的問題。每一個時代有一個時代的外交。爭什麼？怎麼樣爭法都是時代的反映。每一個國家有一個國家的外交，不是因為各國所處的地位不同，還因為各國有其文化的特殊傳統。……除非我們外交得著相當文化信條為其後盾，我們的外交也不會有力的。」

　　傳媒與外交有何關係？如同作者胡逢瑛在《俄羅斯傳媒新戰略——從普京到梅普共治的時代》一書中的「全球化下的俄羅斯外交戰略——梅普共治的時代」一文中提及，俄羅斯把資訊戰略當作是

外交活動的一項重要工作，這早在普京 2000 年執政時期就在《俄羅斯外交政策的基本概念》文件中確定下來。換言之，如何完整、準確、如實地反應出俄羅斯的外交活動，是符合俄羅斯國家利益和廣大俄羅斯民眾的期待的！在《俄羅斯傳媒新戰略——從普京到梅普共治的時代》一書中，作者胡逢瑛也同時闡述了俄羅斯現任總統梅德韋杰夫和外交部長拉夫羅夫的講話內容，俄羅斯的主政者認為，在西方媒體對俄羅斯敵視的傳統意識形態框架下，西方媒體在這場國際關係的角力過程中充當的是新聞宣傳的工具，喪失了新聞專業中公正客觀與平衡報導的原則，這傷害了俄羅斯的國家形象，也傷害了俄羅斯人民的情感。俄羅斯認為，將媒體列入到國家發展和外交的戰略計劃中，是捍衛俄羅斯國土安全和國家利益的重要工作。從胡逢瑛所撰寫的《俄羅斯傳媒新戰略——從普京到梅普共治的時代》一書中，我們可深覺媒體對於國家整體在國際關係中的重要性。

　　本部胡逢瑛助理教授又一力作《俄羅斯傳媒新戰略——從普京到梅普共治的時代》，此一專著為我國在俄羅斯媒體與外交關係的研究領域中增添了新意和資料，讓我們對俄羅斯的國情現勢和文化背景有更多的認識與了解，元智通識教學部鼓勵並且支持這類融合學科的創新研究出版，以提供國人在此相關領域中一個重要且特殊的參考案例。

王立文

元智通識教學部主任、教授

2009 年 6 月 7 日

目錄

全球化下的俄羅斯外交戰略
——梅普共治的時代

胡逢瑛

元智大學通識教學部助理教授

　　2000 年前夕，普京臨危受命發動了第二次車臣戰爭；2008 年 8 月，梅德韋杰夫當選為俄羅斯總統不到半年的時間，便以迅雷不及掩耳的速度對格魯吉亞進行了三天集中強烈的軍事打擊，以回擊格魯吉亞對南奧塞梯的軍事入侵，這項軍事衝突同樣震驚世界。西方媒體仍慣以進行敵對撻伐的輿論宣傳方式，塑造俄羅斯具有軍國主義的邪惡形象。從俄羅斯外長拉夫羅夫的談話中，可以看出俄羅斯外交因應的戰略思想脈絡：合作取代衝突、經濟因素多於政軍因素以及參與國際組織。在俄羅斯因應全球化問題時所擬定執行的外交政策中，其中一項就會考慮到對外宣傳的輿論作用，如何有效、準確地反應俄羅斯外交行為則影響著俄羅斯外交活動的結果。

　　從普京到梅普共治的時代，兩位俄羅斯總統均以戰爭行動鞏固了自己在國家領導位置上的強人地位，樹立了強人的形象。俄羅斯的媒體發揮了關鍵的作用。本書《俄羅斯傳媒新戰略——從普京到梅普共治的時代》，各篇均探討了俄羅斯媒體在俄羅斯強國之路上的作用。此外本書也總體闡述了全球化時代俄羅斯媒體在國家發展與

外交戰略中所扮演的角色，並且試著解讀俄羅斯、中國、美國之間的多邊關係、媒體角色及其與對外政策變化上的互動關係。

「化危機為轉機」以及「以合作取代衝突」的作法可以在俄羅斯的外交戰略中看見。2008年，在梅德韋杰夫當選俄總統的第一年，俄羅斯外交戰略有了新的施力點。高加索的危機反應在俄格的軍事衝突中。俄羅斯備受西方媒體輿論撻伐的壓力，西方國家也以撤資向俄羅斯抗議施壓。此間，從美國向全世界燃燒的金融危機，以出口石油、天然氣為貿易導向的俄羅斯經濟也受重創。2009年4月的倫敦二十國峰會讓俄羅斯找到了建立多極國際體系的著力點。俄羅斯的外交思路是希望藉由全球性的金融危機，與西方國家乃至於美國之間化解軍事對立，也試圖在世界各國普遍發出的中國威脅論中悄悄抽身，中國在俄羅斯低調的過程中就充當世界輿論的箭靶。雖然這樣隱性的企圖不會成功，中國部份者也意識到不能充當重建國際金融秩序的老大，否則容易變成美國這個危機始作俑者的出氣筒。儘管俄羅斯外交部長拉夫羅夫外交辭令軟中帶硬，外交手腕委婉靈活，擅於借力使力，但仍可以感覺出中俄兩國作為鄰居，俄羅斯人對中國潛藏的一向疑慮並沒有消除。在俄羅斯方面，拉夫羅夫的外交戰略，但至少可以緩和俄國國內悲觀的情緒，進一步有效凝聚民眾團結的共識。

俄格軍事衝突後，對於西方輿論撻伐俄國有軍國主義的傾向論述，俄羅斯外交部長拉夫羅夫認為，在俄羅斯人的眼中，西方自己才是信用破產，西方的媒體允許自己充當資訊戰的工具。拉夫羅夫撰文談到與西方關係的危機時，暗批在全球性危機中，美國才是發動戰爭與引發軍事衝突的始作俑者，而俄羅斯的外交傳統卻是以穩定週邊環境來發展國內事物。

壹、拉夫羅夫撰文「與西方關係的危機」

俄羅斯外交部長拉夫羅夫撰文「與西方關係的危機：什麼危機？」刊登於 2009 年 5 月 18 日的《總結》雜誌。該篇文章的全文本人翻譯出來，附在本書中，目的在提供讀者自行解讀判斷的一個參考資料。拉夫羅夫寫到：

「總體上我們對於倫敦二十國峰會所達成的結論還是感到滿意的。在此所得出的決定延續了去年的華盛頓共識，並且鎖定達成的務實結果可用以克服金融危機和世界經濟的『超載』（"перезагрузке"）問題。俄羅斯將會積極持續向前參與這項工作。其中，在倫敦峰會中達成了有關成立穩定金融委員會的決議，由俄羅斯和其他國家共同參與，這為我們建議推動有關改革世界金融結構的進程開啟了新的可能性。

我們期望繼續對有需要的國家提供援助，特別是那些在金融危機爆發後的這段期間內陷入困境的國家。在此我們的主要關注將會首先投放在我們的近鄰——獨聯體國家。我們已經給予了白俄羅斯、吉爾吉斯和亞美尼亞相當可觀的物資援助。我們計劃要深化這些目標，特別是由獨聯體國家組成的歐亞經濟共同體成立了抗危機基金會（Антикризисный фонд ЕврАзЭС），決定撥出 100 億美元來進行金融疏困，其中俄羅斯挹注的資金為 75 億美元。

關於危機對俄羅斯與西方乃至於美國之間的關係產生了何種影響？我們認為應該是促進了相互關係的改善，特別是幫助了美國和西方國家把對俄羅斯關係推進到更加具有建設性的軌道當中運行。這樣的共同合作不僅可以制定正面共同的議事日程，而且可以幫助增進彼此之間的互信以及技術和文化之間的交流。這裡沒有衝突，

相反地，有意義地顯示出危機期間人為政治化的問題退居到第二位，所有國家承認在危機面前大家擁有共同的利益，特別是談論到具體存在的問題時。

與此同時，雖然危機把大家推向更加緊密互動的關係當中，但是若沒有各國政府的善意就無法化解彼此存在的對立關係。俄羅斯總統德密特里·梅德韋杰夫，在與西方先進國家和美國領袖會晤之際，強調俄羅斯準備好與他們進行全方位的合作，包括了貿易經濟關係的合作。我們期待在現有的基礎上邁出步伐，我們預見在公平條件的基礎上，支持俄羅斯加入世界貿易組織，作為承認俄羅斯與世界經濟體整合的基本要素。希望阻撓俄羅斯進入世界貿易組織的障礙能夠清除。俄美關係改善的訊號將會是廢除美國臭名遠播的傑克森·維尼克修正案（поправка Джексона - Вэника），雖然這已經不是我們的問題，而是美國的問題。

一、走出危機：戰爭，會像是 20 世紀的 30 年代一樣？

有個別的專家語出驚人地論斷戰爭的可能性，不過總體而言，這種說法是缺乏論據基礎的。錯誤之處在於，將現在的全球性危機和大蕭條年代類比的人是沒有搞清楚兩個時代之間存在的基本差異。重要的是我們處在全球化的時代，廣泛的意義就是沒有任何一個國家有能力決定國際上任何一個單一的問題。伊拉克的經驗表明，沒有正義的武力只有製造混亂，而無法走出危機的困境。我本人堅信，沒有完全的根據來將現在的危機時期與第二次世界大戰的先前歷史相比較。現在外交的意義大為提升，透過彼此的聯繫網路可以對任何一項問題來尋求和解的最大公約數。透過倫敦二十國峰會的努力，走出危機是可預見的，例如阿富汗問題的國際化協調以促進區域的安全是我們一貫的做法。

　　但這並不意味著世界受到保障而基本擺脫武力衝突的威脅。無法排除有些國家已經陷入使用『戰爭興奮劑』（"военный допинг"）的迷惑手段來使自己的經濟脫困。現在沒有人曉得下一步有甚麼科技基礎來發展全球的經濟，但我不認為軍國主義（милитаризация）是具有決定性的因素。眾人面前還有擺著其他的解決方法，要以穩固發展的理念來確認方向。我們經歷的是全球化方向上的體系危機，為了經濟發展必須有綜合建全的手段，而非採用危險的刺激劑。我們認為，避免戰爭的決定因素就是，解決全球性的問題應當要將克服貧窮納入到國家發展戰略當中。

　　現在的全球性危機不僅提供了一個絕佳的機會重建世界經濟體系，也是構成世界走向國際共同參與議事日程的積極要素。這等於迫使所有國家集體發揮作用。從我們的觀點來看，世界經濟結構的重組將促進國際關係進一步去意識型態化和去軍國主義化，以建立外交的途徑來避免大規模戰爭的爆發。

二、長遠的聯盟者

　　俄羅斯如同大多數國家一樣，執行的是多方面交往的外交政策。俄羅斯在維護國際安全上扮演關鍵的角色，我國的參與有利於全球的利益，並且有助於同施壓的國家建立起戰略夥伴的關係。

　　當前的國際事務也日趨複雜化，困境仍需要有創造性的決策，可以透過外交途徑的框架來解決問題，則無須笨重累贅的軍事政治聯盟。今天談論的是戰略夥伴的共同利益問題，而不是聯合起來針對某些特定的國家。我們認為，隨著冷戰的結束已經沒有軍事結盟的基礎，不應該試圖制定這樣的『非友即是敵』（"или с нами, или против нас"）的對立普遍原則。

　　我們相信，正是因為多邊的外交政策最能夠完整保障俄羅斯在國際事務中的國家利益。今天的成效已經在俄羅斯與國際機制的相互作用中體現出來，像是俄羅斯參與的集體安全條約組織（ОДКБ）、歐亞經濟合作共同體（ЕврАзЭС）、上海合作組織（ШОС）、金磚四國（БРИК）、獨聯體（СНГ）、二十國峰會、七國集團，以及多國會談解決伊朗核與朝核的問題。類似的例子不勝枚舉，可以說俄羅斯在國際事務上扮演著正面且積極的角色。

三、俄羅斯與西方關係陷入危機？

　　事實上，三分之二以上的俄羅斯公民正面評價了我國在國際舞台中的角色，認為俄羅斯的外交政策符合廣大社會的利益，執行的是獨立外交政策的方針。我們歡迎批評我們外交路線的人同我們進行公開的實質內容討論。俄羅斯領導層賦予外交決策透明的特性以及吸納廣大的專家參與到外交政策制定的過程當中。

　　俄羅斯多年努力，致力於恢復俄羅斯過去在國際舞台上所扮演的其中一個領導者角色，符合我們多個世紀以來的外交傳統。想特別強調的是，俄羅斯外交最重要的優先考量，就是塑造外部良好的環境條件來循序發展國內的事物。在此俄羅斯認識到自己對國際事務的責任就是遵守國際法與自己簽定的條約。

　　對此我想倡議簽訂歐洲安全條約，制定歐洲大西洋政策的議事日程，建立一個集體安全的開放體系，涵蓋溫哥華到遠東地區，這是填補冷戰後意識形態真空的重要步驟。

　　當然，與其他國家發生的歧見和這些國家不負責任的領導都不能確保我們的安全。借由資訊戰我們試圖展現我們合法堅持自己的最終利益，在國家安全領域與日常事物中行使自主決策，捍衛自己公民的生存權和國際法的原則。這與去年八月爆發的高加索危機有

直接關係，遺憾的是，真相受到了蒙蔽，傷害了俄羅斯的國際形象，凡此目的要讓俄羅斯參與建構國際政策的角色降低信譽，但在俄羅斯人的眼中，西方自己才是信用破產，西方的媒體竟允許自己充當資訊戰的工具。

事實上證明，在過去的幾個月當中，我們得到了我們西方夥伴們傳來合作意願的訊號。當我們提到了存在於俄羅斯與西方關係中的危機，就會得到這樣的提問：什麼危機？我們的合作比過去更加緊密積極。那些人不久之前還說要凍結與俄羅斯的關係，現在又要與我們解凍。我們準備好在誠懇、公平正義的基礎上進行合作。希望這樣的進程不會被我們政府與北約（HATO）之間的互信缺乏而阻斷。根據法律對於冷戰時期的產物我們被迫要回擊。結果是對於發展俄羅斯與北約雙邊關係的人都受感到挫折。

四、等待新冷戰？

俄羅斯並沒有將北大西洋公約組織毫無根據地看待作為威脅的根源。對我們而言，北約組織就是一個確保在歐洲大西洋區域內聯同我們邊界安全狀態的客觀組成的關鍵要素。僅管情況並非如此，我們的夥伴於 90 年代做出不利於北約中心主義的抉擇，強化歐洲安全會議（ОБСЕ）作為完全區域性的組織。我們與北約互動以深鑿互信基礎，反對歐洲建立分歧的路線。我們希望相信，北約不會有興趣再回到零和結果（"игра нулевым результатом"）的遊戲規精神和邏輯當中，或出現在歐洲大陸區域不同層級的安全當中。

顯然地，每當有北約的成員國家再度使冷戰時期的衝突邏輯觀死灰復燃，恢復到集體聯盟的政策當中，問題就出現了。因此今天當試圖對格魯吉亞進行軍隊武裝重整時，當格魯吉亞要推動加入北約的計劃時，這裡就不能不產生一個問題就是北約的目的為何？我

們記得最後北約在格魯吉亞境內軍演的事例就是 2008 年 7 月兩個星期對南奧塞梯的砲火攻擊。

我們的擔憂坦白直接地講，我們向北約夥伴表明了，北大西洋公約組織的一步步擴張，將使彼此的互動關係複雜化，最終怎麼樣也無法確保區域和全球的安全。俄羅斯不能不正視北約國家對我們邊界軍事建構的進逼：北約擴張伴隨著引進空中巡邏、飛機場現代化，以及在新成員國的領土上建立軍事基地。毋庸置疑，這些方面的問題，從確保俄羅斯國家安全的角度來看，都必須納入到我們的外交政策和軍事計畫當中。

不久之前，我們與北約關係的冷卻，是由於北約對於薩卡什維利政權攻擊南奧塞梯的單一立場，以及在俄羅斯──北約會議上拒絕討論這個主題所引發的，凸顯了我們對話產生了麻煩。但是我們並不準備要衝突。對我們而言，全球性的共同危機和挑戰不允許我們有這麼做的權利。俄羅斯準備好在彼此公平對待的基礎上尋找有建設性的交集點。

未來歐洲軍事政治的穩定有賴於俄羅斯與北約之間達成共同的安全原則，雙方的互動關係必須以系統組成的文件固定下來，1997 年的基礎條款（Основополагающий акт 1997）和 2002 年的羅馬宣言（Римская декларация）。首先就是有關於無法確保特別安全而損及對方安全的責任問題。

我們堅信只有在夥伴們具有政治意願時，俄羅斯──北約會議才能轉為發揮確保在歐洲大西洋安全領域中前景性的作用，且會在當前共識政策體系中構成不可或缺的要素。

談到新冷戰，這是記者或是御用專家慣用的聳動手法和想像出來的成果。在現今全球化運行的世界現實裏，在互跨國界挑戰的情況下，對於這個威脅沒有客觀的論據基礎。意識形態的分裂已經克

服，假如面臨抉擇，在合作之間且在共同利益之下鴻溝並不存在。但是仍有急迫的任務，就是政治上必須明確從兩極對立的狀態過渡到自由、公平、民主的多極體系當中。在當前歷史性的時代裏，必須要強化互信基礎並且達成互諒的共識。我們認為，現在的工作就是要轉型全球治理結構，為確保安全與克服全球金融危機創造必要的條件。

五、「請幫忙解決西方的價值觀」

我們深信，人類文明建立在存在的永恆不變的價值基礎上。不能將其區分成為西方的、非洲的、亞洲的或是歐洲的。它們是共同的價值。假如你同意的話，這應該就是當代社會生活的神經基礎，這是聯繫所有民族、人民和種族團體的黏合劑（"цемент"）。

我的意思就是所謂適用於每個人、所有宗教的傳統價值：誠信、尊重、知恥、負責、勤勞。偉大的英國作家喬治・歐威爾（Джордж Оруэлл）定義為共同的莊重特質（common decency）。

我們並不感到驚訝，當英國首相高登・布朗在 3 月 31 日倫敦二十國峰會舉辦前夕，說出了傳統價值像是救生圈，可以借此漂浮求生存，根據他的話，借此可擺脫全球市場經濟的道德危機。可惜的是，我們的夥伴假裝沒有聽到。不少於二十年我們談到不要歧視波羅的海國家中操持俄語的居民。情況是我們不僅忍受了根本的變化，從歐洲還發展出仇外排外的浪潮。

現在格魯吉亞的政體，委婉地說，不是精神正常的狀態，我們不只一次地提及它攻擊人民的侵略性，進行大規模的屠殺，終歸希望世人必須認清這個事實。關於格魯吉亞的民主和言論自由狀況，歐洲議會專家指出格魯吉亞的文件從不送入議會監督審核，然後對此西方媒體不知為何卻保持緘默。

關塔那摩的秘密監獄，北約對塞爾維亞的轟炸，以清除根本不存在的核武為口號發動入侵伊拉克戰爭（況且，更甚者，拒絕公開準備這場戰爭的檔案），在曾經是蘇聯的這塊領土上策動「顏色革命」（"цветные" революции）──凡此種種不單單是最惡劣違反人權的案例，還是踐踏精神道德的標準，更不用說我們西方的夥伴，包括在倫敦，從來不想對發動第二次世界大戰這段期間的檔案資料解密。這就意味著，是不是有什麼事情需要去隱瞞？

這些現象很危險，以至於產生了連鎖反應：可以如此這般，也可以那般。就開始了竄改歷史，英雄化納粹份子，抹黑把歐洲從法西斯主義中解脫出來的解放者─也就是做這些完全站在善良對立面上的邪惡事情。

典範就是推動民主和人權的最佳手段，關於這個現在在歐洲和美國有很多人在談論。

俄羅斯已經在國際組織的框架內倡議討論關於傳統價值與人權不可切割的聯繫。我們希望這個主題的討論可以持續在聯合國人權會議、教科文組織、歐洲會議上引起許多國家感到興趣的回應。」

貳、梅普共治的外交戰略：化危機為轉機

在世界全面經濟危機面前，俄羅斯的政治、經濟、外交政策開始全面轉型，這種轉型主要是建立在經濟穩定、多參加和主導國家組織、外交設定在獨聯體國家的整體框架上，普京不僅讓擔任楚科奇州州長已達 7 年半之久的俄巨富阿布拉莫維奇離開了州長寶座，而且還公開、嚴厲地批評了俄執政黨最大贊助商梅切爾公司的銷售政策。現在普京的主要策略是在國際組織的框架內，逐步排除西方國家對於獨聯體國家的影響，這其中不包括格魯吉亞的意外行為。

將俄羅斯的危機轉化為機會，這個機會出現的基礎是，西方國家開始忙於內部事務，對外顛覆活動減少，機會的表現是內部改革及對獨聯體國家進一步經貿整合的重大調整。

俄羅斯進入世界貿易組織的主要角色已經從廉價市場和生產基地，轉變為能源價格制定的參與者，對於這一點，俄羅斯外交戰略的智囊已經方向一致，沒有分歧。能源、技術和文化是俄羅斯未來戰略的主要武器。外長拉夫羅夫認為，在全球化的時代，廣泛的意義講，沒有任何一個國家有能力決定國際上任何一個單一的問題。伊拉克的經驗表明，沒有正義的武力只有製造混亂，而無法走出危機的困境。現在迫切需要解決的是戰略夥伴共同利益問題，而不是聯合起來針對某些特定的國家。隨著冷戰的結束已經沒有軍事結盟的基礎，不應該試圖制定這樣的「非友即是敵」的對立普遍原則。但問題是在美國佔領阿富汗和伊拉克之後，就再沒有能力挑起新的戰爭，在格魯吉亞挑釁俄羅斯後，馬上遭到武力對抗，之前格魯吉亞還出現一個營士兵的叛亂。現在看來無論是獨聯體國家還是西方都沒有國家希望軍事挑釁俄羅斯。

俄政府的經濟政策開始凸顯出戰術性特點：政府開始向銀行體系大量注資，最終避免了 1997 年式的金融風暴在俄羅斯再次發生；政府有計劃地讓盧布貶值，則使俄國民眾和俄國公司減少了不少損失；而已經鋪開的俄軍改革計畫，俄軍開始力求自行解決資金問題。俄外長認為，全球性危機提供了一個絕佳的機會重建世界經濟體系，也是構成世界走向國際共同參與議事日程的積極要素。這等於迫使所有國家集體發揮作用。世界經濟結構的重組將促進國際關係進一步的去意識型態化和去軍國主義化。以建立外交的途徑來避免大規模戰爭的爆發。俄羅斯執行的是多方面交往的外交政策。俄羅斯在維護國際安全上扮演關鍵的角色，同施壓的國家建立起戰略夥

伴的關係有利於俄羅斯和獨聯體國家的穩定。正是因為多邊的外交政策最能夠完整保障俄羅斯在國際事務中的國家利益。今天的成效已經在俄羅斯與國際機制的相互作用中體現出來，俄羅斯參加這些國際組織並扮演角色，不僅可以保障俄羅斯的國家利益，而且還對獨聯體國家的發展有著引導的作用。

　　總體而言，俄羅斯應該是認為在與美國進行政治化的合作上不能夠沾光，是無法與西方相抗衡的，只有進行經貿、技術和文化方面的交流合作，俄羅斯才有機會與西方國家進行平等互惠的合作。這樣的外交戰略顯示，俄羅斯外交人士認為當西方國家和美國遇到金融危機時，俄羅斯不應當落井下石，同時也不應當自大。相反需要把俄羅斯和西方的合作導引到技術和文化之間的交流上，在技術和文化交流上，俄羅斯並不會輸於西方，而且這比西方聯手政治化和孤立俄羅斯來的簡單，好效果持續時間長。

參考資料

Лавров С.В. (2009.5.18). 《Кризис в отношениях с Западом: какой кризис?》, журнал, 《Итоги》18 мая 2009 года. (俄羅斯外交部長拉夫羅夫撰文「與西方關係的危機：什麼危機？」刊登於 2009 年 5 月 18 日的《總結》雜誌。)

Концепция внешней политики Российской Федерации (Утверждена Президентом Российской Федерации В.В.Путиным 28 июня 2000 г). (2000 年 6 月 28 日普京總統確認了俄羅斯外交政策的基本概念。)

全球化時代俄美中三國新聞輿論戰發展特點與對外政策變化[1]

胡逢瑛

元智大學通識教學部助理教授

摘要

2008 年是國際體系與國際格局轉型的關鍵一年，美國次級房貸風暴引發了全球性的金融危機，凸顯了美國對大型企業與泡沫資本的放縱，華爾街成為資本主義貪婪面的代表。同年 8 月，俄格爆發軍事衝突，聯合國安理會斡旋失敗，在歐盟調停後，俄格仍走向斷交。國際格局儼然從單極轉變為俄美中三極強權。首先，在俄美關係方面，隨著俄羅斯總統梅德韋杰夫與美國總統歐巴馬上任之後，兩國的外交政策也將會有所變化，新任總統標誌著俄美新型關係的開始。二十一世紀對於美俄兩大超級軍事強國而言是一個需與恐怖分子與災難鬥爭的年代。美國在 2001 年九一一事件之後正式進入了反恐時代，2003 年伊拉克戰爭美國陷入中東泥淖；俄羅斯在 1999 年第二次車臣戰爭後進入了反恐時代。美俄兩國的反恐行動與軍事打擊改變了媒體的新聞生態，愛國主義似乎打壓了新聞自由，成為這兩大意識形態對立強國新聞人的新任務，這一現象著實讓自由主義者甚為擔憂。過去半個世紀以來，國際格局以美蘇為首的兩大軍

---

[1] 本文部分內容已在元智大學通識教學部舉辦的「2009－全球在地文化」國際學術研討會上發表。

事集團的對立劃分而成。蘇聯解體後，美國軍事的單邊行動造成了國際體系的單極化，美國外交上奉行單邊主義，試圖要在北約東擴的問題上進一步壓縮俄羅斯的戰略空間。美俄之間國家利益的衝突從兩極格局轉變為具體發生在東歐、中亞、中東、東亞等區域間的鬥爭，導致了美俄在國際安全與地緣政治上的持續抗衡。例如，北約東擴與在東歐佈署反導彈系統，美國在外交上直接挑逗了俄羅斯堅決的反擊立場，構成了美俄國際衝突的新型冷戰之特點。美國九一一恐怖事件後，迫使美國政府必須與俄羅斯以及中國一同站在反恐的合作立場上。其次，在中美關係方面，中國的經濟崛起加深了美國對中國的依賴與雙邊的貿易摩擦不斷。美國發動媒體輿論戰，抨擊中國要為美國爆發金融海嘯負責，試圖轉移美國國內的焦點。在中俄方面，中俄遠東非法貿易問題透露出中俄關係的緊張性。中俄舖設石油管道始終無法落實，囿於篇幅限制，本文不作討論。總體而言，國際關係雖然擺脫冷戰的架構，但國際問題的發生與議題的研究仍擺脫不了冷戰思維與地緣政治的聯繫。在大國角逐國際領導地位以及維護國家利益的鬥爭下，多極化的國際體系呈現了一種既合作又競爭然後妥協的一種循環關係。從中美俄三國在全球化下的競合關係，可以看到各自國家如何在對外交關係與外交政策方面作出通盤整體的考量，以捍衛與維護本國在地的國家利益。

關鍵詞：全球化、國際關係、外交政策、北約東擴、媒體、輿論戰

壹、俄傳媒盼望雙核體制成型

　　過去一年來，俄羅斯經歷了內外交困時期，此間，梅德韋杰夫是否勝任總統的職務也備受俄傳媒的關注，如果梅德韋杰夫不能夠適時發聲的話，一個沉默的總統一定會被俄羅斯民眾拋棄。現在梅普雙核，一個負責國內，一個負責外交背書的模式已經成型，梅普團結眾望所歸。

　　在國際油價狂跌的經濟低谷期間，俄羅斯還要面對北約進一步孤立的戰略進逼，以及美國在東歐設置反導系統的侵略性舉動。2008年 8 月初，格魯吉亞軍隊乘著北京奧運期間，快速佔據了南奧塞梯首府茨欣瓦利市，引發俄羅斯決定進行快速的軍事打擊，俄格軍事交火，引發國際社會譁然，俄羅斯的軍事是否對外擴張引起了國際社會的關切。今年初，烏克蘭也因為天然氣價格的傳統糾紛與俄羅斯槓上。諸多問題都顯示俄羅斯總統梅德韋杰夫過去一年面對很大的挑戰，但梅德韋杰夫卻明快果決地解決了這些問題，也顯得這位總統越加地成熟與幹練。俄羅斯傳媒對梅德韋杰夫過去一年施政表現高度肯定，這顯示了這位年輕總統已經逐漸獲取了俄羅斯民眾的信任以及通過了俄媒體一年觀察期的嚴格檢驗。

一、俄媒體肯定總統政績

　　俄羅斯最大的菁英報紙《消息報》，2009 年 2 月 25 日刊登了一篇社評文章，標題是：「用不著『見獵欣喜的好心人』的提醒」，文章高度評價了俄羅斯總統梅德韋杰夫的施政表現。該報認為，梅德韋杰夫當選總統近一年是相當不容易的一年，其危機處理能力與

外交表現令人刮目相看，尤其是在堅決反對北約吸納格魯吉亞與烏克蘭的立場上；軍事打擊格魯吉亞向南奧塞梯開火的軍事行動上；俄烏斷氣問題；以及應付金融危機和俄羅斯內政上。

《消息報》評論認為，梅德韋杰夫在許多問題上的處理已經非常獨立且有自己的想法，這與普京強調的重點的確不相同，但這體現出這位總統已經逐漸成為一位了不起的政治人物。許多熱切討論關注總統與總理不和的人，如同獵人般追逐且緊盯著兩人的差異，試圖找出這個國家體制上的漏洞，離間克宮（總統辦公地點）與白宮（總理辦公地點），期望見到俄羅斯體制運作的癱瘓。該報寫到，梅德韋杰夫與普京的確是不同類型的人，但他們倆人擅於異中求同去解決問題，無須那些「見獵欣喜的好心人」提醒，這是國家的萬幸！他們倆並不同於烏克蘭總統尤先科與總理季莫申科的互動關係。若是說梅德韋杰夫不適任總統這個角色的話，這是毫無根據的說法！他的政績絕非因為與普京的政策不同來體現。

外交方面，梅德韋杰夫個人展現了明確且快速的決策能力，顯示了這位總統在危機面前並不軟弱退卻，其堅強獨立的人格特質與決策能力，贏得了俄羅斯媒體普遍的高度評價與肯定，俄羅斯媒體並不急於抨擊與負面討論這位新任總統，目的是為了俄羅斯的內部團結，這應該是俄國內部感受到國際上對俄國巨大的孤立壓力以及對俄羅斯國家發展不明的一種擔憂的恐懼。

二、俄格事件測試俄羅斯警戒線

俄格事件是測試俄羅斯忍耐力的警戒區。俄對格軍事打擊說明了俄的態度，所以歐盟尤其緊張。俄格衝突後，在位於比利時布魯塞爾的歐盟總部，在歐盟現任輪值主席國法國總統薩科齊的提議

下，歐盟 27 國領導人當天在布魯塞爾召開特別峰會，討論歐盟應對俄格衝突的具體方案。歐盟成員國領導人 2008 年 9 月 1 日晚結束了旨在為格俄衝突尋找對策的特別峰會，決定在俄羅斯軍隊徹底撤回到衝突前位置之前，暫時推遲與俄羅斯的雙邊關係框架協議談判。

強化俄羅斯能源外交的獨立性，是梅德韋杰夫衝出國際孤立重圍的重點。去年俄格軍事衝突中，我們看見了歐盟與美國對俄羅斯的施壓。為了因應歐盟逐漸減少對俄羅斯能源依賴的可能性，俄羅斯未來將致力於遠東油管的鋪設，開拓東亞的能源市場。但由於俄羅斯與中國之間缺乏互信，俄羅斯的薩哈林 2 號油管計畫並未涵蓋中國。梅德韋杰夫就職演說中提出他的四個現代化政策，政治改革方面，將在下屆國會選舉中降低國會黨團門檻至 5%，讓屬於自由派的右翼團體能夠再度回到國會中。周邊外交以強化獨聯體關係為優先政策，強化獨聯體的關稅同盟來擴大貿易，吉爾吉斯終結美國使用比什凱克軍機場的合約，向俄羅斯示好。

三、南奧塞梯事件為俄突破外交

格俄衝突爆發後，俄羅斯承認南奧塞梯和阿布哈茲獨立。格魯吉亞隨即正式宣佈同俄羅斯斷交。從格軍入侵南奧塞梯的行動來看，薩卡什維利的作法簡直是玩火自焚，以致於自食惡果。俄格的之間的關係惡化就是從薩卡什維利上台之後，在美國的支持之下，薩卡什維利的政治生涯一路扶搖直上。2003 年，在一場抗議格議會計票舞弊的反抗示威聲浪後，2004 年 1 月，薩卡什維利參選總統大獲全勝，執政後立即奉行親美疏俄政策，極力加入北約。雖然阿布哈茲與南奧塞梯謀求獨立多年，俄羅斯一直沒有正當的理由支援這兩個地區獨立建國，況且俄羅斯對格魯吉亞與烏克蘭顏色革命的抗

議只是再再地反應俄羅斯外交的困境與無力感。這次事件剛好是俄羅斯外交的突破口。

近年來美國積極在東歐尋求國家部署導彈防禦系統，在波蘭、捷克、英國表明意願之後，美國又準備將反導彈系統延伸到高加索地區。格軍入侵南奧塞梯事件，剛好給俄羅斯總統梅德韋杰夫一個展現強硬外交的合理性。南奧塞梯在俄烏之間戰略地位相當重要，一方面作為俄格之間腹地的緩衝地帶，另一方面，俄羅斯軍隊也將近一步駐紮到這兩個地區，整個戰略地位又恢復延伸到中亞地區，緩解了北約東擴的一種危機感。俄格衝突後，梅德韋杰夫在南部城市索契接受電視台採訪，他表示，俄羅斯不希望發生新的冷戰，但對於這一前景並不懼怕。

貳、北約東擴催生新型冷戰關係

過去半個世紀以來，國際格局以美蘇為首的兩大軍事集團的對立劃分而成。蘇聯解體後，美國霸權造成國際體系的單極化，北約東擴與在東歐佈署反導系統直接挑逗了俄羅斯堅決的反擊立場，構成了美俄國際衝突的新型冷戰之特點。北約是二次世界大戰後的冷戰產物，但它沒有隨著蘇聯的解體而崩解，反而以東擴的方式不斷壓縮俄羅斯地緣政治上的戰略空間，讓俄羅斯備感威脅。美國在外交上的挑逗性戰略作法，迫使俄羅斯必須採取強硬的外交方式來回擊。俄羅斯在傳統安全戰略上不論向東或是向西眺望，雙頭鷹的俄羅斯都不能忍受失去戰略上的腹地。尤其是不能忍受烏克蘭與格魯吉亞加入北約，倘若烏格加入北約，這將直接打擊與損害到俄羅斯天然氣與石油輸出的經濟利益，以及俄羅斯黑海出海口的軍事戰略

利益，結果就是直接威脅到俄羅斯的國家生存。俄羅斯拉長戰略線與保有戰略腹地，這是增加俄國進可攻退可守空間的必然作法。

對此，莫斯科國際關係學院阿爾丘莫夫教授（V. L. Artemov）認為，世界由單極走向多極反而更符合世界各國的真實狀況與需求，是國際體系的進步，他不能認同世界走向多極是走向混亂或無政府狀態的看法，俄羅斯憑藉著自身的國力重返世界舞台對世界是正面且積極的作用。這代表著俄羅斯期盼國家重振雄風的普遍願望；也顯示俄羅斯反美、反北約、反單極霸權的情緒。

一、北約東擴壓縮俄的戰略空間

1949 年 4 月 4 日，美國、加拿大、英國、法國、比利時、荷蘭、盧森堡、丹麥、挪威、冰島、葡萄牙和義大利等 12 國在美國首都華盛頓簽訂了北大西洋公約，宣布成立北大西洋公約組織（North Atlantic Treaty Organization - NATO），簡稱北約。其宗旨是締約國實行「集體防禦」，任何締約國同它國發生戰爭時，成員國必須給予幫助，包括使用武力。希臘、土耳其於 1952 年、聯邦德國於 1955 年、西班牙於 1982 年正式加入該組織，此時北約成員國已經擴展到 16 個國家。北約與 1955 年 5 月成立的華沙條約組織（華約）形成美蘇在軍事上與意識形態上對立的標誌，世界格局從此進入了兩極對立的冷戰時代。

蘇聯解體後，歐洲的政治與安全形勢發生了巨大變化，北約開始向政治軍事組織轉變。1990 年 7 月，北約第 11 屆首腦會議在倫敦宣布冷戰結束。1991 年 12 月，北約在羅馬首腦會議上決定與部分中東歐國家成立北大西洋合作委員會。自 1992 年起，波蘭等東歐國家相繼提出加入北約的請求。同年，北約批准了一項原則，允許

它的軍隊離開成員國領土到其他地方參與維和行動。當年年底，北約便決定以軍事力量介入南斯拉夫危機。1994 年 1 月，北約布魯塞爾首腦會議通過了與中東歐國家以及俄羅斯建立「和平夥伴關係」計劃，12 月開始向波黑派出維和部隊。

1996 年 9 月，北約公布了《東擴計劃研究報告》。1997 年 7 月馬德里首腦會議決定首批接納波蘭、捷克和匈牙利加入北約。1999 年 3 月，這三個國家正式成為北約新成員。至此，北約成員國已發展到 19 個。2002 年 11 月，北約布拉格首腦會議決定接納愛沙尼亞、拉脫維亞、立陶宛、斯洛伐克、斯洛文尼亞、羅馬尼亞和保加利亞 7 個國家加入北約。這是北約自 1949 年成立以來規模最大的一次擴大。2004 年 3 月，上述 7 國正式遞交各自國家加入北約的法律文本，從而成為北約的新成員，使北約成員國從目前的 19 個擴大到 26 個。

二、西方體認到烏格入北約將刺激俄羅斯

2008 年 4 月 2 日，為期 3 天的北約第 20 次的首腦會議在羅馬尼亞首都布加勒斯特開幕，與會成員國領導人將重點討論北約擴大、阿富汗局勢和科索沃問題。北約首腦會議 3 日發表聲明，承諾在阿富汗問題上共同承擔長期責任，包括為北約領導的駐阿國際安全援助部隊提供更多兵力，以緩解兵力短缺。在最後一天的會議中，北約與俄羅斯關係成為各方關注的焦點。當天，普京應邀出席了北約──俄羅斯理事會會議。

俄羅斯外長拉夫羅夫在俄《消息報》31 日刊登的訪談中說，格魯吉亞和烏克蘭加入北約會造成地緣政治和經濟方面的後果。拉夫羅夫在訪談中說，美國正在越來越積極地向原蘇聯地區滲透，將烏克蘭和格魯吉亞納入北約就是最明顯的例子。但這兩個國家加入北約將引起

消極的地緣政治後果。拉夫羅夫說，烏克蘭一旦加入北約，需要執行北約標準，俄羅斯和烏克蘭數以千計的軍工企業需要改變目前的密切合作關係，俄方也要考慮繼續合作能否確保本國安全。拉夫羅夫說，集團對立的時代已經過去，現在需要網路外交，需要為解決某一問題而靈活結盟的外交，俄羅斯希望與世界所有地區加強穩定的夥伴聯繫。

英國《金融時報》網站 2008 年 4 月 1 日發表文章，題目是「進一步東擴？分裂的北約在俄羅斯『紅線』前止步」。文中寫到：北約領導人本周三將在布加勒斯特舉行峰會，與此同時，俄羅斯給北約籠罩上的陰影也愈發清晰可見。這次北約要決定是否讓烏克蘭和格魯吉亞這兩個前蘇聯國家邁出加入北約的關鍵一步。美國力主讓烏克蘭和格魯吉亞加盟。前蘇聯的一些國家對此大力支持。但以德國為首，包括法國、意大利、比利時和西班牙在內的西歐大部分北約成員國卻表示反對。這些歐洲國家也同意，俄羅斯在這個問題上高度敏感是有理由的，特別是在牽涉到烏克蘭的情況下。在俄羅斯看來，讓烏克蘭加入北約是一道不能逾越的「紅線」。俄羅斯官員表示他們尊重烏克蘭的獨立，但同時又指出，烏克蘭一向被看作俄羅斯民族的搖籃（烏首都基輔被稱為「俄羅斯城市之母」）。另一個讓莫斯科擔心的是，其黑海艦隊的駐地塞瓦斯托波爾就在烏克蘭境內。對於格魯吉亞加入北約，俄羅斯也認為這是今後的一個不穩定因素。這主要是因為格魯吉亞的阿布哈茲和南奧塞梯兩個地方尋求獨立的問題還沒有解決，而這兩個地方與俄羅斯的關係都很緊密。

2008 年 4 月 3 日，北約秘書長夏侯雅伯在羅馬尼亞首都布加勒斯特出席新聞發布會。夏侯雅伯當天下午宣布，北約暫不啟動與烏克蘭和格魯吉亞的入約談判。根據新華社的報導，北約秘書長夏侯雅伯在會後表示，雙方在北約擴大、美國計劃在東歐部署戰略導彈防禦系統、俄中止執行《歐洲常規武裝力量條約》和科索沃獨立等

問題上分歧依然存在，有的甚至是根本性的。據法新社 2008 年 4 月 2 日報導，由於美國總統布希公開呼籲向阿富汗增派軍隊以及支持烏克蘭和格魯吉亞加入北約「成員國行動計劃」，此次首腦會議的議事日程備受爭議。最後烏格沒有被納入申請方案中。

三、梅德韋杰夫的外交原則

俄羅斯中產階級報紙《獨立報》於 2009 年 2 月 17 日刊登一篇文章，題目是「我們將既鬥爭又妥協」，文中寫到，中國共產黨領袖毛澤東曾經喜歡說：「蘇美兩個超級大國既鬥爭又妥協。它們鬥得越厲害，妥協的幅度就越大。」美俄兩位新總統對於處理未來雙邊關係上，仍維持過去普京和布希總統的戰略空間爭奪戰的外交路線。

俄羅斯總統梅德韋杰夫於 2008 年 8 月 31 日，在俄南部城市索契接受三家俄國電視台聯合採訪時，宣布了俄方外交政策的五項原則，包括：俄羅斯尊重確定文明社會之間關係的國際法基本準則；俄羅斯認為世界應多極化，單極世界不可接受；俄羅斯不希望和任何國家對抗；俄羅斯外交政策優先方向是保護本國公民的生命和尊嚴；俄羅斯關注自身在友好地區的利益。梅德韋杰夫說，俄羅斯和其他國家的外交關係前景不僅取決於俄方，還取決於俄羅斯的朋友、夥伴和國際社會。他還說，雖然俄羅斯並非制裁政策的擁護者，但俄方不排除必要時通過對其他國家採取外交和經濟制裁的特別法律。此外，梅德韋杰夫表示，俄羅斯承認南奧塞梯和阿布哈茲獨立的決定是「不可改變」的。他說，俄方作出這個決定的目的在於「避免下一次種族滅絕」的發生。據他介紹，目前正在起草俄羅斯與南奧塞梯和阿布哈茲之間的「國際協定」，俄方將在經濟、社會、人文和軍事領域對其給予援助。

　　中國社科院俄羅斯東歐中亞研究所在最新出版的 2008 年《俄羅斯東歐中亞國家發展報告》中指出，俄羅斯對於世界的新認識主要有三點：一、單極世界已經破產，美國 10 年內難以再打大規模持久戰；二、世界走向多極，但多極世界的基礎有重大變化，對能源這個自然資源的控制權成為俄羅斯世界一極地位的物質基礎；三、俄羅斯的國際地位和作用將會有很大的提升。在對俄政策上，西方世界已經難以保持團結。

　　為此，俄羅斯確立新的外交指導思想，主要有兩點：一、俄羅斯的外交獨立性是絕對的行為準則；二、俄羅斯外交應採取具有競爭力的主動的政策。當上海合作組織沒有明確表態支持南奧塞梯和阿布哈茲的獨立之後，俄羅斯在中亞國家所搞的安全條約基本上在功能方面和上海合作組織重複，對於這樣的挑戰，上海合作組織需要在條約中考慮加強安全方面的條款，其實那只是書面的東西，不用一定實現，只是要頂住來自美國、歐盟的質疑。俄羅斯外交轉型正在形成，其主要標誌就是「以戰求穩」。所謂「以戰求穩」就是當新任領導人上台之後，不論是獨聯體國家還是其他西方國家，對於俄羅斯新領導人都不十分尊重，這樣俄羅斯領導人非常需要一場戰爭來證明自己的能力和實力，這包括兩次車臣戰爭，也包括 2008 年 8 月爆發的俄格的軍事衝突。

參、美國傳媒為單邊行動背書

　　2003 年 3 月 18 日，美國總統布希單邊對伊宣戰，隨之採取了大規模隨軍記者的舉措，準備有計劃且有系統地報導美軍在伊拉克作戰的情況，試圖操控媒體輿論有利於己方。初期預計約有超過 600 名美國和來自世界各國的記者，以及耗資一億美元用於新聞發布的

費用，一起投入這場名為解放伊拉克的戰役當中。美政府一開始重視這場戰役的程度可想而知。大量佔據新聞版面篇幅的伊拉克戰事報導，是牽動美國國民支持美在伊扶植親美民主政權的強力號召。美國企圖保持在中東地區所有利益的目的昭然若揭。美對伊戰被美政府透過媒體塑造成「民主自由 vs 恐怖專制」的意識形態鬥爭。美政府一向利用傳媒進行崇高的思想宣傳以掩飾其控制中東地區與維護美國家利益的單邊行動野心。

一、美政府主導傳媒訊息戰

自從「9・11」事件之後，美政府就直接將報復矛頭指向本・拉登，不但將他定義為國際恐怖分子的頭號幫匪，並且先發制人打擊包庇本・拉登和阿爾蓋達組織成員的塔利班政權和薩達姆政權。從此永久自由與解放伊拉克就成為美國在國際的宣傳號召。自由民主成為美國際宣傳的主旋律，為其出兵阿富汗和伊拉克尋求合理的借口。打擊極權與專制成為美拓展單邊主義的訴求，伊拉克、伊朗、朝鮮被美定義為發展核武的邪惡軸心國家。美國試圖完全主導與控制中東與東北亞地區的戰略野心暴露無疑。美國有線電視新聞網 CNN 擁有強大的國際新聞團隊，不斷地在為美政府單邊行動背書，啟動向聽眾、觀眾發揮洗腦的作用。

美隨軍記者作為媒體的前線代表，無時無刻不與軍隊一起生活、工作和並肩作戰，因此隨軍記者作為隨軍作戰的觀察員，可以深入細膩且真實詳盡地報導本國軍隊的作戰狀況或戰士平日的生活細節，這為聽眾與讀者提供了多樣、迅速和詳實的戰地新聞。美國的社會大眾可因此成為戰爭發展的評判者與觀察家，增加對本國政府發動戰爭的監督或支持，從而增加了整體國民對戰爭進程的間接

參與權利;同時也可降低政府進行戰爭時可能產生的黑箱操作與一意孤行。反之,記者同時能將來自國防部的態度或指示迅速傳達給軍隊,反映作戰的機動性。

二、記者個人色彩過於濃厚

美國新聞部長懷特曼就表示了隨軍記者的重要功能,他說:在作戰過程中,我們需要保持議題的真相,因為薩達姆是個經驗老到的騙子,對抗他的詭計必須透過專業客觀的第三者的報導。此外,懷特曼還同時強調,隨軍記者可彰顯美軍專業良好的軍事訓練素養給世人看。對此,美國隨軍記者的提倡者、前國防部公關室主任與新聞發言人維克多利・克拉克認為,兩者都是隨軍記者的重要目的。一方面,世人應當認識美軍將如何展現專業作戰的實力;另一方面,記者可以擺脫以往戰地報導的諸多限制,有效且公開接近他們的報導對象,也就是本國的軍隊戰士。不過,密斯金、瑞勒與萊立克在《戰火中的傳媒》一書就指出隨軍記者可能有局限性,該書作者表示,1982 年英國與阿根廷的福克蘭群島爭奪戰,英國隨軍記者不但完全依賴軍隊在戰鬥時的安全庇護,而且還仰賴軍隊提供的食物、住所和消息交換。因此隨軍記者多半會對他們報導的戰士產生好感,使得記者報導英國戰士的偏愛之情溢於言表。美國傳播學者麥可・普佛則認為,美國在伊拉克的隨軍記者不見得會完全正面報導隨軍部隊,但是平面媒體的隨軍記者在新聞報導的敘述結構上卻有所改變,例如文章的視野不夠寬廣,敘述結構不夠完整,內文經常出現斷章取義或信手拈來的插入語,似乎記者個人思想與見解過於濃厚,暴露報導觀點偏頗和消息來源不足的缺點。

　　事實上，英國被認為是第一個開放隨軍記者的國家。十九世紀末，在隨軍記者出現以前，英國報業的戰地新聞相當依賴軍方主動提供的消息，或者是報紙委託軍中戰士定期提供戰地報導。但由於受聘的戰士不懂得新聞寫法，身處戰地導致視野局限，並且軍人還帶有強烈的主觀色彩，再加上軍方提供的新聞經常迎合政府需求、宣揚軍隊威武以及隱瞞軍中弊端問題，導致戰地新聞通常缺乏前線軍隊作戰現況的真實反映。軍隊中弊端問題的存在甚至會打擊到作戰的實力與士氣，並不能使軍隊有效發揮捍衛國家利益的堅強力量。因此若沒有政府有效規劃隨軍記者的採訪，戰地記者本身也只能各顯本事，不是瞎子摸象自行規劃採訪路線，就是與軍隊拉近關係而得到採訪的許可，這樣被動的採訪既不客觀、也不全面，整體缺乏系統的戰地報導也只能斷章取義，反而容易扭曲事實的真相。

三、助軍隊長期駐伊拉克

　　早在 1854 年英國向俄國宣戰的克里米亞戰爭中，倫敦《泰晤士報》的隨軍記者拉塞爾就因為勇於揭露軍中弊端而聞名。美國新聞學者約翰・霍恩博格在《西方新聞界的競爭》一書中寫到：拉塞爾發現了部隊中存在醫療與營養補給不足的問題，傷員和戰士因此處於極度的痛苦當中。結果報導一出，輿論譁然，英政府被迫撤換陸軍大臣，英軍醫療狀況得以改善。南丁格爾也在拉塞爾報導的感召之下，作為第一代隨軍女護士走上前線。時光進入二十一世紀，美國對伊戰爭的初衷是不損一兵一卒而達到屈人之兵，以宣揚美國現代化科技作戰的先進。2004 年年底，當美國防部長拉姆斯菲爾德駐足在一座美駐伊營區時，就有一名戰士當面提問他：為何政府不加強物資運輸軍車的防彈設備，致使許多美國軍人輕易死於游擊叛軍

的突襲炮擊之下。《時代周刊》就指出這是某位隨軍記者建議提出的問題。這個問題經媒體大肆披露以後，才引發出一系列運輸車製造廠商與政府之間利益勾結的問題。美國戰士安全問題也一下子浮出台面。因此，隨軍記者就維護士兵的利益而言，反而有助於美國政府適時解決軍中弊端，反倒是有利於美軍長期駐伊作戰。

歐巴馬當選美國總統後，雖然將美軍逐漸撤離伊拉克，但是歐巴馬增兵阿富汗顯示美國絕不會從中東地區撤出，中東仍是美俄國際利益的衝突點所在。

肆、美操控傳媒對中國進行輿論戰

歐巴馬於 2009 年 1 月 20 日發表就職演說後，正式開啟了美中嶄新的外交關係。然後在此之前，美國媒體早已發動了對中國外交的輿論戰。美國財長蓋特納在參議院金融委員會為其舉行的提名聽證會上說，美國總統歐巴馬相信中國正在「操縱」人民幣匯率，並將「積極通過所有能動用的外交途徑，尋求讓中國在匯率方面做出改變」。中國社會科學院金融研究所研究員曹紅輝說「這可以視為歐巴馬政府在中美經貿關係問題上的首次公開表態。幾乎可以肯定的是，今後美中在匯率、貿易等方面的摩擦和爭端將會增加。」中美未來的摩擦可能的表現形式首先應該在媒體戰上，現在美國媒體和歐巴馬的配合度已經非常高了。

一、美輿論施壓中國成性

自從去年中旬美國爆發金融危機後，美國輿論就試圖將責任外移歸究到中國身上，抨擊中國政府控制人民幣匯率，訛言中國固守

人民幣不升值是導致美國無法極早從經濟衰退中復甦的原因，以此
輿論讓中國成為美國民眾撻伐聲浪的替罪羔羊，好轉移布希政府治
國不力的焦點，這也反映了美國政府影響與操控輿論一貫的伎倆。
美國輿論為歐巴馬上任後的內政與外交鋪平道路，藉由美國國際強
勢的媒體來影響中國對美談判的決策。冷戰期間美蘇對立，美國插
手亞太事務並且深陷泥淖，如何防堵蘇聯赤化亞洲必須要有中國的
協助，中國與蘇聯不論在邊境問題上或是意識形態的建立上，都有
很深的歷史，中俄在歷史上產生了難分難解的恩怨糾葛，對此美國
從來就沒有放棄與中國交好來牽制俄羅斯的戰略想法。美國見縫插
針成為牽制中國與蘇聯的特點，而美國傳媒的任務就是執行美國政
府這樣的對外政策，在輿論上扮演鷹派，立場堅定且從不退縮。自
從歐巴馬上任後，美輿論基本上對歐巴馬抱持友善的態度，期望給
歐巴馬解決內政與外交政策塑造一個良好的環境，而美國輿論給中
國施壓，好讓歐巴馬在對中國政策取得更大的戰略空間。

二、歐巴馬對華政策備受關注

2009 年 1 月 30 日，美國白宮發言人吉布斯證實，新任總統歐
巴馬首度致電中國國家主席胡錦濤，兩國元首在電話中表達了雙方
正式會晤的高度意願。根據新華社的報導，歐巴馬表示，作為世界
上兩個最重要的經濟體，中美兩國加強合作至關重要。美方期待著
同中方在雙邊和多邊場合進行合作，努力穩定世界經濟，應對國
際金融危機，反對貿易保護主義。胡錦濤邀請歐巴馬在雙方方便
的時候儘早訪華，歐巴馬表示期待著早日訪問中國，也期待著胡
錦濤訪問美國。雙方同意今年 4 月在倫敦 20 國集團金融峰會期間
會見。

　　香港美國商會會長魏理庭（Richard R. Vuylsteke）接受中新社記者專訪時，認為「歐巴馬任內的美國對華政策將保持延續性」，過去十年，中美兩國關係早已超越「外交」層面，不斷拓展旅遊、貿易、文化、國際事務等方面的往來，從政府、民間到個人，實現了「全方位的互動」。魏理庭表示，「歐巴馬目前面臨的最大挑戰就是如何應對公眾心理預期」。華盛頓著名智庫專家、卡內基國際和平基金會高級研究員裴敏欣認為按照裴敏欣的觀點，布希後期的美中關係處於一種「意外地平靜」，而歐巴馬則將會使美中關係重新進入「有控制的摩擦」，歐巴馬會在人權、貿易方面，更加注重美國利益。

　　當前美國更是需要中國這位元貿易與外交的戰略夥伴，美中關係的發展如何有新的突破成為歐巴馬上台後首要的外交任務。這點俄羅斯深有體會，美俄之間鬥爭的焦點在歐洲與中亞，美國從來就沒有放棄擠壓俄羅斯生存空間的意圖，那麼中國就成為了美國穩定亞洲局勢的正面因素，但以負面新聞見長的美傳媒不會這樣報導來肯定中國的重要性地位，如同新任國務卿希拉蕊・柯林頓就強調中國的人權問題、政治問題與軍事議題。由此可知美國需要穩定中國與深化美中關係的進一步發展，美國絕不希望朝鮮無核化的問題與台灣問題成為美國戰略上的麻煩製造者，更不希望見到俄羅斯與中國結盟，如此一來美國將全面在戰略地位上腹背受敵。中國必須體認到美國在台灣問題上不會做出太多的讓步，不能讓美國以台灣問題向中國予取予求，兩岸問題必須要有的戰略眼光與宏觀格局。

三、一個中國政策綑綁美中台三邊關係

　　過去半個世紀以來，中國從來就不是美國的首要敵人，如何拉攏中國與維繫中美關係的友好，且共同對抗俄羅斯就成為了美國歷

任總統上任後的首要任務。美國在亞洲需要中國，一個中國政策成為雙方處理台灣問題的平衡點。中國自古以來合久必分、分久必合，隨著中國的崛起，兩岸領導人需有更大的格局與包容去解決兩岸分離的現狀，不能讓美國利用台灣的剩餘價值玩兩面手法，這是中國作為崛起大國的責任，也是台灣尋求國際生存空間的出路。

　　過去尼克森總統在位時與中國簽訂了上海公報，為「一個中國」政策奠定了基礎，卡特總統進一步與中國建交，建交公報更確認了美國對於中國合法代表權的地位，台灣關係法卻讓美國成為台灣的保護國，台灣每年的軍購案做實了讓美國大發武器財的合理性，雷根政府與中國簽訂的八一七公報，使得台灣感受到國際生存空間更為緊迫，促使了台灣必須更向美國靠近，台灣的經濟與安全完全仰賴美國並且受制於美國，美國以平衡台美之間的貿易來維持美國的經濟利益，以銷售軍事武器來控制台灣的國防，以新台幣匯率來平衡台美之間的貿易逆差問題，以台海的分裂來作為圍堵中國的籌碼。儘管克林頓政府時代宣示了「三不」政策：反對台灣獨立、不支持兩個中國與一中一台、不支援台灣加入以國際資格為要件的國際組織，以及「三項支柱」：一個中國政策、兩岸對話、和平解決台灣問題，再再地顯示美國對兩岸分裂現狀的主導性。

　　美國善於利用地緣政治上的特點來制定對外政策，美國在圍堵俄羅斯方面需要中國，在圍堵中國方面需要台灣。兩岸之間的對立與僵持並不利於解決中國百年來遺留的帝國主義侵擾問題，也不利於維護中國的民族尊嚴，期待美國來解決兩岸統一的問題並不實際。「一個中國」政策成為了美國政府綁架中國的緊箍咒，兩岸如何超越「一個中國」、「一邊一國」、「一中一台」或是「兩個中國」等等框架性與對立的條件，最後促成兩岸和解或是合併都考驗著兩岸領導者的智慧。兩岸對立只能讓美國繼續干涉中國人的自家事

務，「鷸蚌相爭漁翁得利」的戲碼將會繼續成為美國對華演奏的主旋律。

五、金融海嘯衝擊與國際體系多極化趨勢

人類從 20 世紀邁向了 21 世紀，此間卻遭受了戰爭衝突、恐怖主義襲擊、罕見病毒傳染、氣候暖化以及全球性的金融危機等等各種的苦難和打擊。各種重大危機與災難的出現，已經威脅到且影響了地球上每個人的生存空間與生命安全，成為了國際社會共同關注的議題。每當在工業化國家首腦聚首的各類國際重大場合中，總會發現許多抗議團體的身影，主事者與抗議者皆構成了國際媒體報導的要素和鎂光燈的聚集焦點，在媒體的推波助瀾下，危機與災難更鮮明地引起了世人廣泛且高度的關注。例如環保的議題與人類的生存息息相關，節能減碳、尋找替代能源、發展綠色產業等各類抗議的行動和口號，都在在提醒了世人應當重視反璞歸真。

金融危機是一種經濟失根的體現，經濟成長建立在虛幻的金融操作上面，這是一種蒙鳩築巢，風至苕折，卵破子死，不切實際的表現。巢非不完也，所繫者然也，說明了金融海嘯的爆發很大的一部分在於國際金融監控體系的鬆散所致。美國放縱的結果，財富被少數國家和金融企業不當取得和累積，導致多數國家的高速所得形同建立在一種泡沫化和空洞化的幻象基礎上，因此搖搖欲墜。許多國家包括中國已經警覺到空中樓閣的危險性，遂採取了擴大本國內需市場、發展建設交通水利工程等實體產業、堅守貨幣匯率的穩定政策等等各類措施，盡可能地減緩全球金融風暴的打擊並且安然渡過危機。金融海嘯本質上反應了人們追求財富的貪婪心態，遺憾的是人們深陷其中而難以自拔。

　　在上個世紀全球化如火如荼的發展過程中，全球的資本、技術、市場、人力、資源逐漸形成了一個緊密結合的金融共同體，西方國家尤其是美國在這個體系中佔據主導地位。在經濟與金融全球化的時代，美國的影響力是牽一髮而動全身。在國際關係中，各國的交往充滿了詭譎、衝突、對立與競合關係，雖然對於全球性的危機問題有了共識，但是各國仍是採取國家利益和自我利益最大化的作法，這也顯示了在國際金融體系結構失衡的狀況下，西方先進國家企圖永遠維持霸權地位且享有一切優勢，因而採取各種操控國際體系和對外擴張的慣用手法；反之，相對被操控者和落後者就會以策略聯盟和自我保護的消極方式抵抗，激進者則採取暴力手段來維護自身的安全和利益。在國際政治經濟領域中，區域合作的深化採取了一種策略性聯盟的作法，顯示了開發中國家反全球化與反霸權的願望和行動。

一、亞洲區域金融體系正在形成

　　全球性的金融海嘯爆發後，亞洲國家貿易的保守主義再度興起，反思行動體現在建構與深化金融體系的制度和運作上面，以減少對國際金融體系的過度依賴。2009 年 5 月 4 日，亞洲開發銀行理事會第 42 屆年會在印度尼西亞巴里島國際會議中心舉行開幕式，60 多名與會者在為期兩天的會議中著重討論應對金融危機方面的議題。5 日，亞銀年會落下帷幕，東盟 10 國與中日韓（10＋3）就今年年底前啟動區域外匯儲備庫達成共識。金融海嘯爆發後，世界各國嚴重受創，雖然有深淺程度的不同。但相對於由西方工業化的已開發國家掌控世界銀行與金融貨幣組織 IMF 而言，多屬於開發中國家和新興自由貿易市場的亞洲各國，則希望以此建立區域的資金救助機制。亞洲國家普遍意識到依賴現存國際金融體系的危險性，主要原因在於：

　　第一，國際貨幣金融組織體系受西方控制：一旦金融危機爆發，相對落後的國家便會立刻面臨融資困難、救助不及時等等的問題。發達國家在現行國際貨幣金融組織體係中居於主導地位，享有較多的權利，而廣大發展中國家則處於邊緣地位，難以影響全球金融事務的決策。國際貨幣基金組織（IMF）的總裁歷來都由歐洲人擔任，而世界銀行行長一職則由美國人壟斷。在 IMF 的加權投票權份額中，美國享有 16.83%，歐盟一共有 32%（其中，德國佔 6%，英國佔 4.9%），中國 3.66%，印度 1.9%，IMF 的重大議題都需要 85% 的通過率，因此美國和歐盟享有實際的否決權。這與崛起中的中國實力不相符合，改革聲浪遂起。

　　第二，貨幣成為平衡貿易逆差的武器：1944 年，布雷頓森林體系正式確立美元取代黃金本位，美國成為世界經濟的龍頭和霸主。1950 年之後，在戰爭等因素的作用下，美國頻繁發生各類危機，濫發美元成為試圖渡過危機的手段，終於在 70 年代導致了布雷頓森林體系的崩潰。1976 年牙買加體系所確定的浮動匯率制度，從根本上看，只是一種過渡性選擇，這一體系延續到今天。美元作為國際貨幣的通行主體，發展中國家在經濟成長的過程中，均對美國貿易完全依賴，並有巨額美元的外匯存底。美國作為世界第一大經濟體，動輒以美元貶值與要求他國貨幣升值的訴求進行貿易逆差的調控，以此降低美國貿易逆差的損失。這樣一來，例如擁有最多外匯存底的中國和俄羅斯就深感不安，深怕所有賺來的美元會在美國貨幣的操控下貶值，反過來造成經濟成長的泡沫化和空洞化。因此在今年四月初召開二十國倫敦峰會前夕，中俄遂開始不斷拋出建立「超主權貨幣」的議題，希望在美國金融危機爆發後，改變現存國際體系以美國馬首是瞻的失衡結構，趁勢佔據影響地位。

　　第三，西方貨幣優勢與債券外交：國際儲備和貿易結算均以西方少數幾個發達國家的貨幣來進行，因此西方國家佔據了貿易和資金使用的主導優勢。提供國際通貨的發達國家的銀行系統可以享受規模經濟效應和其他成本優勢。各國出於國際清償和穩定外匯體系的需要，總是把部分國際儲備貨幣存放在發行國的銀行裏或購買發行國的國庫券和政府債券，使得資金又流回了發達國家的手中，導致發展中國家經濟成長但卻必須大量購買美國國債的外交關係，形成了「窮國借錢給富國」的奇特格局。在自由市場貿易的叢林法則下弱者恆弱、強者恆強。

二、美金融監管體系鬆綁與次貸危機

　　2008 年 9 月，美國第四大投資銀行雷曼兄弟控股公司（Lehman Brothers Holdings Inc 宣布破產。雷曼兄弟是國際性金融機構、投資銀行以及美國國庫債券的主要交易商。2008 年中，受到次級房貸風暴連鎖效應波及，在財務方面受到重大打擊而虧損，在美國財政部、美國銀行及英國巴克萊銀行相繼放棄收購談判後，雷曼兄弟公司宣布申請破產保護，負債達 6,130 億美元，創下美國史上最大金額的破產案。

　　回顧上世紀三十年代，美國爆發了金融危機，造成半數美國銀行破產。1933 年，在參議員格拉斯和眾議員斯蒂格爾的推動下，通過了《一九三三年銀行法》或稱作《格拉斯——斯蒂格爾法案》，該法在投資銀行與商業銀行間設置了一道防火牆，金融業形成了銀行和證券分業經營的模式，摩根財團就是在那時被分成摩根銀行和從事投資業務的摩根士丹利。法案的實施阻止了商業銀行向其他金融領域發展，保障商業銀行避免證券業交易的風險，但也使得非銀行的公司集團紛紛侵入商業銀行的貸款業務，導致商業銀行利潤下

滑。直到 1999 年《格雷姆─里奇─巴利雷法》，又稱為《金融服務現代化法》取而代之，開啟了當代美國金融銀行業的運行規則。對於次級貸款抵押證券這類跨市場、跨行業的交叉性金融工具如何監管產生了漏洞，最終導致次貸衍生品的價值鏈條愈拉愈長，各家投行的槓桿率變得越來越大，金融風險不斷疊加。

上世紀九十年代，美國國會通過了放寬給低收入階層提供購房貸款條件的法案，九一一恐怖襲擊後，時任聯準會主席的格林斯潘又將利率下降到百分之一，而且在隨後長達四年的時間裏維持超低利率，給美國的房地產業提供了繁榮發展的機會，房貸業也得到迅速發展。從 1994 年至 2003 年的這段期間，次級房貸市場以每年 25% 的平均速度增長，整個貸款規模在九年裏增長了十倍。申請房貸太容易了，低收入者甚至可以得到零首付、頭兩年只付低利息不用付本金的優惠條件，輕而易舉地實現當房東的夢想。由於貸款人（主要是儲蓄銀行）得以出售他們發行抵押貸款的付款所有權，由此產生的證券被稱為住房抵押貸款證券（MBS）以及抵押債務債券（CDO）。1995 年，半官方的房利美和房貸美公司，開始購買包括向低收入購房者提供房貸的次級房貸證券。當房價持續下跌導致次級房貸形式惡化後，資本市場資金鏈出現斷裂，最終引發了這場金融海嘯。次級房屋信貸危機是由美國國內抵押貸款違約和法拍屋急劇增加所引發的金融危機。如果不是房貸低利率、房貸證券化、證券產品衍生化，次級房貸不至於有如排山倒海般的破壞力。

三、國際多極體系儼然成型

在美國爆發金融危機之後，各國才意識到美國遭受九一一恐怖攻擊之後，單邊主義的軍事行動完全在入侵阿富汗和伊拉克之後暴

露出來，在小布希主政的八年期間，完全以對外戰爭掩飾了美國跨國企業過度擴張的現象，忽略了金融衍生性商品過度膨脹的危機，在信任美國經濟體質和股票市場的心態下，導致了本國民眾也成為受害者。從這個角度來看，香港《大公報》專欄作者吳非副教授認為，美國政府以軍事行動向美國民眾與全球投資者展示了美國國土非常安全，投資者過度信任股票市場中出現的商品及其價值。政治大學康榮寶副教授在《聯合報》發表評論表示，現階段全球乃至台灣股市的猛烈上升，並不代擺脫了金融危機，這是全球央行一致性地採取貨幣寬鬆政策，游移資本追捧股市希望股市上漲帶動買氣，刺激經濟復甦。

刺激股市上升的確由如為經濟復甦注射了一劑強心針。這一點也反應在今年 G20 首腦會議所達成的共識當中，IMF 要挹注一兆美元幫助各國短期經濟復甦。2009 年 4 月 2 日，倫敦作為主辦方，舉辦了 G20 二十國高峰會議。G20 成立於 1999 年，也就是 1998 年亞洲、拉丁美洲和俄羅斯等新興國家爆發了金融危機後的第二年。當時這些發展中國家為了提昇貿易量來加速經濟的增長，遂急於加入自由貿易市場，結果造成了過度依賴外資的泡沫型經濟。但由於新興市場多屬於從威權體制向自由市場轉型的國家，所以他們自身的金融監管體系非常不健全，經濟體質尚屬脆弱，很容易讓國際金融投資客滲透且進行投機操作，最後導致金融危機的爆發。98 年金融風暴爆發後，當時先進國家已經意識到國際金融市場在全球化下的連動性，擔心轉型國家退回閉關自守的保守主義狀態中，遂將佔據全球市場貿易總額 85%的二十個國家聯繫起來，組成了 G20，共同研議消除貿易壁壘和建立金融危機緊急通報制度的必要性。

一旦金融產業進行虛假的操作之後，金融體系就逐漸膨脹脫離了實際狀況，美國銀行業與投資公司終於不敵房地產價格持續下跌

與美國公民還不起貸款的多重壓力下而首先潰堤。金融危機顯示著美國經濟正在面臨轉型，崛起的中國與重振雄風的俄羅斯積極共同呼籲重建國際體系，國際體系多極化儼然成型。美國爆發金融危機後，被譽為金磚四國的巴西（Brazil）、俄羅斯（Russia）、印度（India）和中國（China）（合組四國英文起首字母為 BRICs，磚之意），與美國意識形態最為對立的俄羅斯和中國，於今年四月初在倫敦召開二十國峰會前夕，遂開始倡議「超主權貨幣」的主張，企圖改變現存國際體系以美國馬首是瞻的失衡結構，並趁勢佔據國際金融體系的影響地位。中俄兩國在國家相互交往正常化之後，似乎找到了一個反全球化和抵抗美國霸權的共同話題以及兩國友好結盟的切入點。雖然這項主張沒有獲得其他各國的重視，但仍具有戰略性的效果。

參考資料

胡逢瑛、吳非（2007）。《蘇俄新聞史論》，台北市：秀威出版社。

胡逢瑛、吳非（2006）。《反恐年代中的國際新聞與危機傳播》，台北市：秀威出版社。

胡為真（2001）。〈美國對華一個中國政策之演變〉，台北市：商務書局。

胡逢瑛、吳非（2009-2-9）。〈俄操控傳媒對中國施壓〉，香港《大公報》。

胡逢瑛、吳非（2005-3-23）。〈隨軍記者粉飾戰爭行為〉，香港《大公報》。

胡逢瑛、吳非（2005-2-2）。〈極端事件考驗俄傳媒〉，香港《大公報》。

吳非、胡逢瑛（2008-10-8）。〈俄美開啟新型等戰關係〉，香港《大公報》。

中國社科院俄羅斯東歐中亞研究所（2008）。《俄羅斯東歐中亞國家發展報告》。

www.XINHUANET.com 新華網國際新聞資料庫。

http://zh.wikipedia.org/wiki/%E5%8C%97%E7%B4%84.

Artemov V. L. (2009-3-19). The Problem of Globalization: the Russian Perspective, Yuan Ze University.

Артемов В.Л (2002), Массовая коммуникация и массовое сознание.Сбор-к статей.Вып.2.

Артемов В.Л. (2004), Массовая коммуникация и массовое сознание.Сбор-к статей.Вып.4.

Известия (2009-2-25). Без подсказки "доброхотов".

梅普體制特點與俄羅斯發展戰略[1]

胡逢瑛

元智大學通識教學部助理教授

2009 年 5 月 7 日，俄羅斯總統當選人梅德韋杰夫在莫斯科的克里姆林宮裡宣誓就職，並且從前任總統普京手中接過象徵國家元首權力的總統旗、總統徽章和核密碼箱等，43 歲的他已成為俄羅斯歷史上最年輕的總統。普京於 5 月 8 日正式出任俄政府總理。梅普體制成型的目的是國際戰略組合？還是經濟組合？或者是政治組合呢？對此我們需要從俄羅斯在國際關係中的美國因素作為切入口，並且結合中國在和俄羅斯交往中的新思維做出分析，再以普京所主導下的蜂窩型、立體交叉結構的官僚體制分析。

俄羅斯現在主要推行「新現實主義」外交政策模式。儘管俄羅斯的政策始終保持著新現實主義傳統，普京仍然堅持俄羅斯應以自己的方式融入西方國家共同體。但伴隨國力恢復和經濟政治狀況臻

---

[1] 本文為與廣州暨南大學吳非副教授合作的中國教育部重大攻關課題和 985 國家項目中的子研究課題。本文在中俄非傳統戰略安全領域展開合作（請參見吳非在王立文教授主編的《全球在地文化探討——通識觀天下》一書中的《全球化下俄中媒體發展對國家非傳統戰略安全的影響》文章，作者同時感謝政治大學俄羅斯研究所王定士教授提供的寶貴思想和意見。

於穩定，俄逐漸背離其新現實主義議程而越來越變成一個希望修正
國際體系的國家。俄認為西方始終延續冷戰思維，孤立、遏制俄。
西方出現了政策上的四大失敗，即政治失敗、策略失敗、認識失敗
和文化失敗，這導致失去了將俄融入國際霸權體系的良機。俄羅斯
政府的經濟政策不得不開始突顯出戰術性特點：政府開始向銀行體
系大量注資，最終避免了 1997 年式的金融風暴在俄羅斯再次發生；
政府有計劃地讓盧布貶值，則使俄國民眾和俄國公司減少了不少損
失；而已經鋪開的俄軍改革計畫，則明顯出現了「向後推遲」、「俄
軍開始力求自行解決資金問題」等特點。

壹、梅普體制的特點與問題

蜂窩型、立體交叉結構的官僚體制其實就是普京結合政黨、政
府、基金會、國家外交安全單位為一體「黨國體制」的再現。對此，
國立政治大學俄羅斯研究所所長王定士教授認為，普京自 2008 年所
逐漸凝聚成的「黨國體制」，在 2009 年俄羅斯經濟危機中迅速成型，
而且普京在新型「黨國體制」下，注意了避免「黨庫通國庫」的問
題，如果在任何問題中出現研究經費增加的情況下，基金會就會成
為其項目的有益補充，而基金會的成立一定建立在國家組建的基礎
上，並且在基金會內部就加入了跨部門成員和國家不願意加入政黨
或者政府的精英。現在梅德韋杰夫和普京在政府改革上分頭出發，
美國媒體進行大量臆測性和干擾性的報導，俄羅斯梅普體制是否能
夠應對危機和美國的騷擾，還需要觀察，到年底應該會有一個基本
結論出來。美國對中國則採用和藹導向性措施，讓中國忙於經濟問
題中，不能自拔。

一、雙核體制的黨國運行特點

梅普體制之所以成為體制，就是在蜂窩型、立體交叉結構的官僚體制下，未來 2012 年，可能梅德韋杰夫就可能被換掉，但普京仍保留總理地位，有可能普京成為總統，總理又成為另外一個人的位置。這樣的雙領導制，並以一個人為核心，可以在未來八年或者十二年間培養俄羅斯在技術和文化上的戰略優勢，因為俄羅斯不可能取代中國成為世界的生產基地，而且俄羅斯處於寒帶，如果環境被破壞，恢復的可能性為零，這樣發展具有俄羅斯特色的經濟、戰略才是普京施政的重點。

現今在全世界國家當中，能夠再次擁抱「黨國體制」的國家應該只有俄羅斯，王定文教授認為，以台灣為例，「黨國體制」中政務官和黨之間建立平台進行溝通對於政策的貫徹和執行是非常有必要的，只是要儘量避免相互的干預，最好的模式就是將政務官和黨的經驗交流傳承，表面上的交流和不交流都會極大浪費台灣的行政、社會和國家資源，台灣作為一個島嶼，是不可能像美國一樣有大量的資源供給民主思想做浪費和實驗的。

王定文教授還認為，當年台灣第一夫人蔣方良女士就帶領一個研究團隊，專門研究蘇聯軍隊中的政工體系，其中最主要的原因在於蔣介石先生所領導的各路軍閥體系的軍隊，其最大特點是：臨陣叛亂和不執行命令。對於台灣軍隊的體系來講，借鑒美國經驗就會出現問題，此時蘇聯軍隊的特點就值得關注，直到現今為止儘管台灣強調軍隊國家化，但台灣軍隊的核心還是蘇聯的模式。另外，1949年到 1987 年前台灣的經濟發展模式基本屬於列寧的新經濟政策的延續，這使得國民黨執政的方向和經驗，至少一部分需要借鑒俄羅斯的經驗。

二、黨國長期執政優劣問題

　　普京出任總理在兩個月內，他不僅讓擔任楚科奇州州長已達 7 年半之久的俄巨富阿布拉莫維奇離開了州長寶座，而且還公開、嚴厲地批評了俄執政黨最大贊助商梅切爾公司的銷售政策。顯然，主抓國內經濟的普京，對於理順俄羅斯的經濟秩序並開始推行其代表俄羅斯長期發展戰略的「普京計畫」，是抱有堅定的信念的。

　　梅普的結合在於讓部分的官僚享受到八年的經濟成果，並且開創未來，如果梅德維杰夫配合度高的話，還應該會連任，但此時普京的權力就會受到阻礙，但換掉梅德維杰夫的話，普京周邊並沒有更好的候選人出現，而且普京親自回鍋當總統的話，未來的接任者可能的權力範圍就無法界定，如果選擇的接班人的能力有問題，或者解決和處理危機的能力出現問題的話，就會重蹈戈巴契夫的老路。可以假設，如果不是普京出任總理，總統由非普京系統的人馬出線，首先這位領導人在處理俄羅斯八年來的經濟成果就會出現問題，就是說，沒有一個官僚或者一群官僚能夠完全享受八年的經濟成果，然後俄羅斯八年的經濟成果如何變為社會發展的動力，仍然存在問題。最後如果遇到經濟危機，那麼這些經濟成果就會在一連串的失誤政策中，喪失殆盡。

　　全俄社會輿論研究中心 2009 年 3 月份的一項調查結果顯示，約 47％的俄羅斯受訪者認為，在世界金融危機中，受影響最大的就是俄羅斯人。儘管較之 2008 年，俄羅斯人對生活滿意度有所下降，但還是達到了 69％。而且，據莫斯科列瓦達中心的資料顯示，普京作為國家領導人，在民眾支持率方面，仍然保持了較高的態勢：4 月底的調查顯示，梅德韋杰夫總統獲得了民眾 68％的支持率，而普京總理則獲得了 76％的支持率。此外，全俄社會輿論研究中心的另一

項調查結果更是顯示，俄羅斯民眾對於梅普體制是滿意的，81%的俄羅斯人表示，他們不會改變總統選舉中的投票決定。

俄總統梅德韋杰夫在接受英國媒體採訪時也曾明確表示，暫時未決定是否參加下任總統選舉，因此，即使是在普京再次出任總理已經一年多的情況下，有關普京謀求提前重返克里姆林宮的消息，仍一直是西方媒體炒作的焦點問題之一。俄羅斯列瓦達中心的研究專家奧列格·薩維列夫看來，梅德韋杰夫應當會幹滿這一任期。他認為，梅德韋杰夫提前離開克里姆林宮，對於俄民眾而言，仍然會是一件需要有所交代的事情。而俄政治技術中心第一副主任阿列克謝·馬卡爾金更是公開表示，只有在危機持續時間超一年、且大多數居民徹底對政府失望並走上街頭的情況下，俄政權才可能會出現某種變化。

對於這一點，葉利欽在 1998 年的經濟危機中就犯過相關錯誤，就是葉利欽在 1996 年再次競選連任後，並不希望自己的權力被俄共分享，這使得葉利欽的經濟政策都儘量向寡頭靠近，但問題是寡頭的願望是壯大自己的企業，而不是壯大俄羅斯的整體國家實力，而且寡頭在俄羅斯民眾心中並不佔有道德優勢，甚至被民眾認為是缺德的人群。政黨的問題就在於有事為了長期執政，而變得自私。政府部門的問題在於部門利益保護，而忘記全局。總統只能夠解決俄羅斯的戰略佈局問題，但對於細節變革的可能性非常低。現在在俄羅斯出現的梅普體制和「新黨國一體體制」非常值得台灣和中國大陸關注和借鑒。

普京在總統任內儘管取得了豐碩的成果，但問題在於普京由於總統身份而不能夠有任何的政黨色彩，對於這一點，普京非常堅持，在蘇聯解體之後，俄羅斯民眾對於政黨基本都抱持負面評價，首先是蘇共的專制統治、政策失誤和人事制度的僵硬。普京在就任總理

之後，普京迅速調整了他和統一黨之間的關係。普京和統一黨的結合點在於，政黨和政府有著本質的區別在於，政府的任何執政官員的都存在任職期限，但政黨卻需要長期執政，如果普京需要長期執政的話，就需要與統一黨結合。

普京總理在執政一年後所形成的新權力結構運作圖

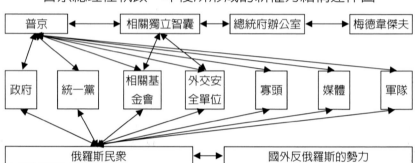

三、梅普體制的跨部會運作特點

2007 年 6 月 21 日俄羅斯政府報紙《俄羅斯報》公佈了俄羅斯和平基金會組建的新聞，11 月 3 日俄羅斯和平基金會正式開始運作，基金會主席由具有外交背景的政治基金會主席尼可諾夫（Никонов В.А.）擔任。在全球化的今天，如果遇到經濟危機，透過世界性大戰來轉移問題的焦點的做法已經過時，如何進行非傳統領域的戰略安全合作成為首要問題。而非傳統領域的戰略安全合作的關鍵點不是政府這樣常規體制可以完成的，就是說政府只是完成非傳統領域的戰略安全合作的基本保障，在某種程度上需要的是跨部門的合作和智庫、基金會的參與下，才能夠完成。

　　政府官員為任期制，如果官員退休後可以將資源帶入政黨，同時政府官員可以在任期內加入政黨，同時軍隊裏的軍官也可以在政黨的智庫中發揮作用。普京利用了政府和政府企業的錢組建了名為俄羅斯和平基金會，俄羅斯和平基金會的基本定位是：政治、教育、外交。比如，專案資金龐大的促進中俄關係發展的「俄語年」，其中的部分專案就是由俄羅斯和平基金會來承擔。該基金會還可以承擔相關的政治任務，保持獨聯體國家對於俄羅斯政策的認同度。比如在台灣的俄羅斯僑民和學習俄語的部分學生就可能接受基金會的資金支持，但資金的支出主要是所在地的外交部門以各種項目進行支出。俄羅斯和平基金會下達的黨直接由駐台灣的常務副代表接受，並負責執行黨所要求的內容。

　　按照普京本人的思路，就是將俄羅斯文化的優勢在基金會的靈活運作方式下體現出來，並且在普京夫人柳德米拉·普京娜的組織下，跨越黨派和政府部門，以各個專案為主軸，直接協調。（第一夫人的角色通常非常重要，但這不是美國和西方國家的特色，只有在俄羅斯、亞洲國家才會存在這一獨特現象。

貳、梅普建立俄羅斯特色的發展戰略

　　最近，俄羅斯總理普京在一些內部會議上就指出一些問題，就是在安德羅波夫時代制定的很多蘇聯的戰略，現在看來都基本上是正確的，但在戈巴契夫時代，戈巴契夫本人為了清除葛羅米柯這樣前朝官員在蘇聯政府的影響，而刻意採用立場一向親西方的謝瓦爾德納澤出任外長。葛羅米柯最大的特點就在於：從來不明顯地依隨任何特定的政治路線或政治派別，只是經常充當一個使者和發言人。葛羅米柯的一個基本原則就是：在蘇聯遇到困境時，要縮小戰

略空間；在順境時，加快擴張的速度，但一定要符合蘇聯經濟發展的速度。

一、梅普借鑒蘇聯戰略的優劣經驗

在「公開性」改革中戈巴契夫和夫人賴莎常常扮演雙簧，但在大原則基礎上確是常常錯誤。舉例來講，在東歐推行民主化進程後，東歐國家接受援助的國家從蘇聯一家增加為許多西方國家，而且西方國家的援助多為現金，使得東歐國家的領導人和菁英都非常滿意，而且對於民主化進行了不切實際的宣傳，使得東歐國家甚至包括蘇聯人都認為，只要推行民主化，冷戰就會消失，大家的生活猶如進入天堂。包括後來俄羅斯總統葉利欽都天真的認為，遠離蘇聯的朋友之後，美國和俄羅斯就會成為自然的盟友了。

蘇聯時期對外援助的特點，是在地進行基礎設施的援助，因為蘇聯專家認為這樣可以保持蘇聯在該國的長期影響。但謝瓦爾德納澤重新調整了當時蘇聯的外交政策後，由對抗西方的傳統路線改為尋求合作與和解，同時減少了對國外反政府武裝的援助。這樣蘇聯放棄了自己援助的特點，而且在不熟悉的現金援助裏和美國抗衡。

現在俄羅斯政府內部存在一個共識就是：在危機面前，俄羅斯的發展不能夠將前任所指定的戰略作為替罪羊，俄羅斯官員需要在更大範圍內實行菁英入閣的計畫。在這樣的共識下，總統梅德韋杰夫開始邀請一些政治積極分子和 36 個非政府組織進入克里姆林宮。俄羅斯現在適度放開自由，而且對於官員實行財產申報。普京則致力於軍隊規模的縮減。儘管俄國家杜馬安全委員會成員古德科夫對此嘲笑為：官僚會對收入申報規定一笑置之，沒有人去核對。其實這是俄羅斯膚淺的菁英的一貫看法，常常希望每項措施都有

效，人民期望更高，但效果更差，甚至會爆發革命。這樣在體制內進行改革，或者稱為改良，這應該是沙俄和蘇聯時期的傳統。只要俄羅斯認真執行改革，那就會產生革命和政變。

二、發展俄羅斯能源型的經濟型態

在美國發生金融危機後，俄羅斯國內的經濟也發生了嚴重的危機，加強中俄的經濟關係成為梅普體制首先需要考慮的問題，梅普體制處理經濟危機問題的方式，首先是讓盧布貶值，這樣可以讓俄羅斯百姓減少對於西方高檔消費品的消費，並且壓低了來自中國商品的價格，這樣在總體消費量沒有太大變化下，俄羅斯本土的製造業的產能得到發揮；然後能源的正常出口，這主要是利用能源出口得到外匯，用來購買俄羅斯能源開發所需要的技術和設備。

俄羅斯的經濟形態本身就是能源型的，中國的主要是廉價制造型，這一本質的形態在未來二十年間都很難有徹底的改變。中國需要做的是如何擴張自己的戰略空間，但這絕對不等於是軍事設備的擴張。戰略空間擴張的速度要快於軍事設備。中國內部軍事企業常常希望發展到像美國一樣的水準，獲得大量預算，讓軍工企業過上好日子。但問題是中國軍事設備的提升和戰略空間的擴展常常是兩碼事，並不合拍。

俄羅斯能源經濟遇到的問題必須採用三個辦法同時進行：首先是國民必須節衣縮食，過緊日子，而不是苦日子；然後縮減政府的規模和權力的範圍；最後，要增加整體菁英參政的規模。對於這三點，梅德韋杰夫和普京都在分頭去做。反倒是中國在這三點上都是在反向進行，這些值得關注。

俄羅斯認為凍土地帶的能源開發未來將會成為俄羅斯的技術優勢，這些優勢未來將會使俄羅斯與美國對抗的主要武器。美國現在開發的綠色能源，但如果美國不講這些綠色能源的開發技術進行轉讓的話，未來包括中國大陸、台灣、東南亞、非洲、拉丁美洲、東歐等國家和地區都會慢慢開始依賴俄羅斯的能源。

俄羅斯在推廣能源經濟的同時，普京相關智囊認為，俄羅斯給國際的印象在某種程度上過於霸道，如何改善這樣的形象，成為普京智囊考慮的問題，所以最終在 2007 年，普京卸下總統職務之前的一年，主要是將俄羅斯所擅長的技術和文化，在某種程度上和外交、安全結合，作為一個打包產品推向世界。

三、俄梅普體制需面對西方輿論干擾

美國對於俄羅斯發展中的戰略干擾是行之有年的，其主要的表現形式，就是在媒體上挑起領導人之間的心結。現在梅德韋杰夫和普京在政府改革上分頭出發，美國媒體進行大量臆測性和干擾性的報導，俄羅斯梅普體制是否能夠應對危機和美國的騷擾，年底應會有一個基本結論出來。當美國遇到危機後，非常奇怪，美國媒體最關心的國家竟是俄羅斯。

美國媒體認為，俄羅斯正在面臨 10 年來最嚴重的經濟衰退：失業嚴重、物價上漲、居民生活水準下降。美國情報顧問公司發佈的風險評估報告認為，現任總統梅德韋杰夫可能會帶著遺憾離開，而普京將會重新領導俄羅斯。另外，俄羅斯聯邦主體內的分裂主義將會盛行，未來出現獨立意圖的地區將占聯邦主體的 20%。 美國始終存在一幫唱衰俄羅斯派，而且這一派的人都相當有背景，其採用的手段，和當初冷戰時期的美國中央情報局詆毀克格勃的手段是一樣

的。梅德韋杰夫和普京整體運行的智囊團隊是一套班子，那麼，俄所面臨最新的挑戰就是：如何在不否認前任的基礎上渡過難關。在蘇聯時期，赫魯雪夫、勃列日涅夫和戈巴契夫都犯過同樣的錯誤。美國在戰略上的陰險和長遠可想而知。

美國對於俄羅斯發展中的戰略干擾是行之有年的，其主要的表現形式，就是在媒體上挑起領導人之間的心結。因為俄羅斯領導人和美國的最大不同就是，美國總統在任四年或八年之後，就會基本退出世界政治舞台，而俄羅斯的領導人則不會，直到死亡為止。

俄羅斯民眾長期以來都普遍認為，克格勃在美國媒體的污蔑下，都變為殺人機械的代名詞，但蘇聯時期的領導人中安德羅波夫和俄羅斯前總統普京都出自克格勃，而且蘇聯和俄羅斯大量的領導人都和克格勃有直接和間接的關係。克格勃就是國家安全委員會，是一個跨部門協調的單位，是保證國家安全協調機制。其實美國的中央情報局（CIA）是和克格勃相對應的單位，但部門級別低很多，在協調力度上比克格勃薄弱，經常在組織活動中出現問題。污名化克格勃是美國中央情報局的主要任務之一，並且這一任務在冷戰中基本得到完成。蘇聯克格勃的主要問題是濫權，並且對於大量的涉外和學術機構及教授進行監聽等活動。

參、中俄關係中的差異問題

2008 年 8 月 31 日，俄羅斯總統梅德韋杰夫在俄南部城市索契接受三家本國電視臺聯合採訪時，宣布了俄方外交政策的五項原則，包括：俄羅斯尊重確定文明社會之間關係的國際法基本準則；俄羅斯認為世界應多極化，單極世界不可接受；俄羅斯不希望和任何國家對抗；俄羅斯外交政策優先方向是保護本國公民的生命和尊

嚴；俄羅斯關注自身在友好地區的利益。梅德韋傑夫說，俄羅斯和其他國家的外交關係前景不僅取決於俄方，還取決於俄羅斯的朋友、夥伴和國際社會。

當俄羅斯和格魯吉亞發生戰爭後，中國並沒有聲援，華東師範大學的馮紹雷教授認為這是中國戰略的錯誤，因為如果中國技術性聲援俄羅斯，必然會在俄羅斯未來發展期間將中國納入盟友的考慮，就是說相當於沒有結盟的盟友。這樣在俄羅斯外交部內認為中美俄之間有著巨大的利益基礎，中國是不可信任的，俄羅斯必須依靠自己的力量發展自救。

一、俄中外交思維的差異性

中國在外交層面上仍然存在一定的問題，就是在中俄關係中如何突出表現，並且在做稍微的退卻。就是說，在俄羅斯和格魯吉亞發生戰爭後，中國可以在外交戰場上對俄羅斯進行聲援並支持俄羅斯的軍事行動，然後再過一段時間後，再向國際社會多做和平的呼籲，並且指出中國並不支持任何的獨立行動。

在俄羅斯和格魯吉亞發生戰爭後，中國太快發表聲明保持中立，並且不支持南奧塞梯的獨立行動，儘管此後，中國的外交部作出修訂，但中國外交欠缺技術性和戰略性規劃是顯而易見的。對此，中國希望在外交以外的部門找出對俄羅斯的不同聲音，比如新華社的新聞分析就具有重大指標意義，但由於新華社直到現今為止，在基層的媒體人對於俄羅斯抱持較為中立立場的媒體人還基本沒有。

因此，中俄關係中的 2009 年的俄語年是俄羅斯國家戰略思維延伸的第一年，其實中國在提出俄語年的計畫中，還沒有意識到這個問題，只是為了延續之前中國年和俄羅斯年的專案，將戰略合作，

轉向為非傳統戰略安全領域，意外之間，和俄羅斯非傳統戰略安全的發展合拍。

在中俄兩國的合作上，俄羅斯需要中國在其採取戰略行動中，進行支持，比如當俄羅斯和格魯吉亞發生戰爭時，俄羅斯是需要中國進行聲援；中國則需要俄羅斯在台灣問題上支持一個中國的政策，另外還需要俄羅斯的能源。可以看出中國對於俄羅斯的需求是立即型的，而俄羅斯對於中國的需求則是間接性的和不長發生的。這與五十年代中蘇的關係完全相反，當時中國需要國際空間，需要蘇聯支援其的軍事、政治、外交等相關的行為，比如中國需要蘇聯支援其進行的八二三炮戰；蘇聯當時需要的則是中國扮演好其作為社會主義家庭一份子的角色，並支持蘇聯作為社會主義盟主的地位。

二、中俄外交存在的問題

在這一點上，中俄在俄羅斯國家年和中國國家年之後，兩國的領導人都發現，儘管國家年非常熱鬧，且取得兩國人民的認同，但在解決兩國間存在的問題上，沒有直接的效果，比如兩國在邊界問題上人民之間的誤會並沒有減少，只是兩邊的民眾都不會提及，另外，兩國媒體之間的合作也並沒有熱絡起來，儘管政府高層不斷接受媒體專訪，包括兩國間的總統和政府總理都和兩邊的媒體表示熱絡。

但問題在於中國媒體直到現在為止，還受到六十年代中蘇交惡，相互媒體叫罵的影響，俄羅斯媒體人則在之後，完全換代，媒體中的「遠東幫」退出媒體，因為兩邊此時已經不需要報導新聞，取而代之的是遠東研究所研究員們撰寫專欄，公開批評中國。1989年儘管兩國關係恢復正常化，但是媒體領導人此時並不喜歡「遠東

幫」再次進入媒體，媒體領導一般比較喜歡的是外語學院直接畢業的學生或者在高加索一代會中文的外交官來做媒體人。比如，俄羅斯三大電視台，俄羅斯國家電視台（莫斯科畢業的研究生）、第一電視台（車臣人）、獨立電視台的媒體人（莫斯科畢業的研究生）都不是「遠東幫」，俄羅斯駐中國使館新聞參贊是高加索人，俄羅斯新聞社為莫斯科人，國際傳真社為高加索人，只有伊塔——塔斯社的分社社長是遠東人。

俄羅斯駐中國前任大使羅高壽為遠東人，但現任大使拉佐夫為莫斯科國際關係學院畢業的莫斯科人，隨著羅高壽的退休，在中俄關係中原來「遠東幫」的勢力最近兩年減弱的速度非常快，「遠東幫」的崛起是因為在俄羅斯遠東地區的科學院和大學有著非常好的語言系，並且在沙俄時代，到北京的傳教士也是以遠東的傳教士為主。

「遠東幫」處理中俄問題中存在的問題就在於，莫斯科與北京間的政治問題常常會和遠東經濟發展和領土保護的問題混淆在一起，就是說如果中俄兩國不簽訂相關領土確認的協定，遠東地區的經濟發展將會非常有限，首先是來自莫斯科的投資規模不大，並且北京方面也不會大規模投資。

在中國長三角和珠三角充分發展之後，東北的開發與發展正在展開，而東北發展的重點將會是和俄羅斯遠東經貿關係的走近。對於這一點，北京與莫斯科的思維完全不同，莫斯科希望東北的發展能夠納入俄羅斯整體規劃的一部分，而北京希望與遠東和相關寡頭單獨來往，這使得莫斯科一直保持懷疑的態度，在中國和俄羅斯油氣管的建設中的問題基本屬於這一類，就是寡頭和遠東的一廂情願，使得即使俄羅斯遠東和寡頭都和中國簽署協議，最終還是會被莫斯科推翻。梅普體制下的中俄關係將會和普京當總統時有著天然

的分別，在普京總統時代，中俄關係比較強調部門對部門的協調合作，2006-2007 年在國家年的框架下，部門間的合作得到了加強。

中俄在利益需求上存在相當的交叉關係，共同利益並不是很多，當然存在一定的經濟基礎，但這不應當是關鍵問題，在全球化的今天，國與國之間的經貿基礎是非常普遍的，只是多與少的問題。

參考資料

新華社國際資料庫。

吳非、胡逢瑛，俄梅普體制面對新挑戰，香港《大公報》2009-5-14。

吳非、胡逢瑛，「新星」事件浮現俄遠東問題，香港《大公報》2009-3-3。

胡逢瑛、吳非，《全球化下的俄中傳媒在地化變局》，台北市：秀威資訊出版社，2008 年。

嶽連國：〈架起一座中俄友誼的橋樑——記俄羅斯第一份介紹中國的雜誌創刊〉，《參考消息》2005 年 8 月 17 日的 14 版。

（俄）B.拉林：《20 世紀 90 年代前半期的中國與俄羅斯遠東：地區協作問題》，符拉迪沃斯托克 1998 年版，第 72 頁，轉引自米‧阿列克謝耶夫：〈中國移民會威脅俄羅斯嗎？〉，《東歐中亞市場研究》2001 年第 5 期。

王維屯：〈俄羅斯民間怎麼看中國〉，《環球時報》2005 年 3 月 23 日第十四版。

В.Г.格爾布拉斯：《中國將以極其實用和冷酷的態度對待俄羅斯》，2002 年12 月俄羅斯政治專家網 http:www.kreml.org.

Е.Т.蓋達爾：《21 世紀的俄羅斯：不是世界憲兵，而是歐亞地區的民主先鋒》，載〔俄〕《消息報》1995 年 5 月 18 日。

С.普里霍季科：《我們不應當怕中國》，載〔俄〕《消息報》2004 年 3 月 22 日。

А.卡巴尼柯夫：《中國人將佔領我們遠東》，載〔俄〕《共青團真理報》2001 年 4 月 17 日。

梅新育：〈我國跨國經營政治性風險及其應對〉，《2005 中國商務發展研究報告》，http://www.china.org.cn/chinese/zhuanti/2005swbg/961979.htm

Л.Бызов："Скорее соперничество"，《ПОЛИТИЧЕСКИЙ ЖУРНАЛ》，2005.08.17.

http://www.wciom.ru/?pt=59&article=1620.

http://bd.fom.ru/report/cat/frontier/countries/china/d044309.

姚世國：〈中俄合辦的第一家報紙──《商務指南報》〉，《東歐中亞市場研
　　究》2001 年第 8 期。王維屯：〈俄羅斯民間怎麼看中國〉，《環球時報》
　　2005 年 3 月 23 日第十四版。

俄羅斯媒體全球在地化特點：

從普京執政時期的反恐任務
與新聞箝制舉措看俄媒體第四權終結的進程[1]

胡逢瑛

元智通識教學部助理教授

摘要

　　自蘇聯解體以來，俄羅斯的政府、立法、司法基本實現三權分立的形式，而媒體居於監督的位置，但政府、立法、司法與媒體卻處於一盤散沙的窘境。「分權卻無責任」，國家在整個 90 年還沒有形成責任政治的環境。當危機事件發生時，不同人以不同的價值觀來進行評價，俄羅斯人的整體價值觀發生了扭曲。普京政府執政時期，以建立一套符合俄羅斯發展利益的傳播體制為目的。

　　俄羅斯在電信與傳媒產業匯流的新通訊時代，對於媒體的職能與發展有了更加嚴格的規定，也就是俄羅斯的新聞自由必須讓位於國家安全與國家利益，民族的尊嚴必須建立在嚴格限制俄羅斯媒體報導內容上面。相關的傳播法規對於涉及媒體報導的部分作出的限制，這樣做的目的是為了任何突發事件爆發時，政府都能夠找到法

---

[1] 本文曾於 2008 年 4 月 8 日在玄奘大學新聞系舉辦的「全球化與在地化新聞學術研討會」上發表。

律依據來限制媒體的行為。自蘇聯解體之後，俄羅斯媒體進入了前所未有的轉型階段。俄羅斯傳媒法以及其他傳播相關法規，構成了俄羅斯新聞體制的基本元素。俄羅斯傳播立法體系的建構可分為兩個階段在進行：第一個階段是在葉利欽執政時期，這是俄羅斯媒體的轉型階段。1991 年 12 月 27 日由葉利欽總統簽署通過的俄羅斯聯邦法案有關於大眾傳播媒體法（簡稱傳媒法），是俄羅斯有史以來第一部關於媒體的專門法案，明文規定賦予俄羅斯境內大眾傳播自由的公民權利。此後俄羅斯媒體開始轉型。第二個階段是在普京執政時期，打擊恐怖主義成為強國政策的核心，俄羅斯媒體回歸國家化，傳播法規成為媒體服務國家的穩定因素，新聞自由陷入了新的控管時期。普京發動了第二次車臣戰爭並且宣示打擊恐怖分子的決心，導致整個國家逐漸進入了政策縮緊的緊急狀態。2006 年 3 月 6 日，普京正式簽署俄羅斯聯邦法案關於打擊恐怖主義法（簡稱反恐法）。該法賦予軍隊武力攻擊、警調單位搜捕的權力，並且明文規定媒體報導可能涉及助長恐怖主義的具體操作項目，俄羅斯等於進入一種不具有正式名稱的戒嚴狀態。

在全球化發展過程中，國家在如何發展本土產業與維護民族文化上再度發揮了作用。隨著俄羅斯的再度崛起，俄羅斯仍是歐洲和中國的最大威脅，俄羅斯研究成為國際課題中不可或缺的環節。俄羅斯媒體發展有其特殊性，這個特殊性對俄羅斯試圖建構新的國際體系有著關鍵作用。俄羅斯媒體所有權的爭鬥證明了俄羅斯要強國必須先要控制媒體。打擊恐怖主義又使得新聞報導受到了新的限制。俄羅斯在反恐這面大旗幟之下，國家受到了冷戰之後首次的新威權主義的侵襲。在本文的研究當中，筆者試圖找出俄羅斯媒體改革的脈絡和軌跡，演示俄羅斯第四權，如何從新聞自由進入到媒體體制的控管階段，最後進入新聞箝制的反恐任務中而終結。筆者想

要特別說明是的是：俄羅斯政權如何在民主選舉機制的正常運作之下，和平地轉移給自己屬意的接班人而不受恐怖主義的干擾是本文想要表達的主要觀點。

關鍵辭：恐怖主義、聯邦法案、新聞箝制

壹、俄羅斯媒體體制轉型特點

自從放棄蘇聯時代國營媒體公有制之後，俄國政府就試圖建立一種結合國家資本、商業經營與公共管理服務制的混合型媒體經營制度，國有電視公共化這個概念的發展大體上經過幾個階段，這一電視公共化概念在葉利欽執政十年期間打下了基礎，普京則負責清除金融寡頭勢力深厚的自由派電視台，它的趨勢特色基本可歸納如下幾點：

第一，政策限制鬆綁，開放媒體市場：大眾傳媒經營的所有權從一黨獨大的壟斷型走向多黨化、多元化和私有化以及金融工業集團的媒體寡頭和國營媒體集團壟斷的方向上來。

第二，媒體管理體制控管的逐步改革：俄羅斯政府以新聞主管機關——俄羅斯聯邦廣播電視服務處、俄羅斯聯邦廣播電視委員會和俄羅斯聯邦出版委員會合併為後來的出版、廣播電視與大眾傳播事務部（МПТР），以及國營媒體事業領導集團——全俄羅斯國家電視廣播公司（ВГТРК）把所有中央暨地方國營廣播電視公司、新聞資訊社（РИА«Новости»）和電視技術中心奧斯坦基諾（ТТЦ«Остан-кино»）同時納入全俄羅斯國家電視廣播公司中統一整合調度管理，來強化政府在資訊空間中的主導地位。

第三，記者角色的轉變：記者角色從恪遵黨意到監督政府，從監督政府到相互制衡，從相互制衡到受政府制約。從蘇聯過渡到俄羅斯政體轉變至今這段期間，記者角色從關心社會與黨的發展到協助政府穩定社會，再從協助政府穩定社會過渡到保衛俄羅斯的國家利益，最近俄羅斯媒體記者還肩負起反恐方面的任務。

一、限制鬆綁，開放媒體市場

1990 年 2 月，蘇共中央全會取消共產黨對國家的法定地位，並實行總統制和多黨制；1990 年 6 月 12 日，最高蘇維埃通過了《出版與其他大眾傳播媒體法》，取消新聞檢查制度與創辦者資格限制；1991 年 12 月 27 日，即蘇聯解體的第二天，俄羅斯聯邦總統葉利欽立刻簽署生效執第一部行俄羅斯聯邦法《大眾傳播媒體法》。

大眾傳播自由的確定與所有權的限制鬆綁[2]帶來了媒體市場化與多元化，但限制性條款的模糊空間存在仍造成政府權力機關與記者的關係緊張，例如傳媒法第四條禁止濫用新聞自由中規定，不允許媒體宣傳犯罪行為，像是號召變更領土、主張國土分裂、煽動種族憎恨、主張色情與其他引起對立憎恨情緒的猥褻言論等，傳媒法第十六條停止傳播活動，賦予媒體所有權者或發行人有權停止媒體活動。傳媒法對媒體限制性的條款尚包括第八條申請註冊大眾媒體、第九條不允許重復註冊、第十三條拒絕登記註冊、第三十一條播出執照、第三十二條撤銷執照等等。不論中央或地方政府機關經常就以媒體內容具有貶損和危害政府形象與利益為由，撤換電視節目或刊物刊登的內容以及解除記者職務或者減少經濟補助來威嚇記者的報導取向。

二、媒體體制控管的逐步改革

1991 年 12 月 26 日，蘇聯解體，俄羅斯新的政治體系開始發展形成，俄羅斯政治學者伊爾欣（Ирхин Ю. В.）認為，任何政治體系

---

[2]　傳媒法第七條創辦人，媒體申請者可為公民、公民團體、企業、機構、組織、政府機關。

中的社會關係都包含著政府權威部門的決策[3]。俄羅斯莫斯科國立大學新聞系教授施匡金（Шкондин М.В）認為，由社會各個成員組成的資訊關係，應該形成一個統一整體的資訊空間體系[4]。

　　俄羅斯執政當局創辦媒體、建立媒體事業領導集團並且持續加強新聞宣傳主管單位統合、分配和管理的功能，這是中央政府在媒體轉型過渡期間逐步摸索出控制媒體的方式。而在這個整體的資訊空間中，俄羅斯政府以新聞主管機關——俄羅斯聯邦廣播電視服務處、俄羅斯聯邦廣播電視委員會和俄羅斯聯邦出版委員會合併為後來的出版、廣播電視與大眾傳播事務部（МПТР）以及國營媒體事業領導集團——全俄羅斯國家電視廣播公司（ВГТРК）來強化政府在資訊空間中的主導地位。蘇聯解體之後，原屬於前蘇聯的中央電視台與廣播電台則分別歸屬於聯邦政府與各地方政府或共和國，在俄羅斯聯邦剛成立的初期，就已經形成大約 75 個電視中心，然而地方政府對於電視中心的管理卻遠遠落後於前蘇聯中央政府的統一管理。這其中關鍵的因素就是地方政府無法籌集到用於電視中心發展的資金，同時電視中心的新聞從業人員對於電視媒體的管理也缺乏必要的經驗[5]。

　　按照俄羅斯大眾傳播媒體法第三十條規定，廣電委員會其中一項最重要的任務就是檢查廣播電視節目是否符合傳媒法的規定，然後再根據各家廣播電視台的具體情況發給節目播出許可證照。此

[3]　Ирхин Ю. В. (1996). Политология, М.: РУДН, стр. 228.（伊爾欣，《政治學》，莫斯科：亞非民族友誼大學出版社，1996 年，第 228 頁。）

[4]　см. Шкондин М.В. (1999). Система средств массовой информации, М.:МГУ, стр. 5-6.（施匡金，《大眾傳播媒體》，莫斯科：莫斯科國立大學出版社，1999 年，第 5-6 頁。）

[5]　Ворошлов В. В. (1999). Журналистика, СПБ.: изд. Махайлова В. А., с.53～55.（瓦拉什洛夫，《新聞學》，聖彼得堡：米哈伊洛夫出版社，1999 年，第 53-56 頁。）

外，如果廣播電視台之間產生任何糾紛，委員會還會介入其間解決糾紛，委員會決定是否幫助廣播電視台在最高法院中的資訊爭議廳進行協定調停，或是有些媒體糾紛還會透過民間機構——捍衛公開性媒體保護基金會（ФЗГ）進行調停。傳媒法第三十一條播出執照中提及，廣電委員會可以因為申請者不符合要求拒絕節目營運的申請與執照的發放，申請者以參加頻道競爭的方式來爭取播出許可執照，廣電委員會具有評鑑申請資格的權力。這一點為普京執政後制訂《部分形式活動登記註冊法》、選擇親政府的電視公司經營頻道以及收回國家電視頻道的舉措種下因數。媒體經營者在頻道資源稀少與發射塔國有的情形之下，只有選擇媒體服務於政府或是退出媒體經營範圍。

1999 年 7 月 6 日，葉利欽頒布命令《完善國家管理大眾資訊》，將俄羅斯聯邦廣播電視服務處與俄羅斯聯邦廣播電視委員會以及俄羅斯聯邦出版委員會（Роскомпечать）合併組成一個單一的新聞宣傳主管機關——出版、廣電和大眾傳播事務部（統稱新聞出版部）（МПТР）[6]。俄國家媒體主管機關以國家行政與技術資源掌控者與分配者的身份在傳播體系中準備逐步收編和整頓媒體的活動。根據總統《完善國家管理大眾資訊》的命令，新聞出版部的主要任務是研議與落實國家資訊政策，大體包括了大眾傳播資訊的傳播與交換，刊物的登記註冊與執照發放，廣告的製作與媒體托播，技術基礎設備的發展建設與頻波規範使用以及協調聯邦各級政府行政機關對廣播電視設備的使用問題等等[7]。

---

[6] Российская газета (1999.7.6). （《俄羅斯報》，1999 年 7 月 6 日）

[7] Указ «О совершенствовании государственного управления в сфере массовой информации». Правовая защита прессы и книгоиздания, М.: НОРМА с 390-392. （可參閱《新聞與圖書出版法律保護》，莫斯科：法規出版社，2000 年，第 390-490 頁。）

　　葉利欽為了讓國家主管機關在參與組織媒體活動的過程中扮演執行調控媒體事業主導者的角色，遂於 1997 年 8 月 25 日頒布總統令《全俄國營電視廣播公司的問題》，1998 年 5 月 8 日，葉利欽又簽署總統令《關於完善國營電子媒體的工作》，正式將所有中央暨地方國營廣播電視公司、新聞資訊社（РИА«Новости»）和電視技術中心奧斯坦基諾（ТТЦ «Остан-кино»）同時納入全俄羅斯國家電視廣播公司中統一整合調度管理，國營的中央電視台俄羅斯社會電視台（ОРТ）與當時最大的商業電視台—古辛斯基（Гусинский）「橋媒體」集團所屬、使用政府規劃出第三頻道的獨立電視台（НТВ）都使用電視技術中心的設備資源，媒體寡頭都立刻感受到全俄羅斯國家電視廣播公司的技術牽制[8]。

　　白宮政府在遵循克宮的命令下，負責執行繼續強化在資訊領域中控制電子媒體活動的政策，遂於 1998 年 7 月 27 日通過了一項行政決議《關於形成國營電子媒體生產——技術一體化》。該項政府決議是延續 1997 年 8 月 25 日總統令《全俄國營電視廣播公司的問題》與 1998 年 5 月 8 日葉利欽簽署的總統令《關於完善國營電子媒體的工作》的實施細則，正式確定了全俄羅斯國家電視廣播公司（ВГТРК）作為國營媒體集團生產技術的最高領導級單位[9]。從葉利欽總統執政的末期到普京當權期間，主政者以立法的方式逐步建立起一個以中央政府的媒體主管機關——新聞出版部（мптр）為中樞控制中心和以媒體事業領導集團全俄羅斯國家電視廣播公司（ВГТРК）為媒體

[8]　Два в одном канале. ОРТ и НТВ теперь зависит от ВГТРК // Коммерсантъ. (1998. 5. 12)（《二合一頻道，社會電視台與獨立電視台現在依賴全俄羅斯國家電視廣播公司》，《生意人》雜誌，1998 年 5 月 12 日。）

[9]　Полукаров В. Л. (1999). Реклама, общество, право, приложение 4, М.: Знак, c123.（波陸卡若夫，《廣告、社會、法律》，莫斯科：標志出版社，1999 年，第 123 頁。）

資源分配者的方式，不斷加強政府在傳播領域中的主導地位，使俄羅斯媒體在一個統一完整的傳播體系下運作。

俄羅斯前總統葉利欽執政初期的傳媒立法專家、前新聞出版部長米哈伊爾‧費德洛夫指出，政府在俄羅斯傳播法建立總體設想當中的地位，在於俄羅斯政府應當大力發展服務於社會的媒體，它的形成必須仰賴於聯邦、地區和自治共和國政府三種領導勢力的整合，只有這三種政府勢力將本以分散的傳播資源整合之後，俄羅斯傳媒才可能在全俄羅斯國家電視廣播公司集團統合資源分配的領導下，完成俄羅斯媒體公共化的目的[10]。這一電視公共化概念在葉利欽執政十年期間奠定了基礎，普京則負責清除金融寡頭勢力深根的自由派電視台。普京於 2000 年就任後的第一件重大的舉動就是重新整頓規劃媒體版圖，讓媒體成為推動國家政策的有利宣傳機制。俄羅斯政府加強傳播領域一體化的做法就是：一方面制訂相應整合的資訊傳播政策，另一方面消弱九十年代中期以後形成的金融寡頭或媒體財閥的媒體經營勢力，同時讓國營天然氣和石油等國家最大的工業集團資金大量介入媒體事業，特別是兼並俄兩大媒體金融寡頭古辛斯基和別列佐夫斯基的電視與電影產業公司。在普京總統執政期間，媒體經營權與頻道使用權在司法與金錢的運用下，逐漸演變成為一場電視媒體經營執照權的媒體資源壟斷爭奪戰。

三、記者角色的轉變

從蘇聯過渡到俄羅斯政體轉變至今這段期間，記者角色從關心社會與黨的發展到協助政府穩定社會，再從協助政府穩定社會過渡

---

[10] Московские Новости (2002.6.11).（《莫斯科新聞報》，2002 年 6 月 11 日）。

到保衛俄羅斯的國家利益，最近俄羅斯媒體記者還肩負起反恐方面的任務。自二十世紀九十年代初起，俄媒體事業逐漸轉型成為扮演相當於監督行政、立法、司法三個國家權威機關「第四權」的社會公器機制，俄羅斯媒體職能從附屬政府機關的宣傳機構轉換成為一個資訊流通且守望環境的獨立階層。所以普京上台後，媒體國家化絕對要高於媒體自由化。

事實上，自由化是俄羅斯媒體人在蘇聯黨營媒體時期渴望獲得的權力。自從十七世紀彼得大帝開始實行西化政策以來，俄羅斯各個領域的思維始終都出現西方派與俄國本土派之爭。在戈巴契夫時期俄共出現了激烈的民主派與俄共派之爭，最後葉利欽的民主派獲勝，促使蘇聯瓦解。解體後的政府與主張第四權的民主派和自由派媒體可以算是理念接近，但是畢竟葉利欽第二任期內政府的績效不振，讓金融工業集團的寡頭淩駕在政府的頭上，社會貧富差距逐漸擴大。因此，普京就任總統之後，便直接追溯以彼得大帝為尊[11]，高唱以恢復俄羅斯國家光榮為己任，普京執政的手法就是一種大斯拉夫帝國主義的國家化：國家利益優先，個人利益次之；政府政策優先，企業利益次之的一種思考模式。

自由多元主義論（pluralism）乃是結構功能學派之下的重要理論觀點，它認為社會務求不同的利益體同時存在，並且取得權力的相互制衡。所以自由多元主義者主張新聞媒體應該具有相當程度的自主性，並且構成獨立於政府、政黨與壓力團體或是行政、立法、司法之外相當於「第四權力」的部門，為達到這些目的，媒體必須要擁有相當程度的自主權，只有當新聞媒體擁有專業的自由權，各

---

[11] 普京總統辦公室內懸掛著一幅彼得大帝的肖像油畫，普京是聖彼得堡人，他曾說過自己最崇拜和欣賞的人就是聖彼得堡建城者——彼得大帝。

個不同的利益群體之間才能藉以相互制衡，來維持社會的動態平衡發展[12]。

而馬克思主義的媒體理論觀點直接挑戰了自由多元主義者對社會權力的看法，認為媒體並非是一個真正自主性的組織體系，而是統治階級用來控制意識形態的工具，它們所表現出來的所有權、法律規範、專業價值都是對主流意義的屈服，其專業理念和工作實踐都是受到政治經濟力量所決定。根據馬克思的意識形態理論，語言符號決定了該社群的意識形態，只要掌握建構意識形態符號的管道——例如大眾傳播媒體，也就是一旦控制媒體的所有權就能控制媒體所製造出來的意識形態，然後就能調控塑造人們的意識形態[13]。普京實行媒體服務於國家概念首先必須重新控制大部分媒體的所有權，這使得自由派的媒體寡頭與專業化記者都對於普京的做法感到憤怒與憂慮。

現任俄羅斯莫斯科國立大學新聞系主任亞欣・紮蘇爾斯基，他的孫子也是俄傳播研究者亞辛・紮蘇爾斯基（Засурский）就強調媒體在公民社會中的作用，他認為媒體在理想的公民社會中對國家發生任何突發事件都能處之泰然，並不斷與政府進行有效的互動溝通，使國家推動的改革能夠一直順利進行下去[14]。基本上，「公民社會」與「民主法治」這兩個概念是俄羅斯在蘇聯解體之後新聞界追求的兩項理念指導原則。雖然前總統葉利欽在爭取國家獨立與政策鬆綁的過程中，曾與民主派媒體是同一戰綫，但是執政者與媒體經營者的利益取向畢竟不同，記者也必須監督政府濫權與揭發政府弊案來滿足閱聽眾的知情權益或甚至是好奇心。這樣自由的媒體遇上

---

[12] 林東泰，《大眾傳播理論》，台北市：師大書苑，1999 年，第 11-14 頁。
[13] 同上，第 16 頁。
[14] http://www.russ.ru/journal/media/98-01-06/zasurs.htm.

國家發生重大政治事件、戰爭或緊急災難時，例如炮轟白宮、車臣戰爭，政體轉軌後的政府與媒體都缺乏在自由時期的合作經驗以及對資訊政策的實踐經驗，例如反政府與反戰的輿論都讓新政府對自由媒體產生一種無可奈何的憎恨感，所以在普京時期，整合媒體是恢復國力的第一步驟。

貳、車臣戰爭與俄羅斯媒體形態的轉變

第二次車臣戰爭爆發的導火線是在 1999 年 8 月，車臣分離分子入侵鄰國達吉斯坦共和國，其目的在於試圖建立瀕臨裏海的伊斯蘭教國家，完全掌握由阿塞拜疆的巴庫經俄羅斯到歐洲的油管，然後最終脫離俄羅斯完全獨立。1999 年 9 月在莫斯科連續發生三起民宅爆炸事件，三百多人喪生。根據俄羅斯國家安全局與內務部調查，是車臣恐怖分子所為，因此俄羅斯當時擔任總理的普京誓言要徹底消滅車臣恐怖分子，以維護國家利益與領土完整。1999 年 8 月～9 月，車臣分離主義分子利用俄羅斯當局忙於杜馬及總統大選之際，相繼在達吉斯坦共和國布伊納克斯克市與莫斯科市連續製造了四起恐怖爆炸事件，造成近三百名平民死亡。車臣分離主義者製造爆炸事件的目的在於攪亂俄國政治局勢，同時攻打達吉斯坦以取得靠海領土及控制俄羅斯石油管道，這些企圖基本上建立在新上任的普京總理乃為一弱勢總理的錯誤概念基礎之上。

車臣分離主義者的恐怖手段雖然一時間成功攪亂俄羅斯的政治注意力，但卻因其對民宅施以「炸彈爆炸」的攻擊平民的動作，而促使了俄羅斯全民的同仇敵愾，並激發了俄羅斯的民族危機意識。葉利欽一方面要徹底拔除車臣恐怖主義分子的分離勢力，一方面也為了 12 月俄國杜馬選舉考量，以反製作為對手前總理葉夫根尼・普

里馬科夫與莫斯科市長尤裏‧盧日科夫可能以此來操縱選情的競爭威脅。俄羅斯新聞媒體在第二次車臣戰爭中扮演著至關重要的角色。自從俄羅斯聯邦的傳媒法明文規定廢除新聞管制，並且憲法明文規定保障不同意識形態的存在，以及保障人民自由獲取與傳播資訊的權利之後，俄羅斯新聞傳播媒體享受到空前的新聞實踐自由，新聞工作者無不以爭取新聞自由與獨立為標誌，以西方媒體監督政府的模式為藍本，希望在俄羅斯複製一套西方式的媒體生態環境。然而俄羅斯媒體工作者卻缺乏對於西方新聞自由的實踐經驗的瞭解，即新聞自由與國家利益尤其是在國家危難時是如何適當地相輔相成一種默契關係，國家應保障言論自由與新聞記者的權力，而媒體工作者應該是具有國家意識，並更應自律，不可濫用新聞自由而主張危害國家安全與極端主義的言論[15]。

一、車臣戰爭中的國家安全與新聞自由

　　筆者來到莫斯科後，從媒體報導與生活環境的氛圍當中，就目睹和感受到 1994 年至 1996 年第一次車臣戰爭的殘酷性。1999 年末，又再度爆發車臣戰爭，然而俄羅斯人與俄新聞媒體對兩次車臣戰爭卻持有截然不同的態度，對車臣人從同情轉為憤怒，是什麼原因讓俄羅斯人產生如此巨大的轉變？

　　1994 年末，俄羅斯爆發了第一次車臣戰爭，結果俄羅斯聯邦軍隊的戰士死傷慘烈，當電視播放出許多難民與大部分俄羅斯家屬哀號痛失親人的畫面時，許多士兵的老母親都痛斥政府為何發動車臣戰爭，使他們的兒子身歷險境甚至喪失生命。1994 年，俄國戰地記

---

[15] 胡逢瑛，《車臣戰爭中的國家安全與新聞自由》，新加坡《聯合早報》，《天下事版》，1999 年。

者在前線採訪到許多戰士都是缺乏作戰經驗的新兵，其中大多數士兵表示不知為何而戰。俄羅斯國會也為了龐大的戰爭預算而杯葛政府，戰爭後國會更是以發動車臣戰爭的罪名年年彈劾葉利欽總統。1994 年～1996 年期間，俄羅斯聯邦軍陷入戰爭的泥淖，如同阿富汗戰爭一樣進退兩難。媒體、輿論與國會在全國掀起了激烈的反戰浪潮，政府在缺乏民意支援的困窘情況下，舉步維艱。直到 1996 年 5月，即在 6 月俄羅斯總統大選前夕，國安秘書長，同時也是總統候選人之一的列別德將軍[16]，與當時車臣共和國總統馬斯哈托夫，共同簽訂了一項和平停戰協議，車臣戰爭才暫告落幕，但這個舉動被俄羅斯軍人及部分政府官員視為聯邦政府向車臣的投降行為。這是聯邦政府做的第一次妥協，此後，車臣獨立運動就沒有終止過。

　　至今普京始終採取最強硬的態度，處理 2002 年與 2004 年莫斯科劇院和北奧塞梯別斯蘭中學的人質事件，這兩次事件一共造成上千人傷亡，從人權的角度而言，普京的不妥協政策是倍受質疑與批評，從俄羅斯多民族共存的角度而言，要如何不傷害民族感情又能維護領土完整是一項艱巨而任重道遠的道路。關於車臣戰爭的爆發與民族衝突的解決之道，與領導人的性格應該說是有相關的。試想，蘇聯的解體與各個共和國的獨立是在戈巴契夫手中發生的。那麼，戈巴契夫具有什麼特殊的民族性格呢？戈巴契夫出生在北高加索地區斯塔夫羅波爾省，這裏有 83%的俄羅斯人，其他的民族是卡拉恰耶夫人、切爾克斯人、奧塞梯人、希臘人、土耳其人、亞美尼亞人等等，根據他自己寫的回憶錄中寫到：「在多民族的環境下生活，可以養成耐心、相互禮讓和尊重的習慣。」他又寫到：「我都不只一次讀到所謂在向新社會過渡中暴力不但情有可原、而且必不可免的高

---

[16] 列別德將軍，1996 年總統大選的候選人之一，總統大選後成為國安秘書長，後任克拉斯諾雅爾斯克省長，最後於 2002 年死於飛機失事。

深理論觀點。革命中確實往往無法避免流血，這是事實。然而如果把暴力當成解決任何問題的萬能手段，號召訴諸暴力，為了達到所謂的高尚目的而對暴力推波助瀾，亦即再次砍光家庭、村莊、民族，那就不可容忍的[17]。」

當時的俄總理普京攻打車臣的行動馬上獲得高度民意支持，因為接二連三民宅爆炸事件使得俄國居民處於極度驚恐與瘋狂狀態。爆炸事件發生之後，居民若接到恐嚇電話或寫著將有爆炸物在地下室的傳單，立刻就會傾巢而出，徹夜不眠，在屋外守候，等待員警檢查之後才敢回家。人們紛紛組成居民自救隊輪流看守家園。在伏爾加河頓市有一棟民宅，被內務部認定地下室的爆炸物無法即時解除引爆，因此主動將整棟樓房炸毀，民眾看著自己的家被炸毀，都忍不住落淚。全國人民無不對恐怖分子所為感到氣憤，因此俄羅斯輿論不再同情車臣，反而轉向將第二次對車臣戰爭視為理所當然。

俄羅斯的新聞界此時也見識到了西方的資訊戰的先進之處。俄羅斯媒體深刻感受到西方媒體新聞自由主義理論的另一面，媒體的真正實力建立在科技與經濟的基礎之上。例如在科索沃戰爭時，西方媒體多播報阿爾巴尼亞族受塞族迫害的情況，以及西方援助阿族難民醫療與物資的鏡頭，那麼塞族的難民呢？對於西方媒體一面倒的主觀報導，俄羅斯媒體此時突然茅塞頓開，領悟到新聞自由之外還有國家利益。因此他們一改與政府完全對立的立場，深入聯邦軍隊報導，與西方媒體進行一場資訊戰，俄羅斯媒體也引發了俄國百姓積怨已深的反美情緒。1999 年以美國為主導的北約軍隊在科索沃發動的戰爭，凸顯了俄羅斯人的反美情緒，當時俄羅斯政府以維護斯拉夫兄弟之名，派遣維和部隊到南斯拉夫幫助塞爾維亞族斯拉夫

---

17 戈巴契夫，《戈巴契夫回憶錄》上冊，北京：社會科學文獻出版社，2003 年，第 28-31 頁。

兄弟，但最後美國還是贏得了勝利。令俄羅斯氣惱的是所有俄羅斯所發起的維和行動的開銷卻靠著賣黑色及有色金屬才彌補回來，俄羅斯在經濟上與外交上並沒有獲得實質的好處，這次維和行動讓俄羅斯人感覺到再度受到孤立。

不同於前次車臣戰爭，俄羅斯媒體這次完全支持政府，不斷播報政府與軍隊堅決與有計劃攻打車臣的言論，俄羅斯戰地記者採訪前線將軍與戰士的作戰情形，與 1994 年車臣戰爭不同之處在於，俄軍皆表示這次對車臣作戰比以往更有經驗和信心。總理普京更飛往前線，發表與恐怖分子奮戰到底的演說，使得俄羅斯聯邦軍士氣振奮且鬥志高昂。此外，為了達到反車臣恐怖主義的目的，俄國電視還播放車臣恐怖分子砍下四名西方記者的頭，放在路邊的雪地上。法國記者被割下手指的殘忍的實況錄影，該錄影是當時車臣恐怖分子錄下來作為談判籌碼。此後，在俄國反恐怖分子的情緒不斷地升高。這次車臣戰爭，政府不允許俄羅斯記者進入首府格羅茲尼採訪，卻讓西方媒體進入採訪車臣災民的情況，其目的為贏取國際社會的聲援與減少對俄國政府的譴責。為此俄羅斯私營電台獨立電台（NTB）的節目《全民之聲》，由俄羅斯名記者電台新聞出版部經理葉夫根尼·基辛廖夫主持，邀請俄國各大媒體記者與西方媒體，就車臣戰爭與媒體的客觀性進行辯論。外國記者一致性地批評俄媒體替俄政府服務，枉顧車臣平民百姓的生命；俄媒體人表示俄政府的主戰決策是完全正確的，不能讓無辜百姓的血白流，攝影棚內現場場面緊張，猶如東西陣營再現。

俄羅斯前外長伊萬諾夫曾表示：「車臣戰爭將是一場俄羅斯與西方的資訊戰。」而媒體的資訊戰猶如俄羅斯與歐美關係的縮影。俄羅斯內政部官員在莫斯科國際關係學院演講中提到，在這場九十年代國際傳播中的資訊改革與資訊戰中，俄國失敗了。簡言之，無論

是在西方世界或是伊斯蘭教世界，每個人所得到關於車臣戰爭的消息，都是來自俄羅斯媒體，部分涉及國家機密與安全的消息全部分媒體洩露出去，國家利益在俄羅斯媒體所奉行的新聞自由中，喪失殆盡。俄羅斯政治評論家亞歷山大‧格爾茨認為，作為一名政治家，俄羅斯的第二位總統是從車臣戰爭的鮮血和泥潭中升起的，正是利用高加索戰爭作為萬能的選舉策略，才使普京避免採用議會選舉而廣泛使用的各種骯髒的鬥爭手段，年輕人就是應該從代理人的困境中掙脫出來[18]。《獨立報》評論員亞歷山大‧格洛夫科夫指出，普京出任政府總理的背景是在達吉斯坦剛剛發生的爆炸事件，普京由此得出結論：如果現在不儘快把它平息，俄羅斯作為完整的國家將不再存在。達吉斯坦戰事的初期正是普京取得「光輝成就之時」，經過長期期待，他終於成為了真正大規模「英雄」事業的領袖，而後來在群眾意識中出人意料地喚起很大的反響，新政府總理霎那間成為了振興全俄羅斯愛國主義和具有歷史意義的人物[19]。

　　直到 2000 年總統大選之前，對於普京所採取的對車臣的軍事行動還分為贊同、中立與反對三股勢力。自第一次車臣戰爭之後，車臣便陷入孤立與半敵視的包圍狀態當中。在 1996 年至 1999 年這段時間，車臣不僅開始逐步成為一個極端的伊斯蘭教國家，而車臣極端分子所追求的國家此時只徒具其表，因為車臣共和國的經濟增長主要依靠扣留人質、敲詐勒索、走私貨物、販賣毒品等不法行為，同時極端分子已經成為國際恐怖組織的一員，這時的車臣已經成為周邊地區的主要威脅。車臣的這種發展道路不僅不符合與其相鄰各州和各共和國的利益，而且也不符合車臣人民自己的利益，車臣人民已變成人質，為沒有統一中心、沒有統一領導、沒有統一政策的

---

[18] （俄）《Итоги》，《總結》週刊，2000 年 3 月 20 日，第 25 頁。
[19] 《獨立報》，2000 年 3 月 28 日。

武裝集團所控制，狂熱者們和來自穆斯林世界的許多國家的雇傭軍成為車臣武裝集團的主體，這些雇傭軍主要來自阿富汗、巴基斯坦、埃及和科索沃，還有烏克蘭西部、波蘭和波羅的海國家。普京對車臣極端分子的不得人心的地方有著清醒的認識，普京曾經說，國家將把所有的恐怖分子都「用水嗆死」，如果有需要的話就把他們弄到「茅廁中淹死」。這都激發了俄羅斯民眾以及強力部門的鬥志，1999年10月至11月對車臣的軍事行動獲得了不容置疑的勝利。不論是政府官員或是杜馬議員在媒體前皆表示支持聯邦軍在車臣的軍事行動。由於1999年底的杜馬選舉與2000年的總統大選，各黨各派人馬無不表示站在國家安全與利益的立場來對待車臣戰爭，目的是要博得民眾好感與贏得選票，但這並不意味著在俄國不存在反戰人士，事實上在全俄有三百個「戰士母親聯合會」，為幫助解決戰士家屬取得有關前線戰士的消息、維護戰士基本人權、解決政府非法徵兵或隱藏戰士死亡民單等問題。基本上戰士家屬是反戰的少數者，然而以俄羅斯的立場來說，在車臣戰爭期間，國家利益暫時凌駕於新聞自由之上是可以理解的，但是戰爭結束之後，維護俄羅斯國家利益，以及協調經濟寡頭和新聞媒體工作者的良性發展關係成為普京內閣的首要工作。

二、車臣戰爭解決國家內外矛盾

　　俄羅斯發動第二次車臣戰爭主要是為了重建第一次車臣戰爭扭曲的國家價值，調整外高加索石油經濟戰略，維護俄羅斯聯邦的主權和領土完整，重新部署國會及2000年總統大選後回歸正常的國家有機的一體管理。當時車臣戰爭的發展基本有兩種可能情況：其一，以戰促穩定，等到12月19日杜馬選舉後，團結黨在選舉中大有斬

獲時，俄軍再發動攻勢逼迫叛軍棄械投降，重新建立親莫斯科的車臣新政府，並計畫遷都第二大城古德梅斯。其二，若戰爭陷入膠著狀態拖至 2000 年 3 月總統大選後，如果普京獲得勝利，會採取強硬手段，不惜任何代價，爭取勝戰，並且不會讓國際勢力介入，接受國際調停；若由溫和派當選，則會採取和解政策，雙方談判確定車臣未來的政治地位問題。

1999 年發生的第二次車臣戰爭，對其他國家而言，車臣戰爭發生的相當突然，因為俄羅斯正處於內外交困時期。對外，由於俄羅斯高層涉及紐約銀行洗錢醜聞案，使得俄羅斯在爭取世界銀行貸款方面，進行得相當艱難，且更糟糕的是，這項尚未取得的貸款已被編列入俄羅斯 2000 年預算中；對內，由於 1998 年 8 月俄羅斯爆發金融危機，受創的俄國經濟仍處於調整與復甦階段。因此，這難免使人產生疑惑，俄羅斯如何籌錢，來應付車臣戰爭所需要的全部開銷。許多研究俄羅斯問題的專家卻認為，這場戰爭是必定要打的，只是遲早的問題。對俄羅斯當權者而言，車臣戰爭應早打早解決，因為這將使得總統葉利欽派的競選班底有掌握全局的能力，葉利欽的權力因素能在大選中發揮最佳效果。換言之，如果車臣分離分子在大選期間進行一系列恐怖活動，選民必會遷怒政府無力處理車臣問題，會再次勾起人民對第一次車臣戰爭不愉快的回憶，葉利欽的競選班子屆時將難以掌握全局。

車臣分離主義者自 1996 年與列別德將軍（當時國安秘書長，後任克那斯雅爾斯克省長，後在一次空難中喪生）簽署了停戰和平協定之後，就從沒有放棄過謀求獨立的企圖。適逢 1999 年 12 月俄羅斯國家杜馬選舉與 2000 年 6 月總統大選，全國上下皆籠罩在選舉氣氛當中，當俄羅斯當局忙於選戰而無暇分散注意力之時，車臣戰地指揮官認為這時可以採取混水摸魚的方式，讓車臣趁機獨立。車臣

戰爭前夕，車臣分離分子在莫斯科及其周圍地區放置炸彈，一方面企圖攪亂俄國政治局勢及全國民心，使本已內外交困的俄羅斯當局更自顧不暇；另一方面則以精兵多路出擊，從不同方向攻打鄰國達吉斯坦共和國。如果將達吉斯坦併入車臣領土之後，車臣就不再是內陸國，而是靠海國家了。車臣佔領達吉斯坦另一重要因素是完全控制從阿塞拜疆的巴庫輸出到俄羅斯及歐洲的石油管道。俄羅斯當局曾經考慮讓石油管道繞過車臣境內，但是礙於經濟問題，則放棄了此一想法。現在石油管道經過車臣，俄羅斯當局必須定期向車臣繳納過境費用。

爆炸事件經過兩星期的事態發展後，全俄風聲鶴唳，人民談「炸」色變。俄羅斯人對車臣軍隊皆以「匪徒」相稱。巴薩耶夫與哈塔普也成為全國上下眾人皆知的匪首，同時俄羅斯高層對車臣總統馬斯哈托夫產生強烈不滿，認為他對手下的指揮官們管理不力，即是基本上默許爆炸事件的發生。經過一系列爆炸事件之後，可以說這已經達到了車臣匪徒的預期目的。事實上，車臣匪徒們恰恰忘記了歷史上有多少強人在俄羅斯民族前栽跟頭。俄羅斯民族就其個人而言，缺乏團結意識且彼此相互蔑視，並且具有大國沙文主義。在和平年代時人民相當渙散，勤勞與俄羅斯人也是無緣的。但是一旦有外族入侵時，點燃了俄民族的危機意識，那麼人與人之間就會變得團結起來，同仇敵愾，整個俄羅斯民族的個性更是在這時顯露出來。俄羅斯人以其驍勇善戰的特性、豐富的天然資源和廣闊無疆的土地，必然擊敗每個入侵者。

總而言之，對付俄羅斯這個民族，就是不要去觸動其人民的整體危機意識。在危機時刻，俄羅斯最容易產生強人與強人政府，因為俄羅斯人對強勢領導的依附程度相當的高。如蘇聯解體之初，儘管人民生活舉步維艱，但對總統葉利欽的支持是有目共睹的事實，

人民內心中希望葉利欽能成為一個像沙皇彼得大帝式的強人，來拯救俄羅斯，而葉利欽本人也多次利用人民的希望來進行全民公投，用民意擊敗了政敵。美國在冷戰後期中所有對俄的外交政策，基本上也保持著不去觸動俄羅斯民族的神經。當美國在對世界各國廣為推銷其人權至上的政策時，唯獨對俄羅斯雷聲大雨點小。如果俄羅斯結合其國家利益與自身現況發展出了一套自成風格的俄羅斯式民主人權，必將在世界上再次與美國衝突，因為俄羅斯在東歐、中東與高加索地區因歷史與地緣政治上的關係，使得俄羅斯必將在歐亞區域安全與經濟合作問題上扮演重要角色，尤其是前蘇聯國家彼此經濟依賴程度很高。即使在這次車臣戰爭中，美國也只是不斷地對俄國喊話，希望俄當局能夠停止攻打車臣，以和平手段與車臣談判，但是俄當局仍堅持己見，以維護國家安全與打擊恐怖分子集團為號召，獲得了高度民意支持，繼續與車臣進行實質上維護國家及政權利益的戰爭。

三、車臣戰爭與政壇效應

經過 8～9 月車臣武裝分子入侵達吉斯坦及俄境內一連串的恐怖爆炸事件之後，受到驚嚇的俄羅斯人便發出了一致喊「打」的呼聲，希望把恐怖事件「打」出俄羅斯境內。在廣泛的民意基礎之上，取得俄羅斯杜馬以最快速度通過了對車臣戰爭的基本草案，在解決車臣問題上，各政黨展現了空前難得的一致性。但是第三大在野黨「蘋果黨」（又稱雅博盧黨）主席雅夫林斯基強調，對車臣的空襲是必要的攻勢，但他本人同時也表示，堅決反對派遣地面部隊進入車臣境內，以避免第一次車臣戰爭失敗的悲劇再度重演。1999 年由莫斯科市長盧日科夫成立的「祖國‧全俄羅斯黨」，其黨領導人之一且

是前總理的普里馬科夫表示，他也反對地面戰爭，因為他懷疑體弱多病的葉利欽是否有能力領導這場戰爭。車臣問題必須解決，在各政黨討論聲此起彼落之際，俄政府卻已將大量的地面部隊投入了前線，展開了十分節制但卻很有效的攻勢。

　　葉利欽宦海生涯起伏不斷，而俄羅斯政治形勢變化連連，使得葉利欽本人經常捲進政治鬥爭當中，但在以往的政治鬥爭當中，葉利欽幾乎每戰必贏，唯獨 1994 年至 1996 年的車臣戰爭，俄聯邦軍隊陷入戰爭泥淖，進退不得。在 1996 年 6 月俄羅斯總統大選前夕，即 5 月中旬，葉利欽主動要求簽署和平協定，終止長達三年的車臣戰爭。葉氏本人也在公開場合及回憶錄中承認，車臣戰爭為其一生政治生涯中的一項重大錯誤。2000 年總統大選即將來臨，葉利欽由於身體狀況原因，卸任已成必然趨勢，但有關總統家庭成員的黑金醜聞卻接連不斷發生，先是獨立電視台報導葉利欽女兒塔吉安娜利用公款在俄羅斯航空公司參股份紅的醜聞，後又馬上傳出葉氏的女婿也捲入紐約銀行洗黑錢的醜聞案件中。按照媒體觀察家的判斷，醜聞都將由 2000 年總統選舉後，對葉利欽家庭最大的威脅。現任莫斯科市長盧日科夫對於葉利欽家庭的行為並不完全支持。盧日科夫曾是 1996 年總統大選時葉利欽最大的助選夥伴，盧日科夫以百分之九十的選票當選莫斯科市長，擁有高度民意支持，在 1996 年總統大選競選期間，莫市街頭到處可見葉利欽與盧日科夫握手的競選大看板，而盧日科夫組建祖國黨後，對葉利欽的批評就不絕於耳。前任總理斯基巴申遭到解職後，新聞界與政界將此解讀為，總理斯基巴申未能有效地阻止普里馬科夫與盧日科夫的結合。可見葉利欽與盧日科夫的矛盾逐漸尖銳化。

　　普里馬科夫遭葉利欽自總理職務解職後 3 個月即加入盧日科夫組建的「祖國——全俄羅斯」黨，普里馬科夫與盧日科夫的政治結

合的目的在於準備進軍年底的杜馬選舉與 2000 年總統大選，普里馬科夫與盧日科夫希望能夠在杜馬取得多數席位，總統選舉該黨在執政後，杜馬與總統能有更好的配合，著手進行改革[20]。

葉利欽啟用一名名不見經傳的國家安全部長普京為總理，各黨派對普京的任命均不以為然，認為總統用一名特工來治理國家，是俄羅斯民主的倒退。葉利欽點名普京為自己的繼承人後，民意調查卻不捧場，普京只獲得了 2% 的民意支持率。而當 1999 年 8 月 5 日，葉利欽召見普京時，葉利欽認為，「普京這屆政府將要在國家杜馬選舉中勝利，而普里馬科夫與盧日科夫所領導的祖國──全俄羅斯黨不斷壯大時的葉利欽總統本人深感不安。」普京本人表示他將服從總統的工作安排[21]。葉利欽在回憶錄中寫道：「8 月份正是俄羅斯放假的時節，對普京的任命將會像晴天霹靂一樣令人震驚。頓時一切都會變得極度緊張。當然，現會出現連續數周的緩衝期，因為人們還不想從寧靜安樂的情緒中甦醒過來，參與到政治裏去。普京有時間做準備[22]。」

普京上任後，首先對車臣分離分子的恐怖行動加以最嚴厲的批評，這在前五位總理中是絕無僅有的。政府提出對車臣採取空襲的軍事「外科手術」，杜馬也很快地通過決議。俄聯邦軍在二個星期的空襲行動後，再以地面軍隊進入車臣，以包圍夾擊方式南進，將車臣分離分子打出車臣首府格羅茲尼，當車臣分離分子不再控制車臣境內的石油管道時，在不影響俄羅斯的商業利益的前提下，俄羅斯

---

[20] 蘇聯解體後，93 年與 95 年的杜馬選舉共產黨都贏得最多席位，而總統葉利欽卻是無黨派人士，在這幾年改革過程中，政府與杜馬經常成一對立局勢，使得許多政策無法在杜馬中獲得通過，延誤了改革進度。

[21] 羅伊·麥德維傑夫，王桂香等譯，《普京時代──世紀之交的俄羅斯》，世界知識出版社，2001 年 8 月。

[22] 伯里斯·葉利欽，《總統馬拉松》，第 355 頁。

聯邦政府軍隊就可專心對付分離分子。隨後在軍事上的初步勝利，使普京的民意調查如鹹魚翻身，從 2%的支持率上升至 16%，在不到二個星期內，又從 16%攀升至 30%，躍居所有總統候選人民意調查排名第一位。

事實上普京的行情上漲並非空穴來風，普京競選團隊的領導人就是葉利欽的小女兒塔吉安娜和總統智囊團親信之一的尤馬申，這兩人在 96 年俄羅斯總統大選時，將選前曾有一度僅有 2%支持率的葉利欽最後拉上總統寶座。塔吉安娜和尤馬申目前為普京帶來龐大的財政支持及打通繁雜人脈關係。俄羅斯主要的電視媒體均與普京展開合作關係，國家電台「俄羅斯電台」和擁有政府 51%股份的「社會電台」（現第一電視台）在明處支持普京；最大私營電台「獨立電台」的董事長古辛斯基（「橋」銀行集團總裁，同時也是總統智囊班底中的一員）在金融上出現問題，為獲得總統財政支持，也在暗地裏支持普京；除了政府以外，傳媒帝國的兩大龍頭：皆是猶太裔的古辛斯基和別列佐夫斯基（四大銀行集團總裁，前獨聯體秘書長，同時也是總統智囊班底成員）是葉利欽重要的親信。

媒體因素在政府出兵車臣的行動中發揮決定性的效應，電視螢幕前展現在老百姓眼前的是：俄羅斯聯邦軍雄心萬丈的作戰信心和其在車臣的節節勝利；總理普京在媒體前表示與車臣恐怖分子周旋到底的決心，這使得人民對普京的滿意程度也節節攀升。筆者當時判斷，電視台所公佈的 30%的支持率基本有媒體炒作的成分，當時普京的實際支持率應當約為 22%至 25%。在普京支持率上升的各項因素當中，並不存在經濟因素，普京當政 4 個月中，俄羅斯的經濟並沒有好轉，人民並沒有從普京身上得到實質的好處，也就是說一旦俄軍在車臣戰爭中失利的話，那將會直接粉碎普京高支持率的短暫神話。

　　此外，克里姆林宮培養的另一個政治明星：國家緊急狀態與救難部部長沙耶古。在莫斯科發生的幾次爆炸事件中，緊急狀態部又全力以赴，使受難居民死亡程度降到最低.沙耶古所作所為贏得了「救難英雄」的稱號，葉利欽總統於 9 月底親自頒授「英雄勳章」給沙耶古。沙耶古聯合了 13 州的州長，組建了「團結黨」（又稱熊黨，這主要是因為該黨黨旗上有一隻白色的北極熊），由於克里姆林宮背後的支持，使得「團結黨」的勢力範圍在一個月內擴及涵蓋了 22 個州。沙耶古清廉的政治形象尤為民眾所稱道，其本人在緊急狀態部任職十年期間，當歷屆總理重組內閣時，他是唯一未遭撤換的部長。沙耶古同時也是媒體寵兒，他的行蹤經常是媒體關注的焦點。俄記者在與沙耶古進行訪談時，經常提問他這樣個問題：「您是災難中的拯救者，您是否可成為一個拯救俄羅斯的民族救星」。可見媒體對沙耶古是欣賞有加的。

　　葉利欽的兩張王牌亮出後，俄大選的選情發生劇變，出局的黨更加明確，而留在局內的黨將在剩下的時間裏奮力廝殺。民粹主義者日里諾夫斯基領導的「自由民主黨」，在 1999 年杜馬選舉中將失去第二大黨的地位。因為在歷次杜馬決議案中，日里諾夫斯基都以杜馬議題為籌碼，而為自己謀得最大利益。平日日里諾夫斯基螢幕形象一般為：在國會裏丟麥克風；電視訪談中用杯中的水潑人；與男女議員扭打一團或跳上主席台破口大罵，醜態百出；上訪談節目時，喜歡答非所問與用非常民主色彩辭彙刺激其他受訪人；日里諾夫斯基為了表現與年輕朋友親近，會去舞廳跳舞唱歌；1999 年白城州長選舉時，日里諾夫斯基以州長候選人身分，與前來參加集會的老先生、老太太破口相罵，此鏡頭畫面至今仍在全俄電台廣為播放，成為日里諾夫斯基除了向對手潑水的另一花絮。但最令自民黨大傷元氣的是：陣前換將與更改黨名，因為選委會認為「自民黨」與犯

罪集團有關，拒絕讓該黨參選，該黨的頭二號人物在選前資格審查中，皆出現問題，日里諾夫斯基因購買了一部與其經濟實力不符的名車，二號人物貝科夫（克那斯雅爾斯克鋁廠總經理）有犯罪嫌疑，後在保加利亞被捕，其他黨員也有嚴重逃稅的事實。日里諾夫斯基只好臨時更改黨名為「日里諾夫斯基集團黨」重新登記參選。

俄共由於近年來在杜馬的表現則太拖泥帶水，真正為人民爭取到的利益是少得可憐，且俄共的票源正在減少，其競選經費來源也非常緊張，雖然俄共以 20% 的支持率居第一位，但它對於杜馬中另外 50% 的地區選票控制則少得可憐，只有 10 個小州而已，所以實際掌握的選票的實力則居第二、三位。如果車臣戰爭無法見分曉的話，那麼俄共可再運用其最擅長的街頭運動，提高選前聲勢，取得第二或第一大黨地位。但是俄聯邦軍若贏得車臣戰爭的勝利，俄共仍會位居第二或第三位，其大黨地位會削弱。「祖國——全俄羅斯黨」也由於盧日科夫在民眾印象中有與黑道掛鉤的嫌疑，民意調查持續走低，該黨在民意調查中居第一或第二位，而普里馬科夫居第二或三位，與俄共黨主席久加諾夫互有高低。而一旦車臣戰爭因素在選戰中發酵，則祖國黨會因為其居中立觀點的優勢，大量吸收厭戰的左派與右翼的票源，可為其政黨議席取得多數議席；並且在另一半行政區的議席中，拉攏能對選民影響的各州長，使該黨在大選中一炮雙響，為總統大選鋪石墊路。祖國黨將面臨背水一戰，與葉利欽聯合是不可能的事，只有站在葉利欽對立面，才能鞏固票源，在杜馬選舉中保持第二或第一地位。「團結黨」（也稱「熊黨」）儘管擁有葉利欽的支持，可利用現有的龐大政治、經濟資源來進行選舉，該黨主席沙耶古自身的政治魅力還是有些不足之處，但由於該黨地方勢力相當雄厚，可在政黨議席中取得第三、四位之後，從地方議席中

奪得第一位，即而成為杜馬實際上的第二大黨黨若車臣戰爭陷入膠著狀態的話，該黨會滑落至第三、四位黨。

1999年12月19日，俄羅斯第三屆國家杜馬如期舉行，約有6,000萬選民參加了投票，投票率接近60%。俄羅斯杜馬由450席次組成，其中225名由選舉區選出（每區選出一名），另外225名則由各政治黨派按比例制產生，並受得票率百分之五門檻的限制。12月19日俄羅斯國會選舉初步的結果是（除車臣共和國明年戰後補選）俄羅斯共產黨得票率24黨38%，占111席位。親克里姆林宮的團結黨得票率23黨68%，將擁有76席次。祖國全俄聯盟黨12黨08%，總席次62席位。右翼勢力聯盟黨8黨71%，29席位。蘋果黨6黨10%，22席位。選舉結果顯示俄國新國會出現改革主流的希望大增，而受克里姆林宮支持的「團結黨」（2002年，當「祖國黨」與「團結黨」合併之後成為「統一黨」）獲得第二高票的選民支持，意味著葉利欽的繼任人選普京邁向總統之路更加平坦。

1999年12月俄羅斯國會大選的重要性在於中央政治權力的重新配置，影響日後政策制訂方向，大選結果亦將影響明年六月的總統大選。此次俄國大選的兩個值得觀察後續效應：中央權力重組，可能引發後續政策更動；地方派系滲透中央，可能引發中央與地方之間權力分配問題。俄新國會產生具幾項指標意義：一、右派力量聯盟蘋果黨、團結黨將在新國會中形成具有積極意義的多數集團，新國會將一改長年被共產黨席位占絕對優勢的新局面。二、中間偏左政治聯盟祖國俄羅斯黨在選舉中受挫可能導致共產黨無法籌組中間偏左政黨大聯盟，對普里馬可夫決心參選總統受到嚴重打擊。三、中間派政團大有斬獲可能連帶改變俄國的政治面貌，並提高俄國持續經濟改革的可能性。換言之，大多數俄國選民願意接受某種形式的民主經濟改革。

參、俄媒體第四權終結過程

　　過去筆者對反恐與媒體之間的關係多有論述，主要是著重在新聞體制上的變革，以及政府如何進行宏觀的控管，普京總統在其第一任期內，政府與媒體之間維持了一種媒體國家化與自由化路線之爭，媒體尚保留著新聞自由中的言論自由。然而言論自由軌跡的逐漸減弱有一段發展的時期。從 1999 年 8、9 兩個月，莫斯科市地鐵爆炸事件和公寓爆炸成廢墟事件，一直到 2002 年杜伯羅夫劇院人質事件，再到 2004 年的別斯蘭學校人質事件的逐漸升溫，都是在普京任內發生的恐怖活動，因此，打擊恐怖主義的反恐行動是普京執政過程中的最大任務，而兩次人質事件的爆發是使俄羅斯新聞自由從普京上任的爭權時期過渡到蟄伏時期，繼之，2006 年 3 月 6 日反恐法通過之後，新聞內容的報導規範受四項法案的嚴格限制：緊急狀況法、戰爭法、極端主義法和反恐法，新聞自由的限制從對媒體體制的改革再到對新聞內容規定的法律要求，普京的媒體改革再從限制新聞體制進入到新聞內容的鉗制階段，於是乎新聞自由又再從蟄伏時期正式進入第四權終結時代。

一、俄羅斯恐怖主義猖獗的類型與特點

　　中國國際戰略學會反恐怖研究中心主任楊暉[23]認為，俄羅斯自上世紀 90 年代中期以來，深受車臣恐怖活動之害。俄羅斯面臨的恐怖主義主要有以下特點：

---

[23]　楊暉，《外國軍事學術》，2006 年第 5 期。

　　第一，以民族分裂為主要動機。車臣民族分裂主義起源有較深的歷史背景，19 世紀初沙俄向高加索地區擴張，車臣人歷經半個世紀的反抗最終被征服，車臣被納入俄羅斯帝國的版圖，車臣人與俄羅斯人之間的矛盾有深厚的歷史根源，這類恐怖主義往往與國內民族、宗教問題以及內部政治鬥爭糾纏在一起，從而增加了打擊和防範的難度，車臣、印古什、達吉斯坦相當數量居民支持恐怖武裝。

　　第二，民族動機與宗教動機相結合。伊斯蘭教極端主義支持以「聖戰」思想建立自己神聖領土，極端派還提出要以伊斯蘭思想為基礎，把北高加索聯合起來，建立「北高加索伊斯蘭共和國」。1998年 6 月，巴薩耶夫當選「車臣與達吉斯坦人民大會」領導人，朝著將車臣與達吉斯坦聯合組成「伊斯蘭教長國」邁出了重要一步。1999年 8 月巴薩耶夫進犯達吉斯坦，即是為實現這一野心而採取的重大步驟。

　　第三，軍事對抗與暴力恐怖活動相結合並具有相當規模。車臣民族分裂主義徹底走上恐怖主義道路有一個過程，即由和平政變到武裝對抗，武裝對抗失敗後徹底走上恐怖主義。1991 年「8 黨 19」事件，以杜達耶夫為首的車臣分裂主義分子發動政變，宣佈脫離俄羅斯聯邦而獨立，並走上與聯邦中央武裝對抗的道路。一方面繼續頑抗，以襲擊、伏擊、爆炸、暗殺、綁架等游擊戰術對抗俄軍的清剿行動；另一方面，在俄境內針對非軍事目標如地鐵、劇院、學校等人群密集場所發起連續的大規模恐怖襲擊，通過頻繁綁架人質、搞爆炸、劫持飛機等進行報復和破壞。俄羅斯當局的反分裂、反恐怖鬥爭也從有固定戰場的戰爭行為，轉變為無處不在的反恐怖、防恐怖行動。

　　第四，國內恐怖主義與國際恐怖勢力內外密切勾結互動。隨著恐怖主義的國際化，各國的伊斯蘭極端分子形成了一個「統一戰

線」，而車臣恐怖分子則是其中的重要組成部分。早在俄聯邦政府出兵之前的幾年間，「國中之國」的車臣本身就成了國際恐怖分子和犯罪組織的「演兵場」和「庇護所」。許多國家的恐怖分子在車臣接受培訓。

第五，具有明顯的國際反俄勢力插手的背景。車臣非法武裝的伊斯蘭支持中心都位於美國的「附屬國」如沙特、阿聯酋、巴基斯坦、約旦、葉門及土耳其等國境內。美國當局最初支持阿富汗「塔利班」，並與恐怖組織「科索沃解放軍」、「馬其頓民族解放軍」等保持密切聯繫等行徑，

第六，恐怖主義與各種刑事犯罪緊密結合。在俄羅斯，特別是在北高加索地區，恐怖主義與刑事犯罪之間很難明確地劃清界限。轉型時期的利益衝突、法制不健全和政權機構軟弱，使俄羅斯社會甚至部分執法機構呈現「犯罪化」趨勢。特別是在聯邦中央失控的車臣地區，更是成了國內外各種犯罪組織聚集的「樂園」和「庇護所」。

第七，怖活動手段殘忍、方式多樣、活動頻繁，防範和打擊難度相當大。俄羅斯恐怖主義還有特別殘酷、崇拜暴力、蔑視生命的突出特點。山地車臣民族的剽悍性格、深重的民族仇怨，俄國歷史上的沙文主義、政治極端主義文化傳統，再加上伊斯蘭教極端思想的狂熱，凡此種種都使俄羅斯恐怖活動表現出極端殘忍、暴烈的特點。

普京上任以來打擊恐怖主義成了維護國家安全與社會秩序的頭等大事。根據《新聞晨報》的整理，1999 年俄羅斯軍隊與車臣反政府武裝再次爆發衝突以來，發生在車臣或與車臣恐怖分子有關的重大爆炸事件層出不窮，以下是有關事件的不完全統計。如下：

時間	恐怖事件
1999 年 8 月 31 日	在距離莫斯科中心紅場僅幾米遠的一個廣場商業中心發生一起嚴重的爆炸案，造成約 40 人受傷。
1999 年 9 月 9 日	莫斯科東南工人居住區的公寓樓發生爆炸事件，這次公寓樓爆炸案造成至少 20 人死亡，152 人受傷。
1999 年 9 月 9 日	莫斯科東南工人居住區的公寓樓發生爆炸事件，這次公寓樓爆炸案造成至少 20 人死亡，152 人受傷。
1999 年 9 月 13 日	俄羅斯首都莫斯科發生公寓樓爆炸案，至少 73 人喪生。
2000 年 6 月 7 日	車臣境內發生第一次自殺性襲擊。車臣首府格羅茲尼附近的阿爾汗尤特村發生自殺性汽車爆炸，2 名俄羅斯特種員警身亡，另有 5 人受傷。
2000 年 7 月 2、3 日	車臣恐怖分子在 24 小時內向俄羅斯安全部隊駐地發起 5 次自殺性襲擊。俄羅斯員警突擊隊在格羅茲尼附近阿爾貢的宿舍遭到炸彈襲擊，至少 54 人死亡。俄羅斯內政部在古德米爾德基地遭襲，6 名俄羅斯人死亡。
2000 年 8 月 8 日	莫斯科普希金地鐵站發生爆炸事件，致使 13 人死亡，90 多人受傷。
2002 年 5 月 9 日	俄羅斯南部達吉斯坦共和國的卡斯皮斯克市在舉行紀念二戰勝利遊行活動時發生爆炸事件，造成 42 人死亡，100 餘人受傷。
2002 年 10 月 10 日	俄羅斯聯邦車臣共和國首府格羅茲尼市一員警分局大樓內發生嚴重爆炸事件，造成至少 23 人喪生。
2002 年 10 月 23 日	40 多名蒙面持槍的車臣武裝分子闖入莫斯科軸承廠的文化宮大樓，劫持了正在那裏演出的演員、欣賞音樂會的觀眾以及文化宮的工作人員近千人。3 天後，俄特種部隊向劇院內施放催眠氣體後，成功地解救了大多數人質，但仍有 130 名人質不幸喪生。
2002 年 12 月 27 日	車臣「人彈」駕車撞向格羅茲尼市政府總部，炸毀了四層辦公樓，造成 72 人死亡，100 多人受傷。
2003 年 5 月 12 日	兩名自殺性襲擊者駕駛一輛裝滿炸藥的汽車，強行闖入俄羅斯聯邦車臣納德捷列奇諾耶區政府大院並引爆了炸藥，造成 59 人死亡，100 多人受傷。

2003 年 5 月 14 日	位於格羅茲尼東部艾理斯汗尤特鎮的一個宗教慶典遭到自殺式炸彈襲擊，至少 16 人被炸死，145 人受傷。
2003 年 6 月 5 日	一名女「人彈」在車臣附近突襲一輛運送俄羅斯空軍飛行員的車輛，這輛車被炸毀，包括女「人彈」在內共 19 人死亡。
2003 年 7 月 5 日	兩名女「人彈」在莫斯科圖什諾機場舉行的露天搖滾音樂會上發動自殺式爆炸襲擊，導致 17 人死亡，60 人受傷。
2003 年 8 月 1 日	一名自殺式襲擊者駕駛一輛滿載炸藥的卡車沖入與車臣接壤的北奧塞梯共和國莫茲多克市的一家軍隊醫院，造成 50 多人死亡，80 多人受傷。
2003 年 9 月 3 日	一列火車在北高加索溫泉療養地米羅拉耶沃迪附近發生爆炸，至少 6 人死亡，俄警方說此事是車臣叛軍所為。
2003 年 12 月 5 日	俄南部斯塔夫羅波爾邊疆區一列旅客列車在接近皮亞季戈爾斯克市車站時發生爆炸，造成至少 44 人死亡，150 多人受傷。
2004 年 2 月 6 日	莫斯科一列地鐵列車在運行中發生爆炸，近 50 人死亡，100 多人受傷。這是莫斯科有史以來最嚴重的地鐵列車爆炸案。俄羅斯聯邦安全局稱，一名潛伏在車臣共和國的沙特伊斯蘭武裝分子可能是該爆炸案的幕後策劃者。
2004 年 4 月 6 日	俄羅斯印古什和國總統賈濟科夫的車隊遭汽車炸彈襲擊，總統本人受輕傷。

二、俄媒體為政權和平轉移護航

　　俄羅斯政權在俄羅斯人的摒氣凝神當中再度和平轉移了！2008 年 3 月 2 日，俄新網莫斯科 3 月 3 日電，俄羅斯政治基金主席、俄羅斯聯邦社會院成員韋切斯拉夫・尼科諾夫向俄新社記者表示：弗拉基米爾・普京的支持對梅德韋傑夫贏得總統大選起了決定性作用。在總統大選結果出爐後揭曉，候選人德米特裏・梅德韋傑夫在第一輪選舉中以 70 黨 23% 得票率獲勝。而俄羅斯媒體卻是對普京順利將政權交到自己接班人的手中起到了關鍵作用。而普京對媒體的

改革和控管卻又是在恐怖主義猖獗的環境下進行的。自蘇聯解體之後，對於俄羅斯強國道路的實現而言，車臣民族分離主義和與其相關的恐怖事件，是攸關俄羅斯政權是否能夠和平轉移以及俄羅斯是否會面臨像蘇聯一樣崩解命運的致命威脅！對此，從西方推動的北約東擴和對車臣叛軍的接觸看來，足以證明西方國家對俄羅斯存在的弱點是有深刻瞭解認識的！

如果說反恐是為了塑造穩定安全的空間環境，那麼，梅德韋傑夫接掌總統大位之後的重點就是經濟改革。在俄羅斯意識形態的空窗時期或是意識形態發展醞釀階段，普京對人民承諾提高生活水準和改善經濟條件就是重點，普京樸實不帶花俏的承諾和作為，使得俄羅斯公民多數願意相信他，這使得選舉過程中沒有什麼激情產生，俄羅斯公民以投票支持普京推薦的接班人來認同普京的決策。俄羅斯媒體認為這是普京和梅德韋傑夫共治時代的來臨。俄羅斯《總結》雜誌在 2008 年第 10 期，刊登了對俄羅斯工業家與企業家聯合會主席亞歷山大・紹欣的訪問，採訪者帕夫洛夫斯基說，普京和梅德韋傑夫「雙核體制」內要推動落實司法改革、稅務改革、退休金保障改革。3 月 5 日的《消息報》則側重分析對梅德韋傑夫的施政綱領，該報撰文說，梅德韋傑夫把自己執政的主要工作方向確定為四個「I」：體制（Institute）、創新（Innovasion）、投資（Investment）和基礎建設（Infrastructure）。而與媒體有關的是另兩個「I」：意識形態（Ideology）──梅德韋傑夫在施政綱領中提出的理想主義建築在自由、公正和人類的尊嚴之上，而實用主義原則是與之相悖的，而叢林法則、所有人同所有人的戰爭──這就是當今國際法的最高境界；形象（Image）也是軟實力的一個組成部分，媒體要為國家形象擔負起重塑的工作。

　　在俄羅斯這個世界面積最大、卻是恐怖災難頻傳的國家，這是在西方先進發達國家當中相當罕見的！俄羅斯的現況和西方已經站在不一樣的水準上而利益相侵、漸行漸遠了！相較於西方媒體在俄羅斯大選之前鋪天蓋地揣測普京是否可能修改憲法自行延任的喧騰報導，俄羅斯媒體卻沒有對普京在選舉中可能有的延任動作進行任何的揣測評論。因此，梅德韋傑夫在幾乎毫無懸念的情況之下，第一輪就以大幅超過半數以上的得票率當選為俄羅斯第三任總統。顯然，俄羅斯選舉的冷基調，與媒體保持一定的自律和緘默是有直接關係的。普京的媒體改革與控管對俄羅斯政權成功轉移到自己選中的接班人手中，證明產生了明顯的成果！從葉利欽總統為普京成功打造總統之路（當時第二次車臣戰爭爆發，葉利欽宣佈提前退位承擔起某種政治上的責任，普京繼任為代理總統，相當被看好的前總理普利馬科夫與莫斯科市長盧日科夫這組超級人馬宣佈退出總統選舉，支持普京打車臣戰爭），再到普京總統為梅德韋傑夫選上總統鋪平道路，從這兩場跨時空的總統大選看來，甚至當中包括一次普京自己的成功連任，要求媒體自律產生了決定性的影響。

三、俄羅斯新聞控管三分天下

　　俄文的 тройка，原意是俄羅斯東正教信仰宗教上的三位一體，代表的是聖父、聖母、聖子，進而演生出三頭馬車的意思。俄羅斯媒體控管的三頭馬車是總統（政府）、媒體、國家安全委員會（КГБ，發成英語就是 KGB）。首先，總統及政府部門是對媒體的體制進行控管，包括管理媒體的資源分配和媒體的發展方向，為此成立有專門的部門和委員會來管理媒體，俄羅斯的出版部門負責管理印刷媒體；文化部則管理電視媒體與意識形態相關的文化產業；而全俄羅

斯國家廣播電視公司負責管理全國的廣播電視台。其次，媒體從所有權來分可分為國有和私有媒體，國有媒體代表的是國家資產和國營企業運營的一部分，成為政府政策的傳達者或是喉舌，商業媒體是代表多元文化的一部分，是對新聞自由的有益補充，例如俄羅斯的報紙市場仍有比較好的成長，商營性大報和黃色報紙都有自己讀者和銷路，廣告市場也在成長當中。再者，國家安全委員會扮演監控全國的情資掌控和避免洩漏國家機密給媒體炒作的職責，而普京曾是 KGB 情報人員，從情治單位的咽喉上就勒住 KGB，成功地避免了洩漏機密給媒體去炒作醜聞而造成可能帶來的政治政黨之間的惡鬥。

　　普京執政之後很巧妙地控制了三頭馬車的進行，在葉利欽總統時期，電視以醜聞來提升收視率的情況已經不出現了，醜化重要政治人物的節目也無法取得生存的空間。若媒體國家化是政府體制改革的重要核心要素，那麼對突發事件、極端主義、車臣戰爭、和恐怖活動報導的條文限制就是針對新聞內容的鉗制而制定的法律環境。兩次人質事件加速了從媒體體制控管時代進入危機新聞控管的時代，俄羅斯右派黨魁、自由經濟學家蘋果黨主席雅夫林斯基聲稱，在別斯蘭人質事件之後，人質事件給普京提供了擴大車臣戰爭和箝制新聞自由的合理性。2002 年，媒體在劇院人質事件之後宣佈新聞自律，普京不滿媒體的報導而制定媒體修正案，內容是規定任何可能制助長恐怖行為的報導都要禁止，在媒體高層和普京正式公開會談之後，普京否決了杜馬快速三讀通過的媒體修正案，媒體的妥協代價就是制定新聞自律條款並且嚴格遵守公約；2004 年別斯蘭人質事件之後，媒體落實自律公約，俄記協聲稱：「公民人權當中的生命安全優先於新聞自由」，這個思路脈落就是：新聞不能影響到政府救援，新聞對危機事件報導中關於恐怖行為者或是受難者家屬的採訪

都因為會妨礙到政府救援而不被允許，這一條款最終落在反恐法當中訴諸於法律條文，至此，俄羅斯媒體關於監督政府濫權的所謂「第四權」制衡機制正式宣告終結。

參考資料

胡逢瑛、吳非（2006）。《蘇俄新聞傳播史論》，台北市：秀威資訊出版社。
胡逢瑛、吳非（2005）。《透視蘇俄傳媒轉型變局》，台北市：秀威資訊出版社。

傳媒全球在地化問題[1]

胡逢瑛

元智大學通識教學部助理教授

摘要

　　全球化潮流激起了世人對文化認同與國族認同的探討思潮。美國學者亨廷頓於 1996 年出版了《文明的衝突與世界秩序的重建》，在他為中文版寫的《序言》中說：「全球單一文化論者想把世界變成像美國一樣。美國國內的多元文化論者則想把美國變成像世界一樣。一個多元文化的美國是不可能的，因為非西方的美國便不成其為美國。多元化的世界則是不可避免的，因為建立全球帝國是不可能的。維護美國和西方需要重建西方認同，維護世界安全則需要接受全球的多元文化性。」

　　從上所述，基本上亨廷頓是站在建立美國單一文化符號或是確認美國文化認同的立足點上，去看待文化認同與多元文化的關係，也就是讓多元文化作為捍衛美國與西方認同價值中單一文化的有益

---

[1] 本文部份內容曾公開發表在元智通識教學部刊物《元智全球在地文化報》、與香港《大公報》，也曾在本部舉辦的全球化與傳媒對話的座談會中提出討論。

補充！從這裏我們可以看見美國學者與美國統治階層的企圖心，因為美國之所以為美國，就是美國對多元文化與多民族的吸納政策，但是相較於世界四大文明古國和歐洲文明的豐富文化遺產資源，美國的文化認同與文化特點就顯得缺乏內涵而蒼白了。這樣一個缺乏明顯特色文化符號的美國，與其目前在世界上所建構出來的超級霸權地位實不相稱！如此一來，建構美國單一文化的企圖就產生出來。全球化進程就成為了美國建構帝國主義式的文化符號與文化認同的契機，只是對於美國社會的移民後代以及與此產生的種族歧視問題成為美國進行文化認同體系和單一美國文化價值的阻撓因素。這樣美國在進行文化霸權時面臨了兩個問題：第一，美國是否繼續深化她的多民族、多文化的多元化政策？第二，美國在進行軍事與商業全球化的擴張當中，是否繼續她的文化殖民政策、亦或是轉變為尊重、甚至融入當地的民族文化當中？

當蘇聯解體之後，全球意識形態對立的兩大軍事陣營，頓時轉變成為美國獨霸的單極世界，冷戰雖然已經結束，北大西洋公約組織在以美國為首的支撐之下，仍在進行其強勢軍事力量的擴張，這是美國與西方軍事霸權全球化的一個現實寫照。全球化在經濟版圖不斷擴張之下被賦予新的內涵，部分美國與西方學者已經為美國的霸權擴張尋找新的理論依據，這引起了許多擁有悠久深厚文明與文化傳統的民族國家感到不安或甚至抗拒！全球化議題已經成為吾人乃至全世界各民族國家所關心的最重要的議題之一。全球化從商業層面中所產生的現象，例如巨型跨國企業所具有的龐大資金流、人才流、商品流、技術流優勢，激起了小本資額的中小企業的憤怒與危機意識，全球化似乎演變成為強凌弱、弱肉強食、適者生存的演化論現象。弱者與小者如何在叢林中找到自我生存的空間與法則，

成為全球化過程中的重要問題。全球化不僅產生了物質表層的商業霸權問題，更引發了文化層面的深層次的反思問題。

關鍵詞：文化霸權、傳媒全球在地化、新聞倫理、國家媒體

壹、全球化的可能性與構成要素

　　元智大學通識教學部部長王立文教授正在構思，如何在通識教育中推動經典閱讀的基礎上，建構中國古典名著的全球化理論。王教授多年研究與教授《孫子兵法》的課程，並且試圖在孫子兵法的基礎上將《水滸傳》推向全球的經典殿堂。當然，王教授認定的前提是：國際上承認且高度評價《孫子兵法》與老子的《道德經》具有崇高的學術地位與實用價值，並且不論是外國人或是各行各業，都能從這些中國經典中找到行事的哲理與處世的哲學。王教授最關心的問題是：如何在全球化路徑不發達的時代中，這些中國文化經典著作可以佔有全球化的地位和影響力，這其中的關鍵要素又在哪裏？王教授分析到：全球化其中的關鍵要素應在於強調原則性，而非細節。

一、地化走向全球化的路徑

　　筆者延伸王立文教授的觀點，認為重視細節並非全然貶意，因為這種細節也正是在地化和本土化的重要元素，是一個時間、空間、地點三維空間內的共同人民，他們所思、所欲、所想的事情，這樣看來，似乎在地化與本土化更接近民主的思維，而民主的內涵也會隨著時代的變化、技術的革新或是人們的喜好而有所變異。在全球化的過程中，若是民主化是一個西方國家對外拓展霸權的口號與手段，那麼，在地化的功用就在於修正全球化的內涵，使它更符合當地文化和人民的需求和使用。這就是民主化轉化為「全球在地化」的過程。王立文教授表示，他在思考如何把全球化從消極「防禦」

的角度轉化為積極「推廣」的角度，筆者認為這具有一定的高度，這恰恰也就是我們國家要走向世界的難度。台灣經歷了意識形態紛爭的階段，台灣的學術界也進入了某種後現代主義的過程當中，百家爭鳴、百花齊放，沒有一種固定的意識形態是人們希望政府或是政黨堅持執行或是對外宣傳的。學術界可以在這個思想的空窗期努力建構新的理論、新的學說。

王立文教授在其主編的「全球在地文化研究」[2]一書中的「全球化要慎防成為失去靈魂的優秀」一篇中提及：全球化是一強大潮流，在其中建立在地化很不容易。要做好全球化有三要素：奠基（Foundation）、方向（Direction）、努力（Effort）。充分全球化的國家也許經濟發展的不錯，但若失去原有文化特質就是失去靈魂的優秀。沒有在地化的全球化即便十分進步，亦是失去靈魂的優秀。

台大張小虹教授在其著作《假全球化》[3]自序中提及：所有的理論都是史料的「理論化」，沒有先於史料的理論，也沒有無法被理論化的史料。《假全球化》中的歷史史料，是用來創造理論的。另外，她在「假全球化之名」[4]的篇章中提及：《假全球化》一書分別從「全球影視傳媒」、「全球商品流通」、「全球帝國運作」、「全球流行文化」四大面向，探討「假全球化」如何假借全球化路徑，鬆動真／假的權力階層，開展「思想連結」與「差異創造」的可能，讓「虛假的力量」全球離散四處流動。張教授書中強調：[5]以《假全球化》為書名，不僅是要以「真／假」作為當前全球化論述中一個未曾出現過

---

[2]　王立文（2008）。《全球在地文化研究》，台北市：秀威出版社，第 29-30 頁。
[3]　張小虹（2007）。《假全球化》，台北市：聯合文學，頁 9。
[4]　同上，第 21 頁。
[5]　同上，第 17 頁。

的新分析範疇，建立並且拆解一套有關真／假二元對立模式的域外，「假」作為「虛假的力量」，亦即「假」作為虛擬創造力的可能。

結合以上兩位教授的觀點，不難發現「假借」全球化之名義、路徑、手段或是資源，任何在地化的事務都有可能轉變成西方世界中所能理解的全球化本身，而內涵卻是傳遞著特殊地域的在地文化。如果，全球化是一種運動，那麼許多異域文化在二十一世紀初都已經在爭奪全球化的「主權」或是「所有權」，這是非常有意思的現象。二十世紀因為有兩次的世界大戰，美蘇兩大帝國分別控制意識形態的解釋權與軍事霸權，然而，在冷戰中卻也杜絕了零星的區域戰爭與衝突，全世界許多國家分別投身兩大陣營尋求保護與謀取利益。冷戰同時也抑制了區域文化與恐怖主義，美國在對外的全球化蔓延過程中使用的思想基礎的演變包括自由主義、理想主義、民主和平論、新自由制度主義等等學說理論；歐洲則是深受古典現實主義、結構現實主義、新現實主義等權力核心學說的影響；其中橫跨歐亞大陸的蘇聯則受到馬列主義學說的影響。「反霸權」成為後實證主義（post-positivism），包括：後現代主義（post-modernism）、女性主義（feminism）、批判理論（critical theory）的核心要素。各個國家、民族、宗教、非政府團體、或是學術界逐漸崛起，或是建構新世界體系或是建構新的學說理論，他們正在影響著世界……。

二、文明衝突與負面國際新聞

冷戰期間，美國與蘇聯有著極大的內部政治經濟制度的不同，卻在對外政策上採取的是一致的國家安全政策，歷史終結論並無法解釋各個國家與文化差異所引發的全球治理（governance）問題。歷史終結論是美國學者福山（Fancis Fukuyama），認為蘇聯解體美國已

經沒有競爭者，自由資本主義這個理想的制度已經取得最後的勝利。[6]事實上，俄羅斯又再度羽翼豐滿，重新站在世人的眼前。

台灣大學張亞中教授在其主編的《國際關係總論》一書中的〈全球化爭辯〉一文中寫到：隨著冷戰的結束，全球化是當前重要的課題。應該如何看待全球化？全球化的定義或是看法可說是眾說紛紜。David Held[7]提出三種研究觀點的面向：超全球主義觀點（the hyperglobalist position）、懷疑觀點（the skeptical position）、轉型觀點（the transformationalist position）。[8]張亞中教授認為：全球化並沒有改變以國家為中心的國際關係本質，但是參與全球化事務的主要行為者已經擴及到非政府組織、公民運動、全球傳媒等非國家組織成員當中，全球治理體系尚未完成，也不盡然符合人們需求，但是他已經在全球事務中逐漸提升重要性。[9]

後實證學派的觀點在於，國際關係中的理論過注重以國家中心（state-centrism）為理論的觀點，關注戰爭與和平以及各種國家在複合互賴經濟關係下的經濟問題，卻忽略在世界上大部地區在貧窮線下生活的困苦人民，受到國家或是群體壓迫下的弱勢族群的聲音到哪裏去了？他們在各種洲際飛彈、國際組織與制度以及全球化進程中有什麼憧憬？[10]

---

[6] 陳欣之，〈新自由制度主義、社會建構主義及英國學派〉。（參照自張亞中（2007）。《國際關係總論》第二版，台北市：揚智出版社，第75-78頁。）

[7] Held, David et al., (1999). Global Transformation: Politics, Economics and Culture..Standford, CA: Standford University Press.（中文譯本：沈宗瑞等譯，2001，《全球化大轉變：全球化對政治、經濟與文化的衝擊》，台北：韋伯文化。）

[8] 張亞中（2007）。《國際關係總論》第二版，台北市：揚智出版社，第334頁。

[9] 同上，第372頁。

[10] 黃競涓，〈國際關係理論中的後實證主義〉。（參照自張亞中（2007）。《國際關係總論》第二版，台北市：揚智出版社，第120頁。）

　　的確，國際關係中的各種衝突已經占據了全球傳媒新聞版面和世人的眼球，負面新聞成為新聞價值的標準，看看美國有線電視中充斥著伊拉克戰爭的報導和各種災難，戰爭已經將國家關係提昇到國與國之間的積極互動合作上來，因為極端宗教與恐怖組織以一種不受國際關係約束規範的姿態正在影響著世界的格局與穩定，國家間必須以一種互賴合作與相互搏弈的關係來抵抗不可控制的要素，這使得各類重要的人權議題遭到忽略。後實證主義者更關切的人權的各種問題，這使得許多非政府組織的角色和作用更加重要。蘇聯解體之後，美蘇意識形態的對立驟然瓦解，但是這並沒有解除以「國家中心論」與國家利益為權力鬥爭的勢力，美國成為世界強權，進行的是單邊主義的外交政策。從而挑戰國際強權包括美俄中等強權的是民族分離主義者、極端宗教主義者、恐怖主義，表現的形式包括區域戰爭、恐怖活動、軍事衝突等等。

三、全球在地化媒體的新聞倫理觀

　　全球在地化（Glocalization）原本是建立在商業擴張的需求之下所產生的新思維與行動模式，已經在二十一世紀全球化過程中成為各個領域的發展特點和必然趨勢。美國自從在一九九六年通過施行九六電信傳播法案之後，媒體資本全球化與跨媒體集團形成了媒體營運的新趨勢，為美國扮演全球影音產品和新聞資訊最大的生產國與輸出國推波助瀾。在美國媒體全球霸權的擴張之下，我們要如何發展出台灣自己的媒體特點是相當重要的議題。新聞與個人生活、公民素養以及國家發展是密切相關的，筆者認為，全球化的思維與行動在進入不同的地點之後，全球化都必須結合在地的本土文化才能夠得以繼續生存發展。因此，如何在新聞報導中真實地反應

出台灣社會和其真實面貌，是我們媒體專業和社會責任之所在。筆者呼籲，新聞事業必須建立在倫理基礎之上，台灣新聞也應全球在地化。

　　新聞自由演進的過程就是反對來自統治階層的控制。西方的新聞自由是從出版自由、到言論自由、再到新聞自由。出版自由是出版商爭取印刷自由的權利，一方面符合出版商出書的商業利益，另一方面書籍作者的新血結晶得以有出版問世的機會，兩者結合達到了出版商機與普及知識的效果。言論自由主要爭取免於恐懼、遭訴訟的自由，新聞記者、作者或報刊發行者不因為撰寫和刊登某種言論而身陷囹圄。新聞自由主要是爭取發行和籌設媒體的自由。因此，從新聞事業的發展進程中可發現，新聞自由演進的過程與爭取出版和發行密不可分，從這個企業經營和市場運作的角度看待新聞事業的話，新聞自由的思維更多的是來自企業主希望要求的市場自由，而言論自由才是傾向屬於記者和在媒體上發表言論者的說話權利，換句話說，媒體經營者和記者之間是有一定工作思維和理念的差距與鴻溝的！

　　自五四運動以來，西方的人權、自由、民主、科學等等思維模式，就開始深深地影響著中國與週遭具有華人文化背景的地區和社會。媒體大眾化趨勢是西方新聞事業對全球的影響，它象徵著媒體從官辦走入商辦、民營的大時代，並且已經在二十世紀末對東歐、蘇聯的共產極權以及東亞威權國家造成衝擊。大眾化新聞標誌著，新聞不再是過去中央和地方聯繫公文往返的官方管道，新聞已經成為聯繫政府、民間團體和個人的公眾橋樑。大眾新聞的屬性和特點就是要公開、透明，這是因為新聞不再屬於國家機密範疇的公文。新聞與媒體：是政府傳達與解釋政令的宣導平台；是媒體觀察、監督政府政策的成果報告，必須要向公眾利益負責；是民眾訊息交

流、情感溝通的聯繫管道；是公眾表達不同意見和訴求共同需求的窗口。

建構具有台灣特點的台灣在地化新聞，首推重視新聞倫理。新聞倫理重視記者的自律精神，也就是孔子所說的「己所不欲、勿施於人」的自省、自覺、自悟的反求諸己的精神。為什麼記者從事新聞這項行業需要重視新聞倫理，也就是講求自律？因為新聞事業是聯繫公民和政府之間的橋樑，因此被視為行政、立法、司法三項政府公權力之外的第四權力，新聞被任何一方操控都是危險的，至今關於新聞的定性和定位還是爭論不休。西方社會在市場經濟和選舉政治之下，強調新聞自由，因此新聞需要高度的自由與社會責任，反對任何法律形式的鉗制和壓迫。但社會責任論者強調媒體是社會的公器，同時媒體也是社會機制中的一個組成要素，它的運行也必須在一定的規範下和軌道上，才不至於會脫序脫軌，而給社會帶來災難。因此記者的自律必須建立在一個社會所遵從的倫理道德的體系之中和在此基礎之上，自律才是至善的、自省的，而非自我壓抑的行為。

西方的新聞民主化和自由化學理，已經在西方商業和媒體全球佈局的霸權影響之下，深入全球開發中國家。媒體高層與記者的悖論來自於權力結構和職責分配的差異。媒體經營者與高層想的是如何利用媒體獲取政治資源和經濟利益，以達到自我利益的最大化，媒體的永續經營概念被短期有效的政商利益所取代；記者的工作在於報導，必須為報導的內容負責。媒體的工作環境完全可以操控記者的報導取向。雖然當前世界的報紙商業化趨勢已經成為大眾化媒體的特點，但電視體制的發展仍相當分歧，資本主義國家仍在亞當斯密和凱恩斯的自由經濟和政府控管之間擺盪。建構具有台灣特點的台灣在地化新聞，首推重視新聞倫理與中華文化。西方學者倡議

公民新聞，就是強調新聞具有號召公民參與提升公民道德和社會參與的職責。中國偉大的思想家孔子說：「非禮勿視、非禮勿聽、非禮勿言、非禮勿動」，如果我們的新聞也能從建構文明尚禮的出發點來看待問題，新聞素質就可以得到提升。

貳、全球 E 化時代的大眾媒體與公民素養

在網路資訊發達的 E 化時代，傳播內容已是無所不包、無所不談。因此個人與資訊世界的傳播關係就像是人和宇宙的關係。一方面每個人在選擇資訊時扮演的是主動龐大的自我主宰者，以自我為中心選擇所需的資訊；另一方面每個人在接收資訊的同時或之後，卻又像是被動無助的旁觀者，資訊無遠弗屆、多不可數，每個人如同瞎子摸象，試圖拼湊出各類事情的全貌和真相，但卻又不可為之。「資訊溝」（資訊差距）存在於各種傳播關係當中，資訊對人們的影響會因為每個人的知識識別能力而有所差異，有些人鼓勵這些差異，也有些人反對資訊與知識差異的擴大化。

不過，當人們對八卦商業媒體給人們帶來的樂趣而言之鑿鑿或是稱道時，這表示需要八卦媒體是人們平日過安定生活時的正常想法，但是這種想法卻會在人們生活中突然出現重大災難和疾病時受到挑戰，那種對前途與問題解決的不確定性和無助感，又會迫使大眾將希望投射在強大有為的政府和有責任媒體的專業客觀報導身上，這就是大眾的現實和無情、也是人性的多樣性和卑微性，鮮少人願意犧牲自我利益和承擔責任就是大眾的特點。所以，任何有為的政府和有責任的媒體勢必在正常狀況下忍辱負重、遭受挨罵且不求回報，並且認識到大眾只有在危難時才會想起你們存在的意義和價值所在。

一、認清媒體與大眾本質

專攻名人的八卦新聞是眾多媒體的最愛，因為不但大眾喜歡看，而且從社會影響力來看，它的影響力是屬於腐蝕人心型式的，所以又不會立即造成國家社會的崩解和災難，對於衡量媒體責任的辨識度低、衝擊力小，名人八卦屬於商業媒體和大眾便宜消費的對象。也由於責任辨識度低、衝擊力小，媒體和大眾容許了這種八卦新聞的存在。但是人們對媒體不是沒有要求的，大眾是屬於又要馬兒好又要馬兒不吃草的一群人，這一群人就如同媒體報導八卦新聞一樣，責任感低且危機意識不足。因為大眾早已習慣視媒體為茶餘飯後的取樂工具，媒體不但對公眾而言公信力不足，媒體自身也視責任為收益的絆腳石，因此一旦國家社會發生重大危難時，這類媒體就無法很好地處理災難新聞，無法發揮滿足人們知情的權利了。所以這就是為什麼在面臨緊急災難事件時，大眾經常對媒體非常失望，大眾不是痛斥媒體過度渲染，就是苛責媒體報導的消息不準確。

大眾會從眾多傳播內容中獲得樂趣，不自主地忽略傳播內容對於個人的影響，由於個人範圍不大，影響層面不大，大眾普遍缺乏危機意識。當傳播內容對一群人產生影響、衝擊時，影響層面會同時擴大。媒體和媒介守門人經常關心傳播內容對誰產生影響，而刻意忽略影響結果如何以及誰來處理這些影響。因此如果傳播內容影響層面大、並且影響產生之後又無法立即受到相關單位的處理，此時就會有人希望對媒體做出要求和控制，希望從媒體的把門這一關開始就可以將負面傳播的影響力降低。這樣的媒體控制與公民素養沒有直接關係，考慮的是在災難和危機面前的社會控制與危機處理。

二、大眾媒體反映公民水準

　　《佛學與科學》學術期刊總編輯王立文教授，筆者曾經向他請教如何看待媒體現況和公民素養的關係，王教授認為是大眾決定了他們想要什麼樣的媒體，媒體的內容也反映了公民水準和素質。王教授還把宗教派別比喻是信息場，每個信息場都代表著不同的網站，信眾可以選擇進入任何一個網站停留，也可以選擇退出。據此，沒有人瀏覽的網站將會消失，沒有人看的新聞就不會有媒體報導，如果資訊搜索者有足夠的自主性和選擇權進入他們感興趣的網站或是選擇退出，這種媒體網站和民眾之間的關係基本上是定位建立在相互需求的基礎上，比如大眾報紙的出現就是滿足普羅大眾喜好小道消息和奇異現象的心理需求，量少的精英報紙的讀者就是相對少數，這些人和媒體位在金字塔的頂端，代表的是分眾市場中的少數受眾和小眾媒體，小眾媒體扮演著改變的動力。

　　如果媒體內容的呈現，是被動反映了閱聽眾和讀者希望看到某些事情的心理需求，那麼媒體的積極主動性是什麼？台灣媒體惹怒名人已經是媒體八卦化的一種現象了，這種現象說明了什麼問題？是媒體原本呈現和普遍反映了台灣民眾性格中最刻薄、見獵心喜的人性中最壞的那一面，也就是說人心普遍險惡，存有喜歡看別人不幸的心態，才有這樣的八卦媒體滿足人們的各種心態和慾望；還是媒體突顯了和擴大了這類八卦現象，使得人們在有限的媒體選擇中助長八卦媒體大行其道？亦或是媒體八卦化之後使得人們再也沒有希望提升媒體品質的信心和願望了？如果說，什麼樣媒體的出現反映了民眾有什麼樣的需求，媒體的屬性和發展方向，也就是在當下社會氛圍和民眾願望驅動下而逐漸形成的，那麼敏銳的媒體人會先知先覺掌握民意的流動趨勢；後知後覺的媒體就是反映了已經普

遍存在的民意；不知不覺的媒體就是忽略民意或是枉顧民意。不論
是極權國家的媒體也好或是民主國家的媒體也好，都代表這些國家
的民眾希望有什麼樣的媒體存在來協助人們實現心中良好生活的
願望。

三、媒體的「四相」與無相境界

自由主義興盛的年代重視個人隱私和自主權，反對輿論和集體
人的意見對個人思想和行動的限制。所以民意如果是一股強勢力
量，那麼少數不同意見的人就非常關鍵，但也無法在一時之間改變
局勢、力挽狂瀾，只能不斷將自己的意見去影響他人、尋求支持，
慢慢使他人接受這樣的意見，讓少數意見也有成為多數共識的時
候。膚淺的事情總是容易完成的，所以膚淺的意見總能佔據大眾思
想的主流，形成了所謂大眾文化和大眾媒體的支柱，一部分媒體如
果能夠重視分眾而不強調大眾口味或是迎合低俗願望，也應該是
滿足一少部份人希望提高公民素養和開拓眼界的一種媒體型態和
制度。

商業媒體有自己凌駕於編輯檯上的大老闆，記者要對媒體老闆
的收益負責，公眾利益不是它們的首要責任，它們只負責取悅自己
的受眾，揭露醜聞、吹毛求疵是增加新聞的娛樂性，監督只是順便；
公民媒體是對社會的公民團體負責，為民喉舌、監督政府政策，新
聞重視有分析性和深度性；國家媒體是政府政策的傳遞者和辯護
者，向全民負責，新聞不是要取悅受眾，而是向人民報告。當國家
安定繁榮時，大眾就會需要多自由少管束，商業取向的大眾媒體位
於金字塔的下層，為大眾提供各式各樣的消息，大眾覺得高興就好，
沒有什麼要求；公民媒體則位於金字塔的中間部分，有責任的公民

團體需要公共媒體的公共場域，做為發表意見和建立公共論述的平台，公民媒體也要肩負提升公民文化素養和公民教育的責任；國家媒體是金字塔的頂端，它的報導需要強調政策分析和深入報導，冷靜處理任何議題，平時少有人覺得需要它，但是國家社會有危難時，國家媒體可以發揮闢謠澄清、團結民心、凝聚共識的作用。當國家媒體擴大時，公眾和大眾的自由領域會遭受到壓縮，當商業媒體大行其道、公共媒體弱小時，那國家社會只有八卦醜聞滿天飛，大眾看到的新聞當然就是這些不實的傳言了。

全球化下的網路化時代，國家媒體能夠具有關懷本土、放眼全球的胸襟，扮演宏揚傳統文化與提高國際能見度的角色。在民意高漲和多元管道暢通的 E 化時代，國家媒體無法一手遮天、愚弄百姓或是進行意識形態宣傳，它的作用應該是正面且積極的，同樣要爭取大眾的認同、信任與支持，只不過它不會是看人熱鬧、說三道四的小報，也不會是主宰人們消費意識的財閥媒體和霸權。如同王立文教授解釋金剛經中的四相：「我相、人相、眾生相、壽者相」。「我相」強調自我，「人相」強調以他人立場看事情，「眾生相」強調以多個團體的立場看事情，「壽者向」強調以天地宇宙看待事情。從「我相」到「壽者向」就是人生修養過程和看待事物的眼界。如果把媒體放在四相的境界來看，大眾媒體就是「我相」和「人相」的境地，因為這種受眾最多；公民媒體和國家媒體則位在「眾生相」，達到「壽者向」長治久安的境界。如同人要有壽命享受果報，媒體生命如果以商業價值為目的，不管公眾的利益，其結果就是媒體倒閉，或著是媒體奄奄一息最後淪為大企業兼併的對象。《金剛經》寫道：「若見諸相非相，則見如來。」如果人們放棄了分別執著，放棄自私自利的念頭，最後可以連相都不要了，達到不生不滅無餘涅槃的般若境界，以追求眾人至善圓滿的生活為目標。如此觀之，國家媒體則

應該超越宗教、黨派,甚至要超越國家的界線和藩籬,以此為最高奮鬥目標。

參、媒體危機

台灣在全球化過程中不應該被排除,而參與全球化進程,必須要有穩定的周邊環境。台灣元智大學對於全球化與台灣發展一直持有不同觀點,認為這次能源價格的危機,是全球暖化及過度環境開發的後遺症。傳媒發展和全球化的互動關係若即若離,新聞資訊的爆炸,使得媒體發展失去方向。但當經濟危機來臨後,反倒是傳統媒體那種令人心穩定的特性凸顯出來,而網路的浮華性和不準確性不利於準確資訊的傳遞。媒體必須杜絕暴利,適當盈利就好。當初台灣的媒體對此就沒有思考好,好的時候發百萬台幣的獎金,現在發幾千都困難。

一、語言貧乏導致文化流失

元智大學的孫長祥教授認為,以閱聽人的角度出發,新聞內容中充滿了各種語言和符號的暴力。文字語言承載著文化傳承與歷史情境再現的作用,因此擔憂新聞語言和文字內涵的貧乏會繼續導致文化斷層與民眾失智的現象。

現在的媒體傳播力越來越強,但是內容意涵不足。缺乏深度與廣度的媒體將可以被任何投機分子所利用。起因是國人對中文的忽略。這樣不重視中文的結果就是,以後最正確意涵的中文必須要由外國的漢學專家來解釋。這等於是一種中華文化的滅亡。媒體應善盡守門的角色,記者素質必須提高。記者在選擇具有暴力特點的新

聞時，要特別注意語言的傳達。當外國的暴力轉變成為國內年輕人的時尚時，這種劣質文化的入侵反而侵蝕的是本國人的文化與道德觀。記者本身如果不能理解許多詞彙和符號的原本意涵，反而起到助紂為虐的反效果。媒體的力量就是一種掌握語境的話語霸權。媒體素質的提升，成為文化保護和道德重建的關鍵。

二、台灣傳媒傾向「全球化」

《中國時報》總主筆倪炎元教授認為，台灣民主化進程中，媒體在如火如荼地邁向多元化與商業化的發展、擺脫威權時代黨營與國營媒體結合的生態環境之後，廣告大餅並沒有變大，因為進入媒體廣告市場的分食者變多了。媒體受到國際與國內經濟變化與金融危機的衝擊與影響反而更大了。

倪總主筆表示，對中國時報未來的發展有些悲觀，全球化與媒體跨國集團化似乎已經是趨勢，併購成為媒體的宿命，文人論政與辦報的時代已經過去了。報紙的成本已經不堪負荷，設備更新與國際紙張上漲都導致報紙必須另謀出路。利用中國大陸媒體同業的現有設備與資源，已經成為台灣媒體不可避免的一種趨勢。

戰國策國際顧問公司執行長吳春來則表示，選舉的技術與通路很多，而戰國策國際顧問公司能夠在市場上生存二十年，主要在於：深入研究客戶的需求與適應市場的變化；其次是對於政黨與政治人物保持一定的等距關係，保持中立與服務；誠信是對於客戶的資訊一定保密；了解民眾對政治與政治人物的想法，並用在政黨形塑和協助建立政黨的品牌與形象上。

三、避開商業邏輯的死胡同

「全球在地化」一詞，應可被看作是全球化衝擊之下所形成的「後全球化」概念。「全球在地化」因此是各地因應全球化與本土化之間衝突時，所產生的一種妥協與融合後所開創出的思路與方向。「全球在地化」或可被視為對於盲目遵從全球化信念的反省，也是全球霸權操縱者必須要面對的一種反文化霸權作用的勢力。在媒體全球化與國家界限在網路世界中淡化的現象發生之後，興起的反全球化力量，呈顯出凝聚國族主義、宗教信仰與民族主義的認同概念，強調「他者」與「我者」之間的二元區隔對立。這與我們試圖在全球化與在地化之間找到對話與合作空間是一樣的道理。在後全球化過程中，本土媒體應該如何因應跨國媒體的兼併與文化意識形態重塑問題，相信是討論「媒體全球在地化」特點的主要目的。

俄羅斯的報業發展長久以來均脫離不了對知識菁英的宣傳和影響，這與選舉時代電視媒體佔據普羅大眾的資訊主流地位很不相同。俄羅斯進入報業市場化的時代後，壟斷現象依然嚴重。從蘇聯到俄羅斯，政府從來沒有放棄以支援大量報刊的方式來培養俄國人民的文化水準。這種定位，在教育與文化媒體策略上，使得俄羅斯媒體難以在完全自由化與商業化的新聞體制中存在。報紙、雜誌仍發揮對部分重大政策的監督與諫言的作用。總體而言，俄羅斯的新聞與出版事業具有提升民族文化與公民素養的多元功能。俄羅斯「媒體全球在地化」的發展趨勢，已經逐漸使俄羅斯擺脫媒體在全球化商業運作邏輯框架之下，給國家社會、政府、媒體人所帶來的無解痛苦。元智大學通識教學部主任王立文教授在公開場合表示，報紙承載著文化與訊息的重責大任，因此報紙的資金來源應該要多元化，宗旨定位要清楚。報紙是盈利的產業，但要杜絕媒體的不合理

盈利，發展出自己的獨特方向與特色，才能在商業邏輯的死胡同中找到出路。

參考資料

王立文（2008）。《全球在地文化研究》，台北市：秀威出版社。

王立文（2006）。《倫理通識與企業社會責任》，台北：商鼎文化出版社。

張小虹（2007）。《假全球化》，台北市：聯合文學。

張亞中（2007）。《國際關係總論》第二版，台北市：揚智出版社。

湯一介（1994）。已經過時的「西方中心論」，評杭廷頓的《文明的衝突？》《海峽評論》，第四期八月號。

Held, David et al.(1999). Global Transformation: Politics, Economics and Culture..Standford, CA: Standford University Press.（中文譯本：沈宗瑞等譯，2001，《全球化大轉變：全球化對政治、經濟與文化的衝擊》，台北：韋伯文化。）

Huntington, Samuel P.(1997) The Clash of Civilizations and the Remaking of World Order.（中文譯本：黃裕美，台北：聯經出版社，1997。）

俄羅斯電視媒體與中央政府：

廣電體制改革與危機新聞處理模式[1]

胡逢瑛

元智大學通識教學部助理教授，香港《大公報》專欄作者。

吳非

暨南大學新聞與傳播學院副教授，香港《大公報》專欄作者。

摘要

　　本文研究著重在俄羅斯電視體制改革為電視媒體與中央政府在處理危機新聞時奠定了可快速溝通的基礎。作者首先探視了蘇聯解體之後俄羅斯電視媒體的發展過程，接著論述了在俄羅斯電視管理體制改革進程中全俄羅斯廣播電視公司作為廣播電視監管單位與企業領導集團的作用與特色，以瞭解俄羅斯電視媒體為何最後仍走上了國家化的道路。在俄羅斯面臨國家領土分裂危機以及高加索地區成為車臣武裝分子盤據和國際恐怖主義滋生的情況之下，俄羅斯電視媒體的職能發生了變化。看待俄羅斯危機新聞學中電視媒體與政府的互動，必須從俄羅斯希望恢復強國地位的心態出發，否則就無法理解為何俄羅斯媒體在憲法與傳媒法賦予新聞自由的環境中還必

---

[1]　本文曾刊登在香港中文大學《二十一世紀》學術期刊 2006 月 6 月第總 95 期。

須自覺維護國家利益，尤其是俄羅斯已經在普京領導之下進入了反恐時代，媒體職能有所轉向。本文最後將以別斯蘭人質事件為例，說明在全俄羅斯廣播電視公司的垂直管理體制的基礎之上，電視媒體與中央政府對危機處理的互動關係。本文認為，在普京總統對電視體制進行改革之後，俄羅斯三大聯邦級電視台在危機發生時將不會考慮收視率的商業利益問題，電視台將選擇重事實報導而輕評論的方式，儘可能地減少激情報導可能造成政府在危機處理時產生的心理壓力，以避免恐怖主義利用電視媒體管道進行對政府與社會的心理打擊，防止總體人民意志與國家領土再次陷入全面崩解的泥淖當中。

關鍵字：電視、管理體制、全俄羅斯國家廣播電視公司、危機新聞
　　　　處理

一、蘇聯解體後電視媒體的發展過程

　　自上個世紀的八十年代末期開始，俄羅斯的電視媒體在一連串的命令與法規出檯後開始發生劇烈變化。俄羅斯的媒體改革始於 1988 年戈爾巴喬夫（Mikhail Gorbachyov）[2]推動、雅科夫列夫（Alexander Yakovlev）主筆的《關於「公開性」》（Concerning Glasnost）改革的文件，文件主要內容是關於不許壓制媒體中存在的批評性意見，出版刊物要定期公佈黨的情況，其中關於黨報《真理報》的地位問題，以及報紙將介紹引進選舉機制的問題[3]。這首先影響了報紙的言論，報紙開始出現批評各個地方政府的文章，各家報紙以計算批評的次數來界定新聞公開性的程度，這種批評風氣首先在知識份子的專欄中展開。當戈爾巴喬夫與蘇共中央全會於 1990 年開始落實「公開性」改革並取消共產黨作為國家法定的領導政黨之後，新聞報導中開始對馬列思想進行攻擊，導致蘇聯意識型態體系徹底崩塌。1989 年 7 月 14 日，根據蘇共中央總書記戈爾巴喬夫發布《關於電視廣播民主化》的命令，媒體改革開始轉向電視。1990 年 6 月 12 日，俄羅斯最高蘇維埃主席葉利欽（Baris Yelsin）通過《出版與其他大眾傳播媒體法》，取消新聞檢查與放鬆媒體所有權限制，1991 年 12 月 26 日蘇聯正式宣告解體，12 月 27 日，葉利欽最為首任俄羅斯總統，簽署《大眾傳播媒體法》立即生效執行。俄羅斯新聞自由有了立法基礎的專門法律文件。

---

[2]　戈爾巴喬夫（Mikhail Gorbachyov）著，述弢等譯：《戈爾巴喬夫回憶錄》（北京：社會科學文獻出版社，2003），第 470-474 頁。

[3]　吳非、胡逢瑛：《轉型中的俄羅斯傳媒》（廣州：南方日報出版社，2005），第 109-110 頁。

　　自八十年代末期到九十年代末期的十餘年期間，俄羅斯政治體制的民主化轉軌帶動了廣電媒體的快速轉型發展。1990 年 7 月，俄羅斯國家電視廣播公司（RTR，俄語原文是 PTP）宣布成立，俄羅斯境內的中央電視台首度出現了雙頭馬車。1991 年 2 月 8 日，戈爾巴喬夫發布命令，成立全蘇國家電視廣播公司，以此來取代原國家電視廣播委員會的職能。蘇聯解體後，隨之而來的是廣電產業的管理結構出現了轉變，以電視台為例，廣電監管機關以企業管理形式出現，電視產業的所有權形式可分成三種：國家全權所有的俄羅斯國家電視台；原蘇聯國家電視台股份化後的社會電視台、現更名為第一電視台，政府機關控有半數以上的股權；商業業電視台像是獨立電視台與第六電視台，前者於 2000 年後已被國營能源企業控股，後者於 2002 年被取消營業執照，頻道被收回成立國家的體育電視台。目前全俄羅斯國家電視廣播公司的經營結構與管理結構基本上是分開的，由國家資本負責投入主要的聯邦電視台，這樣做的主要目的是防止西方資本的介入，現在俄羅斯的電視台基本上都稱為「聯邦的」或「國家的」電視台，作為俄羅斯電視將來走向公共服務體制的過度形式。

　　蘇聯解體之後，原蘇聯時期已經存在的全蘇聯奧斯坦基諾電視台轉為俄羅斯聯邦所有，由於俄羅斯聯邦政府已經有了俄羅斯國家電視台，因此俄政府決定將奧斯坦基諾電視台私有化與股份化，九十年代，銀行家的資金紛紛進入該電視台並且開始建立自己的媒體帝國，媒體開始進入寡頭的時代。1995 年奧斯坦基諾電視台播出的頻道已經改變，節目的內容也同時變為兩個部分，一部分就是白天播出的 2×2 電視台（"Телеканал 2×2"）和晚間播出的獨立電視台（НТВ）。第一電視台當時最大的任務就在於挽救俄羅斯民眾對於電視新聞的不信任感和枯燥的文化娛樂節目的現狀，挽回蘇聯奧斯坦

基諾電視台已經失去的收視觀眾。在這裏有一個問題就在於為何俄羅斯國家電視台不能夠負起這個責任呢？其中最關鍵的問題就在於，在俄羅斯國家電視台和奧斯坦基諾電視台的兩套人馬中的新聞和節目的工作人員，頭腦的思維模式基本上還保持在蘇聯時期，這為俄羅斯政府在貫徹自己的政策時帶來了困擾，那就是俄羅斯國家電視台和奧斯坦基諾電視台在新聞製作上都可以貫徹來自中央的政策，但兩個電視台的收視率都不太高。俄羅斯受眾的娛樂基本上還是以到劇場看戲為主，而新聞的來源基本上還是以報紙為主。在蘇聯解體後的幾年間，俄羅斯的報紙大多數認為俄羅斯政府的行政能力是有問題的，報紙上充滿了對於政府和總統批評。如果俄羅斯電視媒體能夠吸引更多的受眾的話，俄羅斯政府和總統就能夠擺脫這樣尷尬的局面。普京對電視進行改革之後，國家電視台的收視份額以有明顯的攀昇（見下圖）。

2004 年俄羅斯電視台收視率的調查

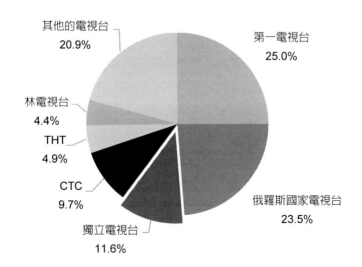

　　俄羅斯的第一批私有商業電視台是從 1991 年起開始發展起來的，由於私有電視台缺少控制及外國資金的投入，使得私有電視台開始進入蓬勃發展的階段。九十年代，俄羅斯媒介環境經歷了東、西不平衡發展的階段，據俄羅斯民間傳媒研究組織公開性基金會公布資料顯示，1993 年在俄羅斯境內已經出現了近千家私有的電視攝影棚及組織，這其中有將近百分之七十是集中在俄歐的莫斯科及聖彼得堡地區，這些私有化的攝影棚既協助所在的電視台向商業化轉型，同時又為電視台提供管理人才。1993 年，莫斯科的第六電視台與獨立電視台正式開播，這為俄羅斯當時的電視媒體結構帶來了多元化的新氣象。莫大新聞系曾參加衛國戰爭的元老級教授尤洛夫斯基認為，這兩大電視台為非國家性、新形式性、獨立性的電視台。1994 年之後，私有頻道如第六電視台和 2 × 2 電視台（現已經退出俄羅斯電視市場的運作）都在不同程度上受到了特定觀眾的歡迎，尤其是年輕族群。第六電視台是 1993 年 1 月 1 日由美國媒體人特德·特納與俄羅斯金融寡頭別列佐夫斯基共同建立起來的，該電視台通過衛星和有線系統播放新聞快報、兒童節目和故事片。2 × 2 電視台是俄羅斯最早實行商業化的電視頻道，它是與超級頻道合作建立的，主要播放美國哥倫比亞廣播公司提供的英語新聞和音樂電視節目。BBC 也向該電視台提供俄語發音的新聞快報，後來莫斯科市政府對該電視台進行投資並進行內部的重組。同時，在莫斯科市還比較有影響力的有線電視台有林——電視台，該電視台由莫大新聞系畢業生林斯涅夫斯基所創辦，電視特快－31 電視台、CTC、首都電視台，以及具有都會電視台性質的中心電視台，該電視台與北京電視台有著密切聯繫。俄羅斯政府對於頻道的數量有嚴格的限制，一個電視台占據一個頻道，因此俄羅斯的電視台都集中在奧斯坦基諾發射塔旁，由奧斯坦基諾發射技術中心負責信號的發射與傳輸，不

論公營或私營電視台都受到技術中心的控制。這個技術控制在普京執政之後更加鞏固了。

二、俄現行電視廣播管理體制概況、特色與作用

俄羅斯政府對於電子媒介環境的總體設想反映在媒體「國有公共服務體制」的形成，這個概念始於俄羅斯前總統葉利欽執政的後半階段。1997 年 8 月 25 日，前總統葉利欽頒布總統令《全俄國家電視廣播公司的問題》，1998 年 5 月 8 日，葉利欽又簽署總統令《關於完善國家電子媒體的工作》，葉利欽以總統令的方式宣布以俄羅斯國家電視台為基礎，擴大成立以國家預算支持為基礎的跨媒體國家壟斷集團──全俄羅斯廣播電視公司，在原有的全俄羅斯廣播電視公司的名義之下擴大規模，這一國家電視媒體的勢力範圍包括：俄羅斯國家電視台、文化電視台、體育電視台、俄羅斯電台、燈塔電台、及遍及八十九個行政區、自治共和國的地方國家廣播電視台和技術轉播中心。這一總統令的頒布表示，俄羅斯聯邦政府已經開始逐漸收回自前蘇聯解體之後各大電視台獲得新聞自由權，同時中央與地方共同建設新聞媒體的構想已經逐漸形成。

俄羅斯國有的電視媒體可以歸為三種所有權的形式：「國家全權所有的國家媒體」，其資金主要來自於政府編列的預算；「國家部分所有的國有媒體」，國家政府機關與民間共同持股，而國家政府占有 51% 以上的股權；「國營能源企業所有的國營媒體」，商業媒體在「國家化」進程中被國營能源企業並購，國營能源有自己的媒體委員會負責旗下媒體的管理與經營。俄羅斯媒體當中唯一由預算編列的國有媒體在俄文當中一般稱作「國家媒體」（national or state media），國家媒體在廣播電視領域主要指的是中央聯邦級別的全俄羅斯廣播

電視公司集團；國家部分所有的國有媒體，例如第一電視台，第一電視台在 1993 年與 1995 年分別進行股份化與重組工作，更名為社會電視台，俄語發音都是 ORT，金融寡頭別列佐夫斯基在 2002 年以前是該電視台最有影響力的個人股東，第一電視台百分之五一以上的股份掌握在政府各個機關與國營企業手中，由於普京不認為社會電視台的名稱與電視台的性質相符合，2002 年遂將其更名為第一（頻道）電視台，這是以該電視台一直處於第一頻道的位置來命名的；第三個部分是國營的國有電視台，由國營能源企業經營，例如前身是寡頭古辛私基「橋媒體」所有的獨立電視台以及別列佐夫斯基羅戈瓦斯汽車集團公司所控股的第六電視台。第一電視台、獨立電視台和已經消失的第六電視台都是普京在媒體「國家化」進程中以國營能源資金注入的媒體。普京在任內全面發展全俄羅斯國家廣播電視公司，由國家編列預算支持該集團資金運作，公司的管理與經營則由專業媒體人負責，公司總裁杜伯羅杰夫由普京直接任命，杜伯羅杰夫再任命地方廣播電視公司的總經理。

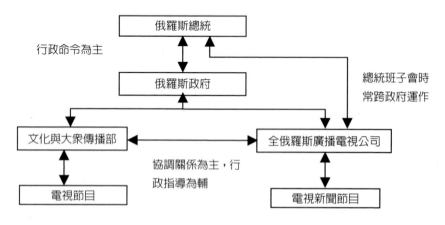

俄羅斯現行廣播電視體制管理結構

　　按照俄羅斯傳媒法的規定，電視播出所必需的許可證必須由廣播電視委員會頒發，電視許可證是每一年都需要審核一次，如果電視台沒來得及申請的話，許可證會自動延長一年。自葉利欽執政之後，各大電視台對於許可證的審核過程都持懷疑的態度，認為傳媒法對於許可證的要求過於寬泛，而使得該項法律都需要依靠全俄羅斯廣播電視委員會來進行具體的解釋與操作。1996 年該項法案的修正案提交到議會下議院杜馬，爭論的焦點就在於：電視節目在轉播過程中會用到屬於國家資產的電視塔，因而國有與私有的電視台必須保證國家的機密不被泄露，電視台經營許可證只是一種控制手段。全俄羅斯電視廣播公司就控制著電視塔的發射權力，也等於間接影響電視許可證的發放或延續。這個權力在普京 2000 年執政之後被更加實際地控制住。俄羅斯後期形成的電視台都采取主持人至上的經營策略，但在各大電視台都有一條不成文的規定就是：主持人有必要在節目播出的前一段時間內將自己講話的書面文字向全俄廣播電視公司提交，這樣國家或各黨派就自然形成了一道無形的新聞檢查屏障，但全俄電視廣播公司對於合資、個人、國家的電視台有著不同的要求，對於合資與個人電視台中側重提高電視收視率的節目一般都會放鬆要求，這是為了照顧這些電視台自身的商業性，但對於俄羅斯國家電視台却有著獨特的要求，如俄羅斯國家電視台必須在每個星期下午定時播出一個小時的《國會》節目，國家政府對此有一定的補助款。自普京執政以來，俄羅斯電視業的發展基本上以國家媒體居主導地位，個人電視台或莫斯科市政府電視台則以豐富社會生活為主，而炒作政府醜聞為賣點的新聞製作方式一般會被禁止掉。

　　有此可見，電視中央集權的層層垂直管理體制已經形成。俄羅斯的威權管理似乎很難在走向強國過程中消失，英國《金融時報》記者 Andrew Jack 稱普京執行的是一種「自由的威權主義」（Liberal authoritarianism）[4]。在西方傳播理論中，援引政治經濟學的概念來解釋政權對媒介的操控，以「國家資本主義」（state capitalism）與「國家統合主義」（state corporatism）對周邊世界如何看待俄羅斯與中國問題仍具有影響力[5]。九十年代是俄羅斯媒體資本運作的時期，國外資本介入電視、廣播、報紙、出版以及各種非政府組織，2000年以後，在俄羅斯政府起訴媒體寡頭之後，國家資本進入媒體，取代寡頭的商業資本，國外資本只能在非政府組織與出版業運作，與此同時，過去政府的官員也在非政府組織中擔任要職，熟悉政府運作，在西方與普京政府之間扮演著一種協調的角色，因此非政府組織經常在俄羅斯與西方國家之間起著與媒體相同具有的協調溝通的功能。俄羅斯現在已經不是「媒體集團化」的問題，「媒體集團化」進程在普京上任的第一屆任期內已經結束了，而未來俄羅斯媒體比較明顯要解決的問題之一，就是在國家媒體如何在過度到公共服務制過程中資金來源的問題，媒體「國家化」進程中國營能源企業資金注入銀行寡頭的媒體，下一步俄羅斯媒體的改革必須會是與經濟改革結合在一起的，俄羅斯經濟結構勢必先要從能源型經濟結構走向全面正常化的經濟結構之後，才能進行媒體公共服務制的改革。[6]

三、俄電視媒體的危機處理模式

　　2004年9月1日，在俄羅斯別斯蘭人質事件，整個事件僵持了三天，最後由總指揮官安德烈耶夫宣告鎮壓恐怖分子的攻堅行動基

---

[4]　Andrew Jack, Inside Putin's Russia (New York: Oxford, 2004), p.297.

[5]　李金銓：《超越西方霸權：傳媒與文化中國的現代性》（香港：牛津出版社，2004），第34-36頁。

[6]　胡逢瑛：〈普京的理想媒體角色：諫臣〉（香港：《大公報》，2006年3月28日）。

本結束。對於這一緊急突發事件，俄羅斯總統普京、媒體工會和電視台之間已經建立一套可以執行的危機處理模式：維持新聞報導的原有時段與時間和危機新聞報導理論：媒體高層達成共識要重事實報導而輕批評評論。電視媒體在這次危機事件中的報導原則基本上與政府所希望的低調處理保持一致。[7]這與原蘇聯時代黨與政府直接以行政命令控制媒體不同的是反應在媒體執中央政策的效率上，例如：普京直接認命專業媒體人杜博羅杰耶夫擔任全俄羅斯國家電視廣播公司集團的總裁，直接與總統保持溝通，無獨有偶，俄媒體工會的領導階層的成員也經常接受普京總統的召見，這種媒體與執政者的直接溝通模式，強化了俄羅斯媒體在執行總統意願和維護國家利益方面達到非常高的效率。這種媒體高層與總統直接溝通模式可以反應在別斯蘭事件中三間聯邦中央級電視台低調處理新聞的態度上。

根據俄羅斯《生意人報》報導，「9‧1 事件」當日三家晚間新聞時段的收視率急速攀升，甚至超過平日很受觀眾歡迎的連續劇[8]。蓋洛普媒體調查俄 18 歲以上觀眾收看 9 月 1 日晚間至夜間新聞的結果顯示，第一電視台新聞品牌節目「時代新聞」每一節的滾動新聞收視最高，其次俄羅斯電視台的新聞品牌節目「消息」系列緊追在後，獨立電視台的新聞品牌節目「今日新聞」的滾動新聞同樣具有強大的影響力。這三家中央聯邦級電視台的新聞時段是分開的，這基本上分散了收視的強烈競爭性，而增加了新聞收看的延續性與比較性。「時代新聞」這個新聞品牌自蘇聯就延續下來，口碑一直相當穩定，雖然經蘇聯解體，電視台多次更名，該欄目長久所建立的新

---

[7] 吳非、胡逢瑛：《轉型中的俄羅斯傳媒》（廣州：南方日報出版社，2005），第 259-263 頁。

[8] （俄）Газета "КоммерсантЪ" №163 (3002) от 03.09.04.（俄羅斯《生意人報》）

聞品牌。「消息新聞」是所屬俄羅斯聯邦政府的俄羅斯電視台的主打品牌和資訊發布的權威渠道，近幾年來新聞欄目收視穩定上升。獨立電視台的「今日新聞」收視處於逐漸滑落的窘境，但欄目在媒體寡頭古辛斯基時期建立的新聞口碑還是保留下來，今日新聞一直是以快速、獨立與刺激著稱。這次在人質事件中獨立電視台第一個發布帶著嬰兒的婦人被釋放的消息，幾分鐘過後，以國家聯邦首席電視台姿態出現的俄羅斯電視台率先播放了事件的新聞畫面。獨立電視台當日也取消原本預定在 9 月 1 日下午 3：40 晚 10：40 對遠東烏拉爾西伯利亞地區以及莫斯科地區晚間的節目，該節目是由索羅維耶夫主持的「接近屏障」脫口秀節目，節目原本要討論北奧塞梯恐怖事件，開播前好幾位受邀訪談的來賓都在攝影棚內到齊了，但臨近拍攝時，主持人突然接獲電視台主管指示，公開說明根據節目製作人列文與總經理庫李斯堅科的要求，決定取消節目的錄製工作。獨立電視台這個突然的舉動，表明了電視台立場上暫時不對事件進行評論的資訊安全動機，而決定以新聞特別報導的方式集中在事件本身的現場報導。這裏可以看見在緊急事件發生之際獨立電視台新聞評論性節目在媒體政治操作上加入國家安全考量的元素在裏面。這是普京執政後要求媒體在國家化與專業化之間取得一個平衡點與達成基本共識的體現之一。

俄羅斯媒體在 2002 年發生的人質事件之後即簽署了一份反恐公約，強調恐怖事件不能作為鉗制新聞自由的理由，但是媒體之間要發揮自律的精神，遵守媒體一致簽署反恐公約救人與人權先於任何公民權利與言論自由的原則。根據俄羅斯生意人報紙報導[9]，這次，俄羅斯媒體工會還緊急在 9 月 1 日發表聲明，希望媒體能夠遵

9　（俄）Газета "КоммерсантЪ" №163 (3002) ,03.09.04.（俄羅斯生意人報）

守兩年前媒體聯合簽署的反恐公約，並重申「在發生極端事件時，救人與保護生命的人權要先於任何其他權利與言論自由」。對於俄羅斯媒體在三天人質事件中的表現，事實上，筆者也上網瀏覽俄羅斯的媒體網站，發現俄羅斯各大媒體網站都將人質事件放在第一關注的焦點，頭條加上醒目的照片，還有專題報導。可以說各媒體官方網站的主要頁面都是人質事件的連續報導，其中兩大聯邦級電視台俄羅斯第一電視台和俄羅斯電視台的網站上也都加設了許多視頻報導。顯然地，相比於兩年前莫斯科劇院杜伯羅夫的人質事件而言，這次媒體與政府對於新聞處理的方式可以看出是經過仔細考量的。例如，俄羅斯媒體報導人質事件整體而言是及時、連續的，事實陳述多於評論，媒體加大了現場家屬的畫面。

不過，在這次事件中仍出現了政府與媒體之間的緊張關係。2004年9月6日，《消息報》總編輯沙基羅夫被解除職務，理由是沒有正確報導別斯蘭人質事件。根據這位前消息報總編輯沙基羅夫本人的說法，遭革職是因為與波羅夫——媒體集團（Проф-Медиа）領導層意見分歧。他認為自己是一位易動情的人，報紙開放的編輯方針使領導高層立場陷入尷尬，最終導致分道揚鑣。波羅夫——媒體集團屬於媒體人與銀行家波坦寧旗下，現在波坦寧已經掌握了消息報的主要控股權，他決定將沙基羅夫解職[10]。消息報另一大股東是國營魯克由石油企業公司。波坦寧是第一位以媒體人身份擔任前總統葉利欽政府管理經濟政策的第一副總理職務的人。看來普京政府又一次拿媒體人開刀，殺雞儆猴的意味濃厚。國營能源企業入主媒體是普京執政後的一大趨勢，可以填補媒體寡頭所遺留下來的資金空缺。這次別斯蘭人質事件的報導紛爭，又造成許多媒體人遭殃，國

---

[10]　http://www.newizv.ru/news/?id_news=10885&date=2004-09-07.

家化與專業化之爭在普京執政後一直處於相互角力的狀態。在這次消息報總編輯遭革職事件中，高層處理的方式將為政府未來反恐事業設定報導方針的強硬模式[11]。對於恐怖主義的報導是電視新聞的紅色警界區，《消息報》又是最有影響力的大報，普京在一片反對聲中仍解除了該報的總編輯。由此可見，媒體高層必須是與普京對危機新聞處理有共識的人。

根據《新消息報》的報導，俄記者協會代表亞辛·扎蘇爾斯基（Ясен Засурский）、韋內季可托夫（Алексей Венедиктов）、特列季亞科夫（Виталий Третьяков）、古列維奇（Владимир Гуревич）、列文科（Евгений Ревенко）聚在一起開圓桌會議[12]。此次媒體會議目的是討論媒體在當代俄羅斯的角色。這當然與在別斯蘭事件中俄媒體態度與立場有關，與會者還有美國前副國務卿泰波特以及布魯金斯研究院的研究員。美國專家在會上並沒有發言。總體而言，會議的宗旨都是在強調記者堅持真相的專業素養：第一，言論自由與新聞的快速性並不能優先於新聞的正確性，堅持事實查證與報導真實性是俄羅斯媒體近期發展的首要原則；第二，不要因為謊言而刺激恐怖分子。獨立報的總編輯特列季亞科夫率先發言，他表達了言論自由應區別於新聞自由的觀點，尤其是在緊急事故中更要堅持這一原則。莫斯科回聲電台的總編輯韋內季可托夫直接表示，在別斯蘭人質事件一發生時，電台立刻出台三項禁令：不要直接轉播恐怖分子的聲音、不要描述軍事行動者的移動位置、不要污辱恐怖分子。韋內季可托夫認為在恐怖事件發生後，記者不要發布道聽途說與未經查證的新聞，因為這可能會激怒恐怖分子。《新聞時報》總編輯古列維奇表示，非常愉快地看見外國電視台已經轉變了報導別斯蘭事

---

[11]　（俄）http://www.newizv.ru/news/?id_news=10885&date=2004-09-07.
[12]　（俄）《新消息報》網站，2004.年9月14日。

件的方式，對此，俄羅斯電視却遲遲沒有轉播。第一電視台消息新聞欄目的資訊部門副總經理列文科對此回應，俄羅斯媒體應當承擔起保護國家電視台的名譽的義務，俄羅斯現在正在處於非常時期，如果電視台要確定一些消息來源，媒體此時還要向反恐怖總部確定一些有爭議性的消息，如：人質的人數、恐怖分子的實質要求。俄羅斯媒體此時的要求是否恰當，是否會影響解決人質問題的進程，媒體與政府還沒有經驗，不過處理危機的官員應該要主動向記者公布確切的消息，這樣記者就不會在危機事件中憑空揣測。對於外界認為俄媒體受到政權的壓力，他認為，他自己沒有感覺有來自政權的壓力，只感覺媒體人要自律的堅持，但媒體如何自律及自律的程度是不好掌握的。莫斯科大學新聞系主任扎蘇爾斯基表示認同韋內季可托夫遏止謊言的見解。他認為，這次事件中部分媒體的報導充滿了不實的消息，與其要強調公民自由，不如先防止謊言的產生，因為充滿謊言的新聞只會助長恐怖分子的聲勢與成功的機率，這會傷害俄羅斯政權和新聞界的形象。

四、結論：電視維護政府政策，報紙監督批評政府

2004 年 9 月 24 日，普京在莫斯科全球通訊社大會開幕會上發表演說，表達了對新聞自由的看法。普京認為，在全球恐怖主義威脅的情況下，媒體不應該只是旁觀者，我們不能漠視恐怖分子利用媒體與民主加強心理與資訊壓力的詭計。明顯地，恐怖主義不能成為損害新聞自由與新聞獨立的藉口。資訊社會中媒體同樣也可以自己形成一種有效的工作模式，讓媒體在打擊恐怖主義這場戰役中有效發揮工具的功能，杜絕恐怖分子利用媒體施壓，媒體的報導不能傷害受難者的情感。新聞自由是民主基石之一，保障民主發展的獨

立性。無疑地，媒體對各級政權的批評是有利的，雖然有時這些批評非常不客觀，並時常帶有感情色彩，不被政權機關領導所喜愛。如同俄羅斯民間諺語所講，打開窗戶很吵，關上窗戶很悶。實際上，俄羅斯在建構透明化與公開化政權的法制環境。但是媒體也應該要被要求承擔責任和報導真相。政權與媒體兩者之間必須相互完成他們應有的任務[13]。現在在普京倡導之下，俄羅斯媒體終究要回到憲政體制之下的媒體，這樣的媒體特點就在於，媒體完全按照法律執行。在沒有法律規範的情況下，政政府與議會主導與媒體協商具體的辦法。媒體精英與政黨的結合，現在已經轉變為媒體經營與政府的結合，此時，俄羅斯媒體的政治化色彩依然沒有轉變，這表示俄羅斯已經進入蟄伏期，它在等待恢復強權國家的時機。普京總統更加著重在如何在法制與新聞自由的環境中，利用總統與媒體高層的直接對話，影響媒體對國家利益與國家安全進行保護，這樣才能使俄羅斯能夠在比較安靜的社會氛圍中再次崛起，邁向追逐世界強國夢的道路上來。事實上，普京對電視廣播管理體制的改革，對於危機事件爆發時能第一時間與媒體高層直接對話，這種中央媒體垂直管理模式對於如何處理危機新聞起到政府與媒體高層直接溝通的作用，可達到不助長恐怖主義的遏止效果。

　　作者在本文中特別強調俄羅斯國家電視台的發展，其中有兩個主要原因，首先，俄羅斯的電視頻道資源受到嚴格的控管，1990年俄羅斯聯邦第一次有了自己的電視台，以區隔蘇聯時期已經存在的全蘇聯的奧斯坦基諾電視台，當時葉利欽當選俄羅斯最高國家機關的最高蘇維埃主席，他並且掌握了這一電視台的人事權。1991年爆發「819」政變，俄羅斯國家電視台並沒有支持戈爾巴喬夫，而是支

---

[13] （俄）新消息報官方網站，2004 年 9 月 27 日。

持了葉利欽。九十年代，金融寡頭控制了幾乎所有的電視媒體與平面媒體，只有俄羅斯國家電視台屬於完全由政府預算撥款而沒有受到寡頭侵占的唯一電視台，這一電視台後來成為了現任俄羅斯總統普京推動強國政策的重要輔助工具，如此一來，俄羅斯的政治改革將會與與俄羅斯國家電視台的發展緊密結合在一起。普京上任之後同時也推動電視的國家化進程，反對普京的俄羅斯媒體寡頭已經逃亡海外，留在俄羅斯國內的都是與政府合作的能源寡頭，但是隨著能源企業在私有化之後再度收歸國有之後，寡頭在俄羅斯基本上已經改頭換面，不再主導俄羅斯的政治發展；其次，俄羅斯的報紙經過九十年代的自由發展之後，立場派系絕對鮮明，例如左派的報紙《蘇維埃俄羅斯報》、《明日報》與右派的報紙《生意人報》都是猛烈批評普京政府的政黨與利益集團的喉舌，報紙目前仍是俄羅斯言論最為多樣化的傳統媒體，不過由於這些報紙色彩鮮明、發行量小且讀者群集中在精英階層，對整體民眾的輿論影響比較小，俄羅斯政府並不限制這些報紙的言論，但是俄羅斯政府對印刷廠與新聞紙進口限制嚴格，使得親政府的商業報紙《先鋒真理報》、《消息報》成為發行量最大且最具影響力的報紙。因此，普京對媒體的控管主要是放在電視媒體上，聯邦級的電視台是唯一能夠影響全俄輿論的傳統媒體，因此普京上任之後重新整頓全俄羅斯電視廣播公司的所有結構與管理形式以及併購私營電視台，結束了葉利欽執政時期寡頭媒體參政的紛亂時代。作者從俄羅斯人強國理念出發來檢視俄羅斯電視廣播體制的改革，以此描繪出俄羅斯電視與政府互動的藍圖。

註：本文是與香港城市大學傳播中心主任李金銓教授合作的課題之一，在此特別感謝李金銓教授。同時特別感謝黎耀強主編給作者提出的寶貴建議，對本文撰寫方向很有幫助。在此作者一併表示誠摯感謝。

Russian News Censorship in the Era of Anti-Terror[1]

Feng-Yung Hu

Yuan Ze University, Taiwan

Abstract

Russia experienced ten years of transformation in the 90's of the twentieth century, when the Russian president Boris Yeltsin implemented the westernized policy. At that time Russian media were commercialized and controlled by the financial and industrial oligarchy. The second Russian president Vladimir Putin changed the media system after a series of accidents designated by the terrorists in the end of 1999. In this paper, the author tries to analyze how the Russian government controls the public attitude to treat any kind of anti-terror operations by passing the federal laws which stipulate the restrictions to limit the media activities and their coverage. After more than ten years' of political and economical transformation in Russia, Russia has entered an anti-terror era in the ruling

---

[1] 本文刊登在 China Media Research 2009 年 7 月。作者要特別感謝總編輯 J. Z. Edmondson 對作者俄羅斯傳媒研究的特別關懷和支持。本文也接受了 Edmondson 總編的建議和修改。在此表示對 Edmondson 教授和 China Media Research 編輯群最誠摯的敬意。

period of the Russian president Vladimir Putin 2000~2008 and after that the dual core ruling system with the following president Medvedev and premier Putin. Since the second Chechen War broke out in1999, the Russian media law system and news coverage of the Chechen War had changed as well. The Russian government regards the Chechen War as the necessary action of fighting against terrorists and maintaining the national interests under the official slogan of national dignity and territorial integrity. It's obvious that Russia has become one of the very countries where extremists and terrorists continue to act rampantly. When Putin assumed his presidency in 2000, Russia officially had entered the anti-terror era. So, after Russia in 1992 started to carry out a very liberal media law in which the feedom of press is protected and censorship is prohibited, how to establish an environment for media activities and their news coverage in the new era might be the crucial mission for the Russian government. The author found out that the regular dialogues between the President and media representatives for finding out the mutual understanding in the crisis of crucial events become the most effective communication model in Putin's ruling Russia and the model will be continued by the president Dmitry Medvedev.

Key words: Russian identity crisis; anti-terror;Law "On Mass Media" ; Law "On Extraordinary Situation" ; Law "On War Condition" ; Law "On Counteracting Extremist Activity" ; Law "On the Fight against Terrorism", censorship

I.The Era of Putin

Introduction: Intensive Relationships among Putin, Federal Laws, Media and the Public in the anti-Terror Era

After Vladimir Putin held power in the Kremlin in 2000, he started to implement his enlightenment policy by building up a very severe federal law system. By doing so, any problem will be resolved by the laws. For media activity, in case of any extremism and terrorism, the authority would have to convene the media leaders and ask them to do good jobs in accordance with the media law and other related federal laws, finding out the appropriate ways for media's reporting crisis events without damaging the authority's image in handling any operations in extraordinary crisis, war, extremism and terrorism.

Maintaining a positive communication channel and dialogue mechanism of the authority with media leaders is very important and is included in the president's agenda. There are four main federal laws signed by president Putin: the Federal Constitutional Law "On Extraordinary Situation" signed on May 30, 2001; the Federal Constitutional Law "On War Conditions " signed on January 30, 2002; the Federal Law " On Counteracting Extremist Activity" signed July 25, 2002; and the Federal Law "On the Fight against Terrorism" signed on March 6 2006.

But how to implement the mission of saving people's lives might be a crucial problem in situations without the participation of the public opinion through the media reports? Does the public really believe the government's decisions in a crisis proclaiming without any sacrifice of innocent victims by using the forces? So, all the problems are attributed to the media's attitude to the news coverage, and that's why Putin attempts to use legal ways to enable the anti-terror actions to be implemented more easily. However, this intensive relationship among the authority, media and the public must be established as the bases of the authoritarian ruling.

On November 1, 2002, the Russian lower house (Duma) massively and rapidly approved amendments to the Federal Law "On Mass Media" , less than a week after October 26, 2002 when the Russian special forces used chemical gas to end a three-day Moscow theatre hostage crisis in which at least 128 civilians died. The Duma's legislation immediately caused a protest from the major media leaders who thought the too broad legislation would slump the country into danger with no prevention of government and society in case of any crisis because of lack of early warning reports by mass media. Under the pressure and the official appeal signed by the Russian mainstream media leaders, president Putin decided to veto the bill in the last minutes. The Russian media's high-ranked representatives promised to find ways to cooperate with the government's anti-extremist and anti-terrorist actions in their coverage. This commitment was the basis of the later Anti-Terrorism Convention, signed both by the media leaders and the Ministers of the press and broadcasting. The Media law system became the compromise and negotiation place between the media industrial committee and the Russian federal government concerning journalists' access to any scene to gather information and report the news. The relationship between media and government turns out to be subordinate dependence under the preemptive and prosecution pressure of the stipulations and restrictions of the federal laws.

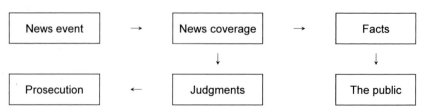

Ps. the communication model of the Russian media news coverage in the era of anti-terrorism as regulated by the Russian Federal laws

The crisis of Russian journalism is that the anti-terrorism clauses might be applied so broadly that the journalists couldn't report the important events and this could damage the public welfare and the national interests. Therefore, the regular dialogues between the President and media representatives and finding out the mutual understanding become the most effective communication model in Russia.

Media Law Amendments Concerning Prohibition of the News Content: Compromise Between Government and Media in the Anti-terror Era

One of the controversial and very severe amendments on Media Law stressed broadcasting and printing news "serving propaganda or justifying extremist activities, including statements of people trying to stop an anti-terrorist operation and justification of such" will be regarded as violation of the Law. This amendment opposition indeed has threatened the Russian commercial media professionals who had been used to the freedom of press after the first Media Law born in Russian history was put into effect in the post-Soviet Russian territory. In other words, in order to avoid prosecution by the court none of the media can doubt or criticize the government's operation in the anti-extremist process and show their sympathy to the extremists or victims who might be involved in the crisis.

However, once the anti-extremist operation ended, the mass media could have lost their first time to report the right event to the public. The problem is, should the public be protected from the fear which might be caused in the first extreme scene through the camera and photographs, or should the public have the right to know the government's action in this situation? What kinds of the details of anti-extremist and anti-terrorist operations should not be disclosed and divulged in front of the camera? What actions should journalists not to take during the process of crisis? What kinds of the journalistic reports are aimed at stimulating the audience rating for commercial purposes? Obviously, Putin tries to use the legal measurements to solve the constitutional contradiction.

In particular, the revised bill would ban the dissemination of information containing statements from people opposed to counter-terrorist operations. In this situation, journalists could not even interview the relatives of the victims and extremists, who might express unsatisfactory words which would be regarded as hampering the actions by the amendments. To protect the officials and assure that anti-terrorist operations proceeded smoothly, the media would not be allowed to publish data concerning the specialized methods and tactics of the security forces during counter-terrorist operations, in particular, operations to free hostages, as well as anything promoting or serving the terrorists and extremists. Furthermore, the journalists would be prohibited from divulging information concerning the personal data about the security services' employees and members of the operational headquarters for conducting counter-terrorist operations, as well as those people who render assistance to the Security Forces, without the consent of these persons. The Law also bans publishing information on technology for making weapons, ammunition and explosives.

These amendments to Media Law required the media acquire accreditation from the authority before their reporting; otherwise the media could violate the Media Law and encounter prosecution by the court. On the other hand, media cannot report any comments or critiques of those who justify and oppose the counter-terrorism operations. Obviously, the amendments are meant to protect the authority. Some Russian liberal media, opposition parties and non-governmental organizations voiced their concern over the Russian media communication situation after the upper house (Council of Federation) on November 13 2002 approved a controversial amendment to the Law "On Mass Media" that would severely restrict the freedom of the press to cover anti-terrorist operations.

About the resolution of the Russian parliament, Grigory Yavlinsky (2002), head of the liberal right-wing Yabloko party in the Duma, said the amendment would "create a basis for the limitation of free speech and the persecution of mass media." The Organization for Security and Cooperation in Europe and the non-governmental organization Reporters without Borders also criticized the bill, warning of the risks of censorship. The Journalists' Union general secretary Igor Yakovenko (2002) then said on radio Echo Moscow (Ekho Moskvy) that the Law amendments would grant the authorities "enormous freedom of interpretation" amounting to censorship. Igor Yakovenko said the legislation would effectively annul the 12-year-old law on the media, which outlines the basic rights of journalists. The amendments would prohibit the media from distributing information that hinders counter-terrorist operations, reveals tactics used in such operations or reveals information about people involved in them.

Most important of all, the crucial and urgent action transferring the media amendments legislation is from the media community's petition. The media leaders on November 13, 2002 signed a petition urging Vladimir Putin not to sign the controversial bill into Media Law and promised to develop an effective code of behavior for reporters covering terror attacks and other emergencies. The heads of the leading TV channels, radio stations and other media outlets gathered in Moscow's Grand Hotel on that day in order to notify the president of their standpoint on the changes to the law on mass media. The Press Ministry's top officials took their seats close to the chairmen of two leading state-run channels – head of the First Channel , Konstantin Ernst, and the head of VGTRK, Oleg Dobrodeyev; NTV's Raf Akopov, Irene Lesnevskaya of Ren-TV, the editor-in-chief of the Ekho Moskvy radio station Alexei Venediktov, the editors of Izvestia, Mikhail Kozhokin, Pavel Gusev of Moskovsky Komsomolets, and Andrey Vasilyev of Kommersant Daily; the president of the Glasnost Defense Foundation, Alexei Simonov sat together with his counterpart from the Union of Journalists, Anatoly Bogomolov. On behalf of the entire media community Ernst harshly criticized the amendments that "can be applied so broadly that they will not have the desired effect". Konstantin Ernst read out the text of the appeal to the president.

Under the pressure from the Russian media leaders, Vladimir Putin decided to veto the amendments signed into law. On December 10 2002, Russian parliamentarians, government officials, and leading media bosses agreed to cooperate on drafting legislation on media coverage of terrorism and antiterrorist operations; this was considered as the compromise between the government and media. Vladimir Putin (2002) harshly criticized the actions of certain media during the taking of hostages at the Theatre Centre on Dubrovka at the end of October 2002. This coverage of events was not an error – it was done deliberately "to increase rating, a capitalization to earn money," the President (2002) stressed. The President vetoed the amendments to the Media Law passed by the State Duma and approved by the Federation Council and proposed to the Federal Assembly and media heads that they should find a balance between restrictions in extreme situations and a society that is fully informed on the actions of the state. Despite the criticism he expressed, Vladimir Putin thanked Russia journalists for showing a civil position, and for their professionalism.

Russian Authority Tries to Change the Liberal Media Law System and Set up Restrictions on Media Activity in Their Coverage of the Process of anti-terror Operations

After the hostage crisis of the Dubrovka theater siege, the Russian State Duma, on November 1, 2002 passed amendments to the Law "on Media" and the Law "on the fight against terrorism", on the third and final reading. Vladimir Putin vetoed the bill due to the petition of the Russian media leaders. The amendments set up to ban the propaganda of terrorism and extremism. The bill introduced new rules regarding the coverage of anti-terrorist operations. In particular, it forbad the use of the media "for criminal activities, the disclosure of state secrets, extremist activities, and the distribution of information about production techniques of weapons, ammunition, and explosives". The amendments also prohibited the dissemination through the media "or otherwise" of information disclosing "special technical methods and tactics of carrying out anti-terrorist operations" and information hampering such operations. The media also should not distribute information aimed at propagating or justifying extremist activities, or of justifying resistance to anti-terrorist operations. The bill banned the media from transmitting statements aimed at resistance to anti-terrorist operations. Media outlets are not allowed to disseminate data about members of special forces, or about command centers for such operations, without their consent.

The Federal Press and Mass Communications Agency intends to defend the right of the media to cover acts of terrorism, the agency's head, Mikhail Seslavinskiy, has said. "It is impossible to imagine that serious major events cannot be covered by the media until an operational headquarters has been set up and the law-enforcement agencies have commented on them," Seslavinskiy said at a meeting with representatives of art, culture and the media. He said that the first document that he signs as head of the agency will be a repeal of the draft law drawn up by the State Duma proposing that the media should cover acts of terrorism on the basis of official information provided by the law-enforcement agencies. Seslavinskiy was dismissed by Putin because of his liberal position.

Nowadays, the theme of terrorism and extremism has so substantially expanded, that it is not only closely connected with social security, but has also influenced media activity concerning freedom of words and speech while a legal framework for counteracting hate crime and hate speech is established by the Russian authority . In compliance with the Federal Law on Mass Media is the Federal Law on the Fight against Terrorism, Clause 15 of which is better known to journalists and their readers under the title "Informing the Public of an Act of Terrorism." The duty to provide such information is not regulated at all. There are, on the contrary, some restrictions. For instance, when conducting an anti-terrorist operation, the public are informed of such activities in form and to the extent determined by the commander of the operational headquarters directing anti-terrorist operations or by a representative of the appointed public relations headquarters.

In accordance with part two Clause 15, it is prohibited to disseminate information which (1) reveals special technical methods and tactics used in the conduct of anti-terrorist operations; (2) could hamper the conduct of an anti-terrorist operation and cause a threat to the life or health of those who are either inside or outside the area of conduct of an anti-terrorist operation; (3) could serve as propaganda for justifying terrorism and extremism, or (4) concerns members of special units or operational headquarters responsible for directing an anti-terrorist operation or its conduct or concerning auxiliary personnel.

In the area of journalistic activity, the press reacts most strongly to restrictions on the spread of information serving as propaganda or justifying terrorism or extremism. According to the interpretation placed on this by the Press Ministry, propaganda in favour of extremist points of view includes granting media time to Chechen field commanders. Moreover, the authorities view such broadcasts as "an abetment to terrorism" stressed Yelena Kandybina.

In addition to the Federal Law on Mass Media and the Federal Law On the Fight against Terrorism, the Federal Law on Counteracting Extremist Activity was adopted in the summer of 2002 and updated in June, 2006. It defines extremist activity (synonymous with extremism, as set out by this law) through a long list of acts of a fairly broad spectrum in terms of their public danger. According to the Article 1 Main Definitions, for the purposes of the present Federal Law the following basic concepts are used:

1) extremist activity (extremism):

   a) activity of public and religious associations or any other organizations, or of mass media, or natural persons to plan, organize, prepare and perform acts aimed at:

- forcible change of the foundations of the constitutional system and violation of integrity of the Russian Federation;
- undermining security of the Russian Federation;
- seizure or usurpation of power;
- establishment of illegal armed formations;
- exercise of terrorist activity or public justification of terrorism;
- incitement to racial, ethnic or religious hatred, and also social hatred associated with violence or with calls to violence;
- debasement of ethnic dignity;
- exercise of massive disturbances, hooliganism and vandalism motivated by ideological, political, racial, ethnic or religious hatred or animosity, and also motivated by hatred or animosity towards any social group;
- propaganda of exclusiveness, supremacy or inferiority of individuals based on their attitude to religious, social, racial, ethnic, religious or linguistic identity;
- preventing legitimate activities of government authorities, election commissions, and also legitimate activities of officials affiliated with the above authorities and commissions, combined with violence or threats to use violence;
- public slander targeting a person holding an official position in the Russian Federation, or in a subject of the Russian Federation, while on official duty or in connection with his/her official duties, combined with accusing such official of actions listed in this article, provided that the fact of slander has been determined in judicial proceedings;
- use of violence against a representative of government authority, or threats to use violence against a representative of government authority or his family in connection with his exercise of official duties;
- attempt at the life of a government official or public figure, with the purpose of terminating this person's official or political activity, or as revenge for such activity;

- violation of human rights and civil liberties, affliction of harm on health and property of citizens in connection with their convictions, racial or ethnic origin, faith, social status or social origin;
- production and/or dissemination of print, audio, audiovisual and other materials (products) designed for public use and containing at least one characteristic listed in this article;

b) propaganda and public demonstration of Nazi attributes or symbols, or attributes and symbols similar to Nazi attributes and symbols to the point of confusion;

c) public calls to exercise of the above activity, and also public calls and pronouncements encouraging the above activity, justifying or supporting the exercise of activities listed in this article;

d) financing the above activity or any other support with planning, organization, preparation or exercise of the above actions, e.g. by providing finance, real estate, education, printing facilities, logistics, phone, fax and other means of communication, information services, and other material and technical means;

2) an extremist organization is a public [non-governmental] or religious association or other organization effectively liquidated or banned by court for extremist activity, based on grounds provided in this Federal Law;

3) extremist materials are documents designed for publication or information on other carriers which call to extremist activity, justify or support the need for such activity, including works by leaders of the National-Social Working Party of Germany, the Fascist Party of Italy, and publications, justifying or supporting ethnic and/or racial supremacy, or justifying the practice of military and other crimes aimed at complete or partial extermination of a certain ethnic, social, racial, national or religious group.

Therefore, the Federal Law on Counteracting Extremist Activity has at least two targets: one is to punish any media groups and religious associations, using any means including articles, print, audio, audiovisual and other materials (products or documents designed for publication or information on other carriers which call to extremist activity) supporting extremists (including forcing change in the constitutional system, violating integrity of the Russian federation, seizing power, establishing armed formations, exercising or publicly justifying terrorism, propaganda of exclusiveness, supremacy or inferiority) and planning (by providing finance, real estate, education, printing facilities, logistics, phone, fax and other means of communication, information services, and other material and technical means) the extreme activities that have been indicated in the federal law. The other is for protecting and legitimizing official figures and activities in extremist situations (preventing legitimate activities of government authorities, public slander targeting a person holding an official position in the Russian Federation, or in a subject of the Russian Federation, using violence against a representative of government authority, and so on). So media reporting falls into the threat of arbitrage.

Alexander Verkhovsky, the director of SOVA Center, thought that this excessively broad definition is combined with excessively tough sanctions against organizations and media outlets (it is important to remember that the law targets primarily groups, rather than individuals). Any organization may be closed by the court, even without prior warning, and its further activity banned in any form, just for one incident of "extremism" (while there is also a procedure for issuing warnings). The same applies to media -- even though you are almost certain to find something which can be labeled as "extremist" among hundreds of articles published by a typical newspaper. Organizations are supposed to publicly denounce the activity of their leader if such activity is found to be extremist. Organizations can be suspended for up to six months in an out-of-court procedure if they are as much as suspected of extremism. Should a suspended group continue its operation, administrative liability may apply; should a banned organization carry on, its members face up to two and its leaders up to three years in prison under art 282-2 of the Criminal Code.

In particular, in early 2006 as part of the restrictive amendments of the NGO legislation: someone convicted for extremism cannot participate in NGO activities. The reform of electoral legislation in the autumn of 2006 also made a reference to the concept of "extremism." It goes without saying that extremist activity may cause a candidate to be banned from elections. Besides the Federal law providing legitimate power for the official handling the extremist activities, an anti-terrorism bill that would allow Russian military to shoot down hijacked airliners was signed into law by   president Putin on March 6, 2006. The bill was perhaps the first to define terrorism in legal terms as "an ideology of violence. It gives the Russian Armed Forces the power to fight terrorism at home and across the border.

Another horrible hostage situation was connected with the Beslan hostage crisis, which happened on September 1-3, 2004. In September, 2004 Putin addressed the World Congress of news Agencies, stressing that journalists must ensure that in no circumstances do their reports from where events are taking place harm people who have become victims of terrorist acts. He also suggested that the information community itself can develop a model of work that would enable the media to act as an effective instrument in the fight against terrorism and would rule out any, even involuntary, possibility of helping terrorists in their aims. Terrorists often make cynical use of the possibilities offered by the media and by democracy in general to launch repeated psychological and information assaults on their audience in order to influence them in their own interests.

Vladimir Vasilyev, head of the Duma Security Committee, told journalists that the law stipulates many stages that an order to down a commercial airliner would have to go through before it is actually carried out. The bill was introduced by lawmakers in December. 2004 after the Beslan hostage siege. In a controversial bid, it initially proposed that the government be given the power to implement a "terrorist threat regime" which would curb civil liberties and press freedoms. Law enforcement authorities would have the power to monitor telephone calls in the area and even confiscate electronic means of communication. The most widely-debated aspects of the bill were provisions regulating the media. But with the "terrorist danger regime" struck down after the bill passed a second reading on February 26, the new law does not restrict press freedoms, and rights activists viewed these changes as concessions.

Crisis Communication Model: Regular Dialogues between the President and Media Representatives in the Crisis of Crucial Events

According to this tension between media and government concerning the media amendments approved by the two houses for anti-terrorism actions, if the bills turned out to be law, the Russian journalists and editors should first of all self-censor their contents of the news stories in any extreme crisis to prevent themselves from violating the law and being prosecuted. However, from the position of the Russian government which is responsible for operating any kinds of anti-terror activities, building up a law mechanism would provide the government with a legal foundation to negotiate with the media leaders and all the Russian media ought to obey the Laws in case of extreme activities. In this situation, the Russian government could recover soon at any time from influence which might be caused by its anti-terror operations in which innocent hostages might be sacrificed. Any media might have their licenses suspended and be asked to stop their activity by Federal Laws.

If we assume that transparent news coverage is beneficial to people's judging the fact of any event, then the main Federal Laws are used to reduce media's critiques and public debate. From this point of view, any anti-terrorism amendment which would be signed into Law on Mass Media might be regarded as the failure of the liberal media, or at least as of the negotiation and compromise between the government and media, which had been used in the free communication environment in the 90's of the last century. So this is the obvious characteristic and reflection of the country from a totalitarian regime, transforming to the democratic regime, but under the threat of the new authoritative ruling regime.

Communication model in the ruling of Yelsin

| News events | → | The public | → | The governmment's action |

2. Communication model in the ruling of Putin

| News events | → | The Dialouge between the President and the media chiefs | → | The Public |

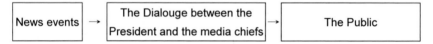

II.The Era of Medvedev

The Problem of Globalization and Russian Transformation

In 1991 the USSR collapsed, and Russia formally entered a post-Soviet Union era in which democratization and liberalization might be the vivid characteristics in the process of transformation. As the American scholar Samuel P. Huntington(1991), tenured professor in the Harvard Government Department, describes in his book *The Third Wave: Democratization in the Late Twentieth Century,* more than 60 countries have experienced democratic transitions since 1974 as the global trend, and defines this as the third wave of the democratization which also happened in Eastern Europe and the USSR in the late 1980s and the early of 1990s.

From this point of view, democratization is one of the most important activities and is regarded as part of the wave of globalization, and this phenomenon has enlarged its power from the economical area into the political area concerning the transition of national regimes in these countries. Under the wave of globalization with the characteristic of democratization, Russia changed her political regime and then experienced the crisis of cultural identification and social infrastructural inequality extending to the labor unemployment in the 1900s of the last century.

Generally speaking, as Huntington defines it, the wave of democratization started from the late 1970s with the transitions in Spain and Portugal and then extended to many Latin American countries in the 1980s, and gathered momentum in the 1990s, engulfing Eastern Europe, the Soviet Union, and some regions of Africa and Asia. But the issue of democracy remains a controversial, even a threatening idea in many countries, for example, in Russia. A lot of new social and economic problems occurred. The ruble lost its value after the Russian currency and market were liberalized. The Russian people lost their jobs and became very poor. In this situation, it is important to know the reason why Russia would change her westernized direction after a ten-year reform. I define the feedback of the phenomenon of globalization as the Russian style glocalization consequences.

The Crisis of Russian Cultural Identification in the Russian Psyche

What views of the impact and results of democratization and democracy might occupy the mainstreaming status in the Russian political decision-making mechanism ?

The result of Globalization in Russia first had its impact in the transition of the political regime. Yuri Fedorov(2000), professor in the Moscow State Institute of International Relations, Ministry of Foreign Affairs of the Russian Federation (MGIMO), points out in his paper *Democratization and Globalization: The Case of Russia* that democratization involves opening up their culture to different ideas and their economy to the global market and global competition. Fedorov stresses the importance of cultural attitudes, and this is what he calls the Russian psyche. The slow progress of democracy in many countries is often attributed to the poor articulation of interests in the political process. Fedorov shows, however, that Russia had the opposite situation. Many important groups believe their interests would be threatened if Russia joins the community of democratic countries and the global economy.

As I had studied in Russia for many years in the 1990s , I agree with the viewpoint of Yuri Fedorov, who has shown us the political tradition and characteristics of the Russian psyche within the structure of the Russian political elite. It is very important information for those countries which have experienced or are experiencing the impact of globalization and the process of democratization, that the Russian political elites very clearly understand if the Russian government adopted the westernized policies too much, Russia would have to sacrifice her tradition of culture and many other conceptions which had been formed and completed in the Russian society. If the Russian government could not solve the economical problems and living standard of the Russian people, the Russian people would lose their confidence in themselves and in their country. This situation happened in the ten-year period during the process of Russian transition after the Soviet Union collapsed. But how to resume the Russian cultural identification and set up the Russian new ideological system was the major mission for the Russian former president Vladimir Putin when he took his Presidency in 2000. Moreover, the following current Russian President Dmitry Medvedev continues to implement Putin's will.

Social Problems and Structural Inequality

In addition to the political transformation and the crisis of cultural identification in the Russian psyche under the wave of globalization and democratization, Russia experienced the crisis social infrastructural inequality extending to the labor unemployment in the 1900s of the last century. The paper *Russian: Globalization, Structural shifts and*

Inequality, which was written by the researchers of the Institute of World Economy and International Relations Alexander Vorobyov and Stanislav Zhukov(2000), analyzed the relationship between the liberal economic market and the social policy, especially concerning the labor problems, and emphasized the social shifts and inequality in six sections: post-Soviet social and economic chaos, external liberalization, dual economic structures, shadowization of economic activity, and segmentation of labor markets.

In the age of the Soviet Union, the communist country adopted the collective economy and national planed economic project. The price of the products did not reflect the economic cost. In the 1990s, while the Russian President Yeltsin accomplished a very liberal policy in the economic area, the national money currency and market was exposed to the world economy market and world prevailing prices, and the Russian people could not afford the imported products. When the Russian domestic prices of all kinds of resources, including gas and petroleum, could not follow up the world prices, the foreign investors and companies bought these resources in irrelevant prices.

After Russia became familiar with the games of the capitalist economy, and in the period of transformation of the 1990s, and after Russian talents became developed and governmental institutions had been designed for the liberal economic market, Russia started to adopt her glocalized policies. From 2000 up to now, the world prices of petroleum have been going up, Russia has earned a lot of money and has attempted to resume her national competition by editing a welfare budget for improving the living standard of the Russian people. By doing so, the Russian government can build up its political prestige and resume her national identification on the world stage.

Global Banking Crisis and Russian Financial Measures

How will Russia cope with the global financial banking crisis? It might be connected with the Russian diplomatic strategy. Russia's stock market is deeply influenced by US factors, because Russia's financial system has been also involved in the US subprime mortgage crisis with the Russian Central Bank owning US$100 billion of mortgage-backed securities in the two American mortgage giants Fannie Mae and Freddie Mac that were taken over by the US government. Investors have also pulled billions of dollars out of Russia because of concerns over escalating geopolitical tensions resulting from the military conflict between Georgia and Russia. American investors withdrew their capital from Russia, punishing Moscow for the war in Georgia. Concerning measures against financial crisis, the Kremlin might adopt more liberal policies to broaden Russian companies and liberalize the national banking system for investing overseas. The Kremlin might also build up a ruble reserve currency region to make Russia another world financial center compared with the US, the EU, and Asian hegemony like Japan and China.

Russia's economy is heavily dependent on energy prices, especially oil which has lost more than a third of its value since its record peak of USD 147 on 11 July 2008. By September 2008, the RTS stock index plunged almost 54%. As the article *Market Plummets Despite Oil Cuts*, published in the newspaper *Moscow Times* on 27 October 2008, was written by the staff writer Ira Iosebashvili, the government has pledged more than $200 billion to support the economy, including injections of $86 billion into the banking system, after the war with Georgia and falling global markets led to capital outflows since August that have been estimated at more than $60 billion.

Under the global financial crisis, the Russian government could process more regulations over the Russian giant companies which are usually called oligarchies. Prime Minister Vladimir Putin criticized Mechel, one of Russia's leading mining and metallurgical companies, which wiped out billions of dollars of its market capitalization. As the Moscow Times reported on 27 October 2008, in August, Mechel postponed the offering indefinitely, shortly after attacks by Vladimir Putin on its coal pricing policies and accusations of tax evasion which wiped out half the company's value in three trading days. Following Putin's comments and a subsequent anti-monopoly probe, Mechel agreed to cut domestic coking coal prices by 15 percent from Sept.1 and agreed to pay a fine equivalent to 5 percent of its 2007 coking coal revenues. Mechel plans to revive a preferred share issue and that would more than double the amount of shares on offer as Global Depositary Receipts.

The Kremlin has encouraged Russian companies to invest more actively abroad, but this has caused alarm in Western nations, which are traditionally suspicious of Moscow's intentions. As Reuters reported on 8 June 2008, the Russian president Medvedev said Russia is now in the 10th year of an economic boom fuelled by soaring prices for its oil and gas exports. Russia is now a global player and understands its role in supporting the global community. Medvedev said other countries had nothing to fear from Russian investment in their companies, since it was "neither speculative nor aggressive," but purely based on pragmatism. Russia would soon adopt a plan to become a global financial center and make the ruble a regional reserve currency, Medvedev said. The Russian leader said that recent Kremlin moves to liberalize the domestic gas market and reduce taxes on the oil sector would help stabilize global energy markets. Russia is the world's biggest gas producer and its second-biggest oil exporter. According to Russian's largest financial newspaper Izvestia on 28 October 2008, the Russian Central Bank will acquire more liberal conditions to invest abroad after the global subprime mortgage crisis.

References

Alexander Verkhovsky (2007). Report at the OSCE Supplementary Human Dimension Meeting on Freedom of Assembly, Vienna.

Artemov V. L. (2002). Mass communication and the mass consciousness, No.2, MGIMO.

Artemov V. L. (2005). Mass communication and the mass consciousness, No.4, MGIMO.

Artemov V. L. (2009). The problem of Globalization: the Russian perspective, report in Yuan Ze University, Taiwan.

Dobrenko V. I. (2005). Globalization and Russia, Frontier of Sociology, No.37.

Gateway to Russia (2002). Russian authorities, media ready to cooperate on drafting key laws.

Gazeta.ru(2002).Media calls on Putin to veto new curbs.

RIA Novosti(2004). March 22.

Russian media(2002). Opposition voice concern over the reporting restrictions. AFP, November 13.

Sarah Karush(2002). Free-speech advocates urge Putin not to sign anti-terrorism legislation that limits media's rights, Associated Press, November 14.

The Moscow news(August 8, 2006) in English edition.

Yelena Kandybina(2002), Coverage of the Chechen War in the Russian press – a legal expert's viewpoint, Special Report for Prague Watchdog. Yelena Kandybina is the lawyer at the Center for Journalism in Extreme Situations.

http://www.gazeta.ru/2002/11/21/Mediacallson.shtml.

http://www.kremlin.ru/eng/priorities/events21888/2002.shtml.

http://xeno.sova-center.ru/6BA2468/6BB4254/8F4D1DA?print=on.

http://www.kremlin.ru/eng/priorities/events21888/2004.shtml..

The Relationship Between Putin's Media Reforms and His Ideological Tendency[1]

Feng-Yung Hu & Fei Wu,

GuangZhou JiNan University, China

Abstract

In the post-soviet Russia, the Russian media reforms characterized as the deregulation of national media policy, privatized national-communist party media, and rapid concentration of the commercial-industrial oligarch's capitalism in the ruling era of Boris Yelsin in the 90's of the last century. On the contrary, after Putin took his office in 2000, nationalizing mass media and multiplizing ownership of commercial media to deconcentralize the Russian oligarchy media might be one of the obvious characteristics in the era of Vladimir Putin. According to these two different media development directions, we assume that the Russian media reforms must be associated with the Putin's ideological tendency in the scope of globalization and national

---

[1] 本文曾刊登於國際學術期刊《跨文化傳播研究》(Intercultural Communication Studies, U.S.A),2007。

interests.   In this paper the authors will first of all analyze the media controling institutions. Secondly, we want to know what's the Putin's ideological tendency in balancing the different attitudes and positions toward the globalization.

Introduction

Vladimir Putin was selected as the Russian president in 2000 march, and from that moment Russia formally entered an era of Putin, the man who has the background of KGB but leads the Russian people fighting against the terrorists and separatists in the Russian territory by launching out an intensive military campaign in Chechnya during his occupying the position of the Russian prime minister before the parliamentary election of Duma in 1999 and the Presidential election of 2000.

While Boris Yeltsin implemented the liberal policy which reflected in the freedom of the press, regular elections and free economical market system but produced so-called financial-industrial oligarchs who controlled the Russian media and national energy enterprises, which had been privatized in Yeltsin's governance period. As the successor of Yeltsin, Putin has his own viewpoint of national development, which differs from Yeltsin. Putin ever expressed publicly that the Russian politicians whom he adores are the Peter I and Andropov. In the process of nationalization, Putin in the right hand controls the national energy enterprises which can be the tool of manipulating foreign exchanges and imlementing the Russian foreign policy, and on the other hand Putin controls the mass media especially the broadcasting which can be the effective weapon to shape the new Russian ideological system in the process of his strenthening country attempt.

In 2004, some editors and journalists of the most popular daily newspaper Izvestiya, supporting arrested Mikhail Khodorkovsky , the former president of the oil company Yukos & bank of Menatep, left the Izvestiya newspaper organization, and the protest event arosed an earthquake in the press. So, whether the Russian media elites support Putin's ideology of national development will be the stable factor of the Russian society. The purpose of this paper represents that the Russian media and economical elites still want more power for self-controlling media under the Putin's media manipulation.

We assume that the freedom of the press and media globalization meet Putin's economical and cultural policy for the integration with the European countries, on the contrary, the Russian political elites tend to adopt the conservative attitude anti the globalization, because they assert that Russia has rich natural resources and gets nothing from the economical globalization. For example, the foundation of the Counter-Oligarchic Front of Russia (COFR) was he first officially antiglobalistic Russian movement. This new organization is headed by the two Left Front leaders, Boris Kagarlitsky and Alexey Nezhivoi. COFR has chosen its first target TNK-BP and its partner Alfa Group, headed by Mikhail Fridman, calling them "an example of the most harmful and dangerous oligarchic structure." We can find these kinds opinions of anti-globalization in some other articles which were written by the Russian intellectuals and politicians, were published in the Russian newspapers. Due to the limit of the research time and fund, the authors will not list all these related articles but only provide an viewpoint of analyzing the relationships among the Russian president Vladimir Putin, media elites, political elites and intellectuals who make up the mainstream of the Russian policy-making.

Vertical Broadcasting Controlling Institution

The mass media reform is going under the nationalization with the stimulation of the globalization. In our study of this paper we assume that Putin thinks there isn't much more contradiction between the nationalism and globalization, because one crucial factor fostering globalization to solve the contradtion is fighting the Russian oligarchies, who basically empower the oils, banks and communication areas. So, fighting the Russian oligarchies will first of all solve the problem of concentration of the commercial capitalism. The national capital will be the main support for the media development and fewer part of the foreign investment would the supply for multiplizing the media ownership market. Here appears a disputed conception that is national media monopoly is the protection of the national and social interests, but commercial media monopoly is the purloiner of the natural resources. The Russian government's mass media controlling institution can be focused on the three aspects: natural resources, information sources, and governmental subsidies.

Concerning of the broadcasting controlling institution:

Firstly, The government controls and monopolizes the TV towers of broadcasting, in other words, all the national and commercial media corporations rely on the contracts with the national TV tower technological transmitting center "Octankino" and its distributions in the regions.

Secondly, The government controls the channels and issuing licenses of broadcasting, in other words, if any broadcasting appliers or owners can't meet the government's reqirements, the government will not provide or prolong the licenses of Broadcasting. So, we can say that the broadcasting is limited to the national broadcasting companies and thoses commercial broadcasting companies, possessing good relationships with the government. The broadcasting market strongly relies on the government's regulation and control.

Thirdly, The leading broadcasting company - the All-Russian National TV and Radio Broadcasting Company controls the budgets and personnel assignments of all the distributions of the regional national broadcasting technological centers and companies. In other words, the centralization of media controlling and management of the federal government is formed and much more strongly strengthened in the ruling era of Putin than in the era of Yelsin.

Technical Print Controlling Institution

After the Russian media were deregulated for free developing, the recent seven years president Putin has taken more attention to the management of media market and organization operation. But how to take charge of media in the democratic ways that cannot effect interests of media and oligarch might be the big challenge for Putin. In Russia what was a common sense that had existed in Soviet Russia was almost the media staff and personnels who graduated and were recruited from faculty of Journalism at Moscow State University and foreign news reporters from Moscow State Institute of International Relations. If Putin controls media through the direct way in Journalism faculty's class-setting that must make the staff of media and oligarch combine together anti the disputed governmental administration fighting for the freedom of the press. So that would be the stupid way for the civilian society. One way left for the president Putin controlling media was technical ways.

Cocerning of the print controlling measures: firstly, the government limits the quantity of printeries and equipments with the color print to the limited national printeries. Secondly, the government controls the prices of the news papers. The national printeries can get cheaper prices of the domestic produced news papers, but the commercial printeries usually use the imported news papers which have much higher prices than the domestic paper. Thus, the newspapers' printing relies on the national printeries. Those newspapers with color printing get more advertisements and attraction from the readers. Since the disaggregation of Soviet Union, the Russian oligarch ignored controlling printeries and paper factories, because oligarch considered that will cost much money in updating and renewing the equipments in printeries or paper factories. When the government controls the prices of news resources and increases the import tariff, the imported news papers and equipments would add the cost of production. The commercial newspapers become much more reliable on the good relationships with the government and that will influence on the media coverage and news content.

Since Soviet Union broke down, the Russian government carried out their first media law that called the most freedom media law. But most the Chinese media analysts still consider that the breakdown of

Soviet Union and confusion of Russian status tied with the freedom of media. Since 1998, at five years timing table, the Russian government put 2 billion US$ in printery equipments' updating, but all these money was only used in 30-40 national printery factories. As feedback the national printeries must strictly abide the requirements of the government, which are more strictly serious than were asked by the government of Soviet Union.

According to the report, the Russian governmental media capital capability was only 6 billion US$, and at 2008 it will be promoted to the 7.5-8 billion US$. So we can say that the development of Russian media was not as the way of media market, and it still remains the characteristic of Soviet Union that only we cannot see directly these means. As the Russian media law writes that building up one newspaper only needs one month and not more than 1000US$ for applying, and one TV station should take three months but need strictly auditing by the Ministry of Finance. So at this situation, the Russian government cannot supervise media as the time of Soviet Union.

Printery is essential element in the producing process of newspapers, and it controls the profits of newspapers. As the rules of media law, the Russian government cannot interfere media operation. So since 1996 the Russian government began its management in printery. For example, in 2000 Russian printeries of different types of ownership were almost 6000, and after two years increased1000 again. But all these printeries were used as private and commercial publications that they only can print advertisements and books rather than newspapers. In Russia printery can be defined as three types: national or central government's printery, local printery and nongoverment's or commercial.

National printeries, belonging to the Department of print and mass communication of the Russian federation, exist 37 departmentalism. In 1999 Department of print and mass communication came out one policy named Government Supporting Printery finished 2000. After the plan carried out 3 printeries can accept duty of full color printing, and 4 printeries can print half-colored newspaper. So almost Moscow and local published newspapers are printed by central government's printeries. Nongoverment's printeries only print 27% newspapers which belong to the government. There exist 1100 local printeries that take 31% quantity duty of local newspapers. Because the local government wants more independence from the central government. But the problem was local printery lack of money in updating equipments. So the central government's printeries control the print market.

In general saying that government's printeries make up not big number in quantity but they take charge of most of the print with money and influence. By now 80% printery equipments need updating that still effect the normal development of the Russian newspapers. Although the Russian newspapers' printing still in low level, and the Russian media reforms have been giving people impact of myth. This will embarrass Russian media in globalization.

Different with big sum of printery, for the paper factory in Russia only exist three big companies named Volga, Kandabog and Salicom paper industry companies. So monopolized condition is very popular and exists in paper production. Papers are sometimes only as lower market price supplied for government's printeries. Some anti government's magazine organizations sometimes import papers with lower price and print their magazines from Finland directly that can avoid interposing from government. In 2001 three paper companies produced 1.715 million tons for newspaper much more than 0.58 million tons in 1997. For the Russian government's printeries use papers only with the price of 420-450 US$ per ton that lower than international paper price of 550-600 per ton. But nongoverments' or those newspapers which have bad relations with the government often use higher price paper of 620-700 US$ per ton. After 1998's Russian financial crisis, the price of paper did'n change so much. Another situation was also very interesting that most government's newspapers always pay money on credit that can pay in cash in the medium or end of year. But for small or anti government's newspapers, they cannot get much material benefits that cause most of newspapers bankrupt. In 2004

Russian media advertisement capability was about 6 billion US$ and newspapers attract 1 billion US$ in advertisement. So we can say that the advertisement market still belong to those newspapers who have good relations with the government because of the government's controlling print institution of printery, printery equipments and paper prices which decide the existence of the newspapers.

Globalization and Russian Media Development

Russian professor R. F. Matveev (2006) in his article "Several methodological and theoretical problems of globalization" divides the trend and reality of globalization into several aspects: military, religious, ideological, philosophy, juristic, moral and econimical aspects. He assumes that the past historical and empirical experience of globalization presents us more military, religious and ideological expansional factors than the juristic and moral aspects. He said pure economical factor has no meaning to the global process. However, Matveev thinks that "Eurocenterism" and "Christianization" with expansion of totalitarian attempt make up the essence of globalization. But he still also stressed that every process has its positive and negative aspects, otherwise, we will produce new conlficts and sink into the intensive relationship, even run into catastrophe.

By the viewpoint of R. F. Matveev, we're going to undersatand how the Russian elite estimates the positive and negative impact of globalization on Russian media and cultural identity. From this dichotomy framing globalization, we might see the extremist opinion on each side. Moreover, from the Peter I implemented the policy of europeanization, Russia has been facing the dipute of route of state development between the europeanization and slavonization. Thus, in Russian elite there are two attitudes and positions to examine the globalization to the Russian state developement. One direction is supporting Russia joining the trend of globalization, the obvious action of which is to take the European standard to implement Russian reform, at the same time integrating with EU and strenthening the Russian political influence on CIS from its joining into NATO. The other direction is to set up Russian model, not depending on the foreign technology and international trade market, in other words, Russia should build up own market system from the world market system influencing Russia's both these two directions existing in the field of the Russian political and media elite. From the viewpoint of building up its own world market system, the Russian president Vladimir Putin, who took part in the SCO in Shanghai, expressed his global energy proposal with the giant energy company Gazprom. Energy resource is the most poweful weapon for Russia implementing his controlling the world political and economical system.

The paper concludes several opinions, published in Russian media, including the Russian newspapers, magzines, televisions, radio, agencies and internet, so that we can better understand how the Russian elite looks at globalization, because their view points might influence the Russian policy-maker's decisions on the Russian state direction of development.

How does the Russian elite understands globalization of Russian media?

Firsrt of all, the Russian media collaborate with foreign media groups in media business to integrate with world market system and to weaken the Russian financial-industrial oligarch's control over the Russian media.Russian media regard the first step or the most visible characteristic of media globalization is the collaboration with foreign media groups in sharing the holding stakes in Russia or on the contrary seting up the Russian media branch to expand their own presence in other countries. After Vladimir Putin took his post being the Russian president in 2000 year, he began to weaken the financial-industrial oligarch's control over the many important areas, including the media industry and oil business.

From 2000 year to 2002 this period was the process of the Russian private television companies nationalized. The Russian newspapers

Vedomost on the 24 December of 2002 reported about the revoke of license of two biggest commercial private television companies NTV and TV-6. Now the industrial group Gazprom is the owner of the NTV. After that, the Russian governmnet controls the three biggest national and federal TV companies: they are RTR, TV-1 and NTV. The chairman of the U.S.-Russia Investment Fund Patricia Cloherty said that Five private Russian broadcasters, including REN-TV, share 36.2% of the national audience today. So how the government copes with the private broadcasting companies after the end of oligarchy rule?

After the Russian governmnt nationalized the biggst and most influential private TV company NTV and clear up the stakes of media tycoon in the First channel TV-1, it seems to be that Putin is preparing to liberalize the less than 40% broadcasting market to balance the media development. From the news of RTL's buyiny part of REN-TV, let foreign biggest media group invest in the Russian media market might be the ideal way to keep the Russian media collaborated with the world media system. By doing so, on the one hand, the Russian government can reduce the influence of the oligarch on media and politics, especially during the period of the elections. The Russian government is still the owner of the three biggest national-federal broadcasting TV companies, which are the most authoritative source of the massive audience and has occupied more than 60% the broadcasting audience. On the other hand, the Russian government has no capacity to eat all the broadcasting market, joint-stock broadcasting company can solve the problem of capitals and at the same time can learn the management of the developed media companies and suck the personnels with ability from the foreign media companies. The news resource from the joint-stock companies can be shared as well. It may help Russian media companies build up a more transparent and efective management institution. So collaborate with foreign media groups, especially with the European media groups is the good way to intergate with the western countries and to balance the Russian simplistic national broadcasting market for enhancing the competitiveness.

We would like to take for example of this news source of RIA Novosti about the joint-stock corporate model in media business. RIA Novosti political commentator Alexander Yurov (2005) wrote an article tiled "Foreigners move into Russian media business " saying: *Europe's largest commercial broadcasting holding, RTL, is to buy a 30% stake in the Russian television company REN-TV…… This will give RTL and its parent company, the German media giant Bertelsmann, a blocking stake in the Russian channel. If the Russian regulators approve the deal, which would go ahead by the end of the year, this would be the first time a foreign investor has owned a significant share in a Russian television company.* He still wrote "*However, when Anatoly Chubais, the prominent Russian politician and head of Russia's largest energy company RAO UES, bought 70% in REN-TV in 2000, it cost him $30 million. And now, under pressure from the state, which wants RAO UES to streamline its non-core assets, the new deal has been initiated. The company is being forced to give up its share in the media business, ….*"

The author thinks that the deal was the aim of the Kremlin to centralize the information flow in Russia. He wrote " *Kremlin must therefore have endorsed the acquisition and that its aim must be to centralize information flows in Russia. Yet this thinking clearly contradicts the processes that are underway in the Russian media market. What some would call the "cleansing" of the Russian mass media has not prevented increased foreign investment in the Russian publishing industry. Last year, the publishing house Axel Springer launched Forbes, Newsweek Russia and Wallpaper in Russia. And since the Finnish company Sanoma Magazines bought over the Independent Media publishing house, Russia has seen collaborative publications by Izvestia and the New York Times and by The Moscow Times and the International Herald Tribune. By the autumn, Russian versions of the Economist (in collaboration with Independent Media) and Business Week (a Rodionov publishing house project) will be on the shelves. Meanwhile, the Russian media is expanding its presence in Europe: the Ekho Moskvy radio station has announced it wants to open a branch in*

Ukraine, and the business daily Kommersant is launching a local publication there. Vedomosti, another business daily, also has its sights set on Ukraine. So it seems that the main trend in the Russian media business is globalization."

Secondly, the TV and radio companies build the Public broadcasting station to integrate with the European media institution and European civilization In Russia part of intellectual elite who supports Russia integrating with Europe regards themselves as European, and this European cultural identity is obvious in media intellectual, media elites and journalists. The Russian famous media law expert Mihkail Fedotov, interviewed by the Nataliya Rostova of the Russian newspaper Nezavisimaya Gazeta, is the project designer of the Russian national public station draft saying that Russia should integrate with the European civilization, so the Russian broadcasting company VGTRK should let the national television RTR to be the public television which will make the national interests accord with the public interest. He thinks that the national interest should not differ from the public interest and this is the democratic country should have this characteristic.

Conclusion about Globalization and Media Nationalization

According to our study, we thought that anti-globalization emotion occurred among the political elites, but economical elites and media owners prefer more globalization to attract foreign investments, advaced technology and brainpower talents to run the world market. Putin's attitude toward the globalization as the coordinator and policy-maker is quite important. We observed that Putin keeps strengthening the power of the national media in the process of controlling institutions to control the media market structure and at the same time allows the commercial media to collaborate with the foreign media corporations in ownership and staff exchange to weaken the concentration of the Russian oligarchy capitalism that might influence and interfere the policy-making process.

From this point of view, Putin might support the globalization process step by step and take use of globalization to multiplize the Russian commercial oligarchy media market but the national media institutions remain playing the role of controlling media of the mainstream of information flow in Russia. In the process of media production industry, the news coverage is the end of that process influencing the public opinions, but technology is the fundamental infrastructure. For Putin, controlling the technological institutions would be much better than the content censorship, and between them will be the negotiation among the president, political elite and media elite.

References

Andrey Kolesnikov(2006), Putin Brings Iran into the SCO, Kommersant, June 16,2006. http://www.kommersant.com/page.asp?id=682607.

Alexander Yurov(2005), Foreigners move into Russian media business, 06/07/2005, http://en.rian.ru/analysis/20050706/40855251.html.

Charikov A. (1998). Russia: Country Report. In: *Country Reports: Recent Developments in Media Broadcasting and Media Research*. GEAR Annual Conference, Stockholm, 9-13 May 1998, pp.52-54.

Sparks C. and Reading A. (1998). Communication, Capitalism and the Mass Media, London: Sage.

Два в одном канале. ОРТ и НТВ теперь зависит от ВГТРК // Коммерсантъ (1998. 5.12).

Матвеев Р. Ф(2006)., Некоторые методологические и теоретические проблемы глобализации // http://liber.rsuh.ru/Conf/Globalization/matveev. htm. Валентин Федоров, замдиректора Института Европы РАН, экс-губернатор Сахалинской области, Глобализация как фактор отставания России, 《Izvestiya》 May 5 2006.

Наталия Ростова ("Независимая газета", 2 июля) ГОСУДАРСТВЕННЫХ СМИ НЕ БУДЕТ?. // Каскад (Калининград).- 04.07.2002.- 114.- С.7 Государственных сми не будет? http://www.ruj.ru/index_74.htm.

Russian Antiglobalists Make Business Plan, 《Kommersant》 Dec. 06, 2005.
http://info.paper.hc360.com/html/001/001/001/15035.htm.
http://www.mptr.ru/.
http://www.fapmc.ru/.

Russian Crisis Communication: Interaction Between Federal Televisions and President Putin in the Beslan's Hostage Crisis*[1]

Fengyung Hu

Abstract

On 1st September of 2004 at a southern Russian school in Beslan, which is located near Chechnya where the rebel-insurgents are actively appearing, suddenly occurred a hostage-held tragedy. Thousands of school-children, parents and teachers were captured by gunmen for three days without being allowed eating food and drinking water. In the process of Beslan's hostage crisis, the three biggest Russian federal televisions and central government's crisis handling techniques spurred disputes around their intentionally hiding the truth of how the rescue action was planned and implemented. It's worth to mention that Russian Media Union on that day formally announced an urgent statement, emphasizing obeying "anti-terrorism agreement" signed two years ago, and reaffirming that "in case of any extremity, saving and protecting

---

[1] The paper was published in China Media Research 2007-3.

people's lives prior to any kind of other civil rights. Freedom of words will be regarded as the most important news principle". From that statement, we can assume to say that the logic is: the freedom of words is only part of civil rights, but saving and protecting people's lives prior to it. Obviously, media self-censorship here is the first measure that would be taken into consideration in the crisis. In the circle of news manipulating process, then the government might release some instructive information to influence the reporting direction of media and tune up the coverage principle without any authoritarian force. Finally, Putin's public address in television after the Russian special military force's shooting action was shaping him as a savor, stabilizing and conciliating people's emotion. In this paper Putin's rhetoric skill would be analyzed as well in order to see the whole manipulating circle in the news running system. We found out that after Mr. Putin took his position in the Russian presidency, the Russian politics from that moment formally entered the Putin's ruling era. One of the most obvious characteristics of relationship between Putin and television is that Putin's image of television is a hero of crisis-handling and crisis coverage should not be critical to the government but focus on the rescue of the government in any extreme situation. In this paper the Russian media coverage running process in the Beslan crisis case is represented and analyzed. [China Media Research. 2007;3(1):91-102].

Key words: crisis handling mechanism, federal televisions, Russian Media Union, self-censorship, Putin, rhetoric communication.

Crisis, Media Coverage and Putin's Position to the Terrorists

The Beslan crisis, in which the gunmen had used tactics bearing the hallmarks of past Chechen rebel attacks, gave the president of the Russian Federation Mr. Putin one of the hardest challenges in his second term presidency in Kremlin. Putin was slumping in dilemma ： Should he risk a slaughter by following his past practice of sending troops to end such sieges, or try to save the children by breaking a long-held vow not to negotiate with so called "terrorists"? In the end, on third September the armed confrontation between special troops and gunmen was ended by bothside's starting shooting due to two exploded grenades causing a lot of hostages running out of the building where they were bound with explosive bombs by the terrorists.

After this event ended, Putin was trying to influence on the media coverage of how to explain the government's striking operation in this lengthy hostage crisis. The interactive relationship between the Russian three biggest electronic media and Putin's authority caused our attention. In this paper we'll see that the main federal televisions on which the massive audience relies on receiving information at that time had to cope with the government to overcome the extreme crisis, and at the same time to reduce any passive impact on damaging social solidified atmosphere with Putin' hero image and prestige in Russia. The news reporting model in cooperation with the government in extreme situation had been set up after this crisis since Putin rebuilt the Russian state and commercial media groups' territory from his first presidency in 2000. Media become the key instruments to smooth and implement his executive decisions.

After the terror just happened in Beslan, Putin rushed back from a Black Sea holiday to Moscow on Wednesday and cancelled a planned trip to Turkey. At the same time, the gang spoke by telephone in the morning with a well-known paediatrician, Lev Roshal, who helped negotiate the release of children during the deadly Moscow theatre siege in 2002. There was no progress of the talks. Previous hostage tragedy in Moscow was ended with big loss of life. This time in the process of negotiation, the talk with the gang was again charged by paediatrician Lev Roshal, and he said to the media that the gunmen had rejected offers to deliver food and water to hostages, but they had assured Roshal the children were still fine. None of negotiations was successful in the crisis without satisfying gang's requiring releasing Chechen prisoners. Valery Andreyev, head of the FSB security service in North Ossetia province, had no choice but to answer the questions of journalists "Why the special troops used forces to end the crisis?" Andreyev said： "There is no question at the moment of opting for force. We were intended to have a lengthy and tense process of negotiation." By the way, the Chechen rebels staged a similar attack on Chechen capital Grozny just a week before a candidate hand-picked by the Kremlin was elected as regional president. "The planners of the terrorist attacks wanted to make Russians feel the 'Chechen hand' can reach them in a bus, on the metro, in a plane and in a busy street – anywhere," Kommersant daily wrote.

The media coverage running process
in the crisis with the influential factors

The crisis event at the Beslan school

↓

Russian Media Union's urgent statement

↓

The government's instructive information

↓

News is tuned up: more facts, less critiques

↓

High supporting rate for the anti-terrorism action

The triangle relationship among the media, government and the public

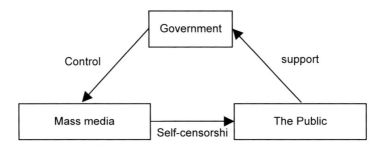

The High Rating of the Three Russian Federal TV Concerning the Beslan Hostages

Putin had taken this Chechen rebels for terrorists and emphasized that any kind of attack to the Russian people will be regarded as terrorism for granted. This connection was confirmed in Putin's formal speech televised by all the TV channels at 6 o'clock in the evening on forth September 2004. The content of speech is analyzed in the following part of the paper.

According to the report of a Russian newspaper "Kommersant" on the crisis's day, the audience rating of the biggest federal televisions' evening news raised rapidly higher than popular soap operas.[2] The evening news program "Time" of the First Television (TV-1) got the most audience rating, the second place occupied the evening news program "Vestia" of the Russian Television (RTR), and the next following one was the evening news program "Today" of the Independent TV (NTV). The concrete rating and proportion was showed as following:

---

[2] Газета "КоммерсантЪ" №163 (3002) от 03.09.04.

The rating & proportion of the three evening news programs of the three Russian federal TV

Channel	Program	Broadcasting time	Audience rating (%)	Proportion (%)
First Channel	Time	21.00	13.26	32.56
(TV-1)	Late Time	22.51	10.02	28.14
	Midnight Time	00.00	4.9	25.77
Russian	Vestia special report	20.00	10.02	27.8
Television	Vestia special report	21.59	7.96	20.12
(RTR)	Vestia special report	22.59	6.42	18.42
	Vestia special report	23.59	3.78	19.17
Independent	Today	19.00	5.86	19.71
TV	Today	19.57	10.03	27.97
(NTV)	special report			
	Today	20.55	10,29	26,72
	special report			
	Country & world	22.00	7.25	18.43
	Today	22.57	5.18	14.38
	special report			
	Today	0.30	2.37	20.31
	special report			

The rating and proportion of the three evening news programs of the tree biggest Russian federal televisions

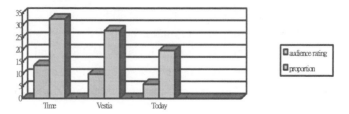

As we see, the broadcasting time of the three televisions is arranged separately, and this reduces the direct competition among them, at the same time enhancing audience's watching will and options.

"Time" of the First Channel Television (original Social public Television) was regarded as the most authoritative news program brand from the Soviet Union era. Although the First Channel TV was experienced the Soviet Union's collapse, the Russian transformation of Yelsin's ruling era and Putin's authoritative ruling period, "Time" is still the main information source and reliable news program among the Russian people because of its serious and accurate reporting. The 51% ownership of the First Channel Television is controlled by the state organs and the 49% belongs to the personal found and corporations.

The Russian Television is the state national media, which was founded by Yelsin's order in 1990, playing the role of federal central government's propaganda mechanism channel. These years the central government was trying to promote audience rating proportion of "Vestia" in order to control the influence on public opinion. The Russian Television is managed by the Russian leading media group—All Russian National Broadcasting and Television Company (VGTRK), the leader of which is nominated and assigned by the Russian president. The Russian Television is the best propaganda channel to the Russian authority for its not controlled by the Communist Party of U.S.S.R and the Russian media oligarchs formed in the Russian political transformation process. The Russian television is regarded as the best platform by the Putin's authority in transforming broadcasting system into the public service system. Due to the limited capitals and political motives, the Russian government has no ways implementing the idea immediately.

"Today" news program of former commercial Independent TV, which was belonged to the media oligarch-Gysinskye, was famous for his fast and sentimental news and independent reporting from the government, and losing his competitiveness in media market after Putin's authority started arresting media oligarch-Gysinskye, who was accused of tax evasion. Now Independent TV is mainly controlled by the state gas corporation "Gazprom".

In Beslan crisis, Independent TV was first of all releasing news without video concerning a released woman hostage holding a baby. Just several minutes after this, the federal state television-Russian TV was broadcasting the event totally in Beslan. Russian TV got the first permission to deliver reports by using the satellite transmission devices. So the government controlled the situation by controlling broadcasting process and technology. By the way the First Channel Television didn't set up special reports. People knew few from the television. News reporting was required not making comments before the situation was clear. Self-Censorship existed in this crisis. In a word, national security and national interest were taken into consideration in the first place in this case and media market benefit and freedom of speech were forced to concede in the second place compared to them.

In the 90's of the 20th century, Russian media experienced transformation in the process of the political regime's transition. Under the deregulation of the media policy, Russian media had a lot of space practicing freedom of speech. The government was often criticised by the commercial media. The authority thought that the first Chechen War was lost by media' opposite manner which had influenced the public opinion, asking the central government signing peaceful agreement with the Chechen rebels. So far the three federal televisions have not set up the all day full-run news channel in the Russian language for lacking fund and limited channels on the one hand, but most important of all, the government didn't want to release the satellite resources for keeping the censorship of media context on the other hand. Take the Beslan case for example, on first September of 2004's hostage crisis, Russian Media Union, under the control of the media management representatives, announced an urgent statement, emphasizing obeying anti-terrorism agreement signed two years ago, and reaffirming that in case of any extremity, saving and protecting people's lives prior to any kind of other civil rights, and freedom of words will be regarded as the most important news principle. In other words, news self-censorship was put into effect. TV news reporting in the crisis was limited to the limited reporting time, Media Union's statement for self-censorship, and state control of authoritative, political, economical and juristic procedures.

Theories Concerning Relationship Between Presidential Power and Political Rhetoric

The role of president is very important in a nation of presidential system, which was researched by Denton and Hahn in *Presidential Communication*, published in 1986. Among these nine aspects including constitution code, institution, multi-role, talent, behavior, decision-making, system, political course and symbol-cognition, symbol-cognition was regarded as the most important part to president in political communication.

Dan Nimmo, an expert on political communication, considered that "politics is talk". He thought that a statesman is known by talking as well as by his statements. Mass media have been focusing on the talking and activities of a statesman and of political groups at any time. By the way, even a silence, as a kind of expression with political motives, might be regarded as a piece of news. Besides, David Bell in his publication *Power, Influence and authority* suggested that there are at least three talking methods with political meaning as following:

— Power talk: dominating other's behaviors with intimidations or promises.
— Influence talk: influencing other's behaviors with personal credits and reputations.
— Authority talk: dominating other's behaviors with orders.

Political talk and communication mean handling with political symbolic language skillfully. There are three elements in communication of political symbolic language: symbol, objection the symbol represents and the interpretation to the symbol. The relations among them are explained in the picture below, depicted by Ogden & Richards (1923) in *The Meaning of Meaning.*

Interpretation

Direct relation   Direct relation

Symbol   Objection

Indirect relation

    The president of the United States always plays the role of debating basically for his policy in the management of a country, mentioned by Allen Smith and Kathy Smith in his book of *The Rhetoric of Political Institution* that was published in 1990. He also believed that debating art or speaking skill is the chief principle, whose functions are most obvious in the democratic society. The speech art and political communication which president possesses are the sources of his supreme powers, which could define, rationalize, legalize, persuade and enlighten something. What the president has said or done hides or communicates something in political process. His words, behaviors and rhetoric should be calculated and evaluated. Meanwhile, occasion and scene where published with words should be taken into consideration.

    The researches of language art could be traced back to *Rhetoric*, which was wrote by Aristotle, a famous philosopher of ancient Greece. He defined that language art was the ability of discovering ways to persuade others in any cases, which stresses persuasion with ration, sensation with emotion and admiration with morality.

    Richard Neustadt (1964) described in the *Presidential Power : The politics of Leadership* that presidential power is a kind of persuasion within system of authority-diversion, since the media channel is the most convenient way for president to clarify and explain the decisions. In the case of authority-division and media comment, president always makes use of debating communication to establish his professional prestige and purchase public support to smooth the execution of decisions.

American Scholars Denton and Woodard (1985) summarized in *Political Communication in America* that personal significant characteristics and public images are so necessary for a president including integrity, maturation, zealousness, resolution, dignity and equanimity as well as wisdom, foresight about nation's future, abilities to solve problems and judge quarrel with affluent knowledge.

In the book *Language as Symbolic Action,* author Burke considered that disseminator has two methods to clean up evil. One was self-condemnation and expectation and another was transferring evil. At first, one expects himself trying harder by the way of painstaking, doing away with evil, and gaining rebirth. Then, he tries to find out a scapegoat, which will be the target spurned by everyone. Burk thinks that the advantage of scapegoat is to create an outside enemy and reduce the disagreement inside. This view reminds us of that there are many examples about creating public enemies to gain the public's agreement in our history.

Thus, with introducing some conceptions of the above definitions of rhetoric, we would like to analyze the original speeches of Russian president Putin in the following passages. We can study his debating art by making use of theories of symbolic language to see his arranging the content framework. We can acknowledge how the President Putin called for fight against terrorism and united his Russian people to overcome the sadness caused from the crisis in Beslan.

The Context Analysis of Putin's TV Speech and Action for Finding Massive Support

Recording to this self-examination's asceticism and imputation dualism, we analyzed the TV speech addressed by Putin at Moscow time 6 pm, September 4th. In the beginning of Russian president Putin's speech[3],

---

3 http://www.1tv.ru.

he tried to cause audience's sympathy and the same manner accorded with him. So Putin used self-condemnation communication skill for reducing people's anger about the victims in the Beslan hostage crisis after the Russian special troops starting fire with the terrorists. Then he found out the attributes of crisis causes, orienting on Chechen rebels producing the hostage terror in order to threaten all the Russian people. Finally the Russian president asked for unity to support the government in striking terrorists. In his speech we can find out Putin's rhetoric in political communication process. The public address's structure could be divided into four parts as following:

1.Part of self-condemnation and expectation

a. Part of self-condemnation

Putin started his 15 minutes' televised address with the words: "There have been a lot of melancholy cantos and events in Russian history. We are living in a complex environment formed after a great country's disgregation, because this great country has lost gradually its ability of adjustment in the quick development of the world. But it seems that we have not prepared well for many changes in our lives. Why?

We do not have measures to cooperate with the condition or level of the social development in the political system, because we are living in the period of economic transformation. We are living in an environment in which the interior conflict is acute and there are antagonistic moods among folks in Russia. In fact, these conflicts or antagonistic moods are suppressed by the Soviet Union leaders' ideology. We stopped paying attention to the state's safety, and indulged corruption corroding our judicatory and legal system. Besides this, our country had been the strong system to protect our national territory, but now suddenly we cannot protect ourselves from the east to the west.

We do not react in time in whatever situations. We showed our weakness."

b. Part of self-expectation

"Now, first of all, I want to express my support and the same feeling to those who lost their children and relatives. Please reminisce the people killed by terrorists in last days."

"No matter how difficult it was, we still kept the core of the great USSR successfully, the new country we called it the Federal Republic of Russia."

"We are looking forward to a change, better and better."

"We have spent many years to build up a new, modern and actual boundary protection. And it needs roubles. If we professionally try it out in good time, it will be more effective."

"As the president and the chief executive of Russia, a person swearing to defend the territorial integrity of our country, and as a Russian man, I strongly believe that we have no choice, because these men in front of us are blackmailing and frightening us."

"On this condition, we really can' t and shouldn't live without vigilance as before. We must build up a more effective security defense system, and require an active action of legal routine department to deal with newly emerged threats."

"It is more important to activate people's sense of the national danger. The events, which happened in every country, demonstrate that the most effective way to counterattack terrorists is the combination of a strong country and an organized, united citizen society."

"Dear countrymen, obviously, the men who sent gangsters to make odious crime are to corrupt our nation, frighten the Russian people and expand the bloody civil strife in the North Caucasia.

At the same time, I want to talk about these following points:

Firstly, we will prepare a suit of overall measures focused on strengthening the unity of our country soon.

Secondly, I think we must build up a new interactive system of military force and connection, which is in charge of controlling the situation of the North Caucasia.

Thirdly, we must build up an effective danger solution system, containing new methods to deal with the actions of the legal routine departments.

And I especially emphasize that all the enforcement measures will be completely conformed to our Constitution.

Dear friends, we experienced the very difficult and humiliating moment together. I want to thank all the people who showed the spirit of endurance and citizen responsibility.

With our morality, courage and human unity, we showed powerfully in the past and we will in the future. Tonight, I saw this spirit once more. Although we suffered from tragedy and pain in Beslan, people showed the spirit of how human to be human.

We shouldn't be defeated by the sadness of losing relatives. The purpose of gangsters made us more closely and forced us reviewing many things.

Today, we must stand together. Only by this, can we defeat our enemies."

2.Part of imputation

"It is very difficult and distressing to tell. A horrible tragedy happened on our land. Everyone was very suffering during these last days. Our hearts are fluctuating with the Russian city Beslan. We do not only meet the murders but also the helpless children who have no ability to resist the armed attack. But someone is attacking. "

"Someone is coveting the profits and wants to take a share of spoils and someone wants to pour oil on the fire. There must be the thought that Russia is threatening them because it is a great country which has many nuclear weapons. So we have to clear this mind of doubt."

"In fact, terrorism is the means carrying one's point."

"Just as I mentioned many times, we have been attacked by riots or terrorism not only once. The terrorists totally lose their human nature and the crimes they do is unprecedented brutal. This is defiance not only to the president, the government and the congress, but also to the whole Russia and its people. "

"Terrorists think they are stronger than us, and they believe they can intimidate us by their brutality. They think they can disintegrate our will and collapse our society. It seems that we have only one choice now, beating back or agree with them. We surrender, destroy them or filch Russia to expect the terrorists can give us peace. "

"The problem we are facing now is not attack by individual terrorist, but the threat from the international terrorism. In this cruel and large-scale battle, our people's lives are taken again and again. "

3. The structure of president speech's framing context

As we have discussed above in this paper, political speech is regarded as a kind of public communication, which is made of convinced speech, information speech and entertainment speech. Since public speech is a single disseminator to amounts of audiences with language or non-language manners, media as mass communication tools make the influences of speech greater than the case of no media. Public communication consists of five programs: construction, arrangement, phraseology, memory and publication, mentioned by Haper (1979) in *Human Communication Theory*.

The paper divided Putin's speech into four parts: evil-self-condemnation-imputation-expectation, including short leading topic of ascribing evil, self- condemnation about disaster, re-ascribing in details, expecting the ending. Construction is simple enough to memory; phraseology is definite enough to show attitudes: to enemy firmly, while to people pitying and promisingly. The publication day followed the disaster finished reflected Putin's activeness, power and determination.

    a. The first part——ascribing evil. Leading topic of ascribing. " It is very difficult and distressing to tell. A horrible tragedy happened on our land. Everyone is very suffering during these last days. Our hearts are fluctuating with the city Beslan, Russian.

We do not only meet the murders but also the helpless children who have no ability to resist the armed attack."

b. The second part——self-condemnation. The main part is self-condemnation, alternately with expectation to encourage people and arise people's evil-cleaning, re-starting.

c. The third part——re-ascribing evil. Re –ascribing in details, drawing a clear line between enemy and us. Take the Putin's words as an example: this is the attack to our country. Terrorists think they are stronger than us, and they believe they can intimidate us by their brutality. They think they can disintegrate our will and collapse our society. It seems that we have only one choice now, beating back or agree with them. We surrender, destroy them or filch Russia to expect the terrorists can give us peace.

d. The forth part——expectation. The main part is expectation, companied with self-condemnation. The purpose of putting the expectation in the final part is putting forward the government for solving the problem in order to recover the powerlessness of government against terrorism in advance. Addressing consolation and writing a new page of raising hatred for the common enemy is the viewpoint of Putin, the last sentence in Putin's speech is: "today, we must stand together. Only by this, can we defeat our enemies."

4. Action-symbolic cognition: Putin flied to Beslan to see the wounded children

On 4th September the Russian president Vladimir Putin flied to Beslan, the republic of North Ossetia of southern Russia, where he came to the hospital and visit wounded children immediately. Then he carried on a conversation with the leading official of anti-terrorism headquarters, who was negotiating with Chechen's terrorists, grasping hundreds hostages in the No.1 junior high school of Beslan. Russian State TV channel and the First TV channel both broadcasted Putin's live picture transcribed previously. The author also watched this video from First TV website to analyze Putin's action-symbolic cognition .

First of all, the content of the TV picture showed that Putin at first visited the wounded in North Caucasia hospital, where also was cured the school director of No.1 junior high school in Beslan. Her health condition was becoming stable. Then, Putin came to the children hospital to visit the wounded children who had fallen asleep.

In fact from TV scene, then we could clearly see the face expression of Putin when he was gently touching a child, showing his care and mercy. That child felt being disturbed, and turned about to sleep again. Meantime TV screen showed without background explanation, only you just heard the sound of many cameras taking photographs, and naked feeling can be touched by reporters, wounded, officials and audiences. From TV Putin looked so sad, coming out of ward, lowering his head.

In the following the content of TV news reporting was Putin's classic speech with officials of anti-terrorism headquarters. It could be attributed as follows:

－The hostages' event influenced on the whole Russia: Putin pointed out that event wasn't the first time that North Ossetia was attacked, but terrorists began hurting children. Then Putin turned back to the president of North Ossetia and said to Alexander: the whole Russia felt painful for you and your republics, and got the same humiliation as you did. The whole Russia would thank you and pray for you.

－Define the conception of Russian terrorists: Putin considers the purpose of this event was to spread out international enmity and maliciously destroy stability in Caucasia area. Thus all the participants or cooperators with the similar affairs will be taken as terrorists or their gangs. Putin ordered to blockade the traffic and boundary of the North Ossetia for cleaning up the Chechen's gangsters totally.

－Provide all medical treatment on time to show government's duty: Putin expressed that Shayegu, who was the Russia urgent rescue minister, would stay here to deal with carrying the wounded to the hospitals and providing instant rescue. Putin called the name and the first name of Zasuohov and said: we will try our best to rescue the children and help them to get well. We will send the wounded children for treatment as soon as possible and by the way you need, as long as it can help the children to get well. No matter adults or children, we could provide them with any proper treatment place in our country.

The president of North Ossetia said to Putin: people suffered from tragedy these days, we cannot save the lives killed by terrorists even we try our best. We are all sad and feel the same with you. But we appreciate president's supports.

From the dialogue between Putin and Zasuohov, according to the negotiation process, Zasuohov who took short talk with Putin seemed hiding a little complain about innocent lives sacrificed in the Russian government's three-day lengthy rescue action. For example, Zasuohov didn't appreciate for the national leader's care, but put it in the end of talking. He emphasized that the people had a rough time at first, implied that the medical care couldn't save the dead lives. Zasuohov showed some dissatisfactions which referred to the Russian government's attitude in dealing with the problem, such as the warranty of the negotiation with the terrorists and so on.

Putin also knew dissatisfaction of Zasuohov, but he replied that special troops OMOH also sacrificed many soldiers in the process of rescue action. This was the most terrible things that special troops lost so many lives in dealing with terror events in the last 20 years, as this event came up to us very quickly, just liked the storm, and our inner department of special troops showed the brave spirit.

It appeared that Putin considered the evil was terror event itself, and this disaster was also the unprecedented sacrifice which had happened for the special troops. At that day, there were two planes of instant rescue department carrying the wounded to Moscow for treatment. It seemed that Putin tried his best to solve the problem of medical care, in the other part this will help himself remedy the no-compromise policy of the government to treat the terror, in which many hostages had already sacrificed.

Discussion

In Beslan hostage crisis, the Russian governmental strategy of manipulating media was very clear at that moment. Although the Russian Media showed so many views and pictures in reporting hostage event in time, the Russian government didn't take measures to restrict live TV transmission. We also saw from TV news reporting that a female journalist of the First TV was gathering news in the live place when both sides began battling on fire. Putin's media strategy in this case was opening information channel to show the rescue firing action in disaster to the whole world. By doing so, on the one hand, the Russian government could show its tolerance of not interfering media interview rights, and on the other hand, let the world see the terrorists' lack of humanity and the hard work of the special army in the three days rescue assault. Even America and the NATO all couldn't criticize the Russian government at that moment, but expressed their pity and the will of helping rescue, and left the opposed political problems behind.

However, the Russian government controlled the situation by controlling broadcasting technology and licenses. People knew few from the televisions. News reporting was required not making comments before the situation was clear. Media Self-Censorship existed in this crisis. In a word, national security and interest was taken into consideration in the first place in this case. Media market benefit and freedom of speech disappeared compared to them. The Russian state televisions played an apparatus role after Putin's media nationalized process. In the process of Beslan's hostage crisis, the three biggest Russian federal televisions and central government's crisis handling techniques spurred disputes about their intentionally hiding the truth of negotiation with the terrorists. From the first day of the extreme situation, the government's media manipulating mechanism started running. Firstly, Russian Media Union on that day announced an urgent statement, "emphasizing obeying anti-terrorism agreement signed two years ago, and reaffirming that in case of any extremity, saving and protecting people's lives prior to any kind of other civil rights and freedom of words will be regarded as the most important news principle". In other words, freedom of words should not hurt the saving live, if in that case, media should be regarded as the responsible agent for the sacrifice. So that statement was a crucial signal for media self-censorship in the beginning of the crisis, which led to few detailed TV news released to the public. It might jeopardize the right to know of the citizens, which is protected by the Russian democratic media law in the format of the freedom of communication in the Russian territory.

Finally, Putin's public address in television, after the Russian special military forces' shooting action ended, was shaping him as a savor, stabilizing and conciliating people's emotion. In the 90's of the 20th century, the government was often criticised by the commercial media. The authority thought that the first Chechen War was lost by media' opposite manner which had influenced the public opinion for asking the central government signing peaceful agreement with the Chechen rebels. So the Putin's media strategy has two hands: one hand is technically controlling media resource, such as the ownership and license of broadcasting, and the other hand is maintaining the contact with the Media Union and related media non-governmental organizations to influence journalists' news reporting principles in any extreme situation. In a result, in the process of news running, the news coverage would focus on the event itself but not the comments: more facts, less critiques. The end of the communication process is the public's positive feedback for the governments' urgent measures. So the theory of media function and their role was publicly expressed by Putin many times and it would influence the news principle of the Russian media coverage. Theoretical issues still make the Russian journalists slump into the ideological dilemma.

References

1. Газета "КоммерсантЪ" №163(3002) от 03.09.04.
2. http://www.1tv.ru.
3. Ворошлов В. В. (1999). Журналистика, СПБ.: изд. Махайлова В. А..
4. Грабельников А. А.(1995). Средства массовой информации в современном обществе: тенденции развития, подгатовка кадров, М.: Изд-во РУДН.
5. Два в одном канале. ОРТ и НТВ теперь зависит от ВГТРК // Коммерсантъ (1998. 5.12).
6. Егоров В. В. (1999) .Телевидение между прошлым и будущем. М.: 《Воскресенье》.
7. Закон СССР о средствах массовой информации, М.: Юридическая литература, 1990.
8. Засурский И. Я. (1999). Масс-медиа второй республики, М.:МГУ..
9. Засурский Я. Н. (2001). Средства Массовой Информации России , М.: Аспект Пресс .
10. Ирхин Ю. В. (1996). Политология, М.:РУДН.
11. Комментарий Конституции Российской Федерации (2000). М.:《ОМЕГА −ЭЛ》 .
12. Полукаров В. Л. (1999). Реклама, общество, право, приложение 4, М.: Знак.
13. См. Правовое поле журналиста. Настольная справочная книга, М.: Славянский диалог, 1997 .
14. Российские СМИ на старте предвыборной кампании// Среда, 1995, No 3, с. 13~18.
15. Российские средства массовой информации, власть и капитал: к вопросу о концентрации и прозрачности СМИ в России, М.: Центр «Право и СМИ», 1999. - 80 с. - (Журналистика и право; Вып.18).
16. Симонов. А. К. (1998). Средства массовой информации, М.:Галерия.
17. Согрин В. (1994). Политическая история современной России 1985 - 1994: от Горбачёва до Ельцина,. М.: Прогресс-Академия.

18. см. Шкондин М.В. (1999). Система средств массовой информации, М.:МГУ.

19. Правовая защита прессы и книгоиздания, М.: НОРМА.

20. Blumler, J. (1990). Western European Perspectives on Political Communications: Structures and Dynanmics. European Journal of Communication, Vol.5.

21. Blumler J.(1977). The Political Effects of Mass Communication, Open University Mass Communication and Society Course, Unit 8, Open University.

22. Deutsch, Karl (1963). The Nerves of Government: Models of Political Communication and Control, New York：Free Press.

23. Easton, D. (1965). A System Analysis of Political Life, New York: Wiley.

24. Easton, D. (1965). A Framework for Political Analysis, N.J.: Prentice-Hall.

25. Easton, D. (1953). An Approach to the Analysis of Political System, New York: World Politics.

26. Gitlin, T. (1980). The Whole World is watching, University of California Press.

27. Keane, J. (1991). The Media and Democracy, Polity Press, Oxford.

28. Seymour-Ure, C. K. (1974).The Political Impact of Mass Media, Constable, London.

29. Sparks C. and Reading A. (1998). Communication, Capitalism and the Mass Media, London: Sage.

30. 胡逢瑛、吳非（2005）。《透視蘇俄傳媒轉型變局》，台北市：秀威出版社，2005。

31. This paper was represented in the Conference of IAMCR-2005 and got Grand Award. IAMCR is first grand association of UNESCO.

The Problem of Globalization: The Russian Perspective[1]

V. L. Artemov

Tenured Professor,

School of International Journalism of Moscow State

Institute of International Relations (MGIMO)

of the Ministry of Foreign Affairs of the Russian Federation

Hu, Feng-Yung

Assistant Professor of College of General Studies of Yuan Ze University.

Ph.D of School of International Journalism of Moscow State

Institute of International Relations (MGIMO)

of the Ministry of Foreign Affairs of the Russian Federation

First of all I'd like to underline that, although we in Russia are not unanimous in our attitude towards the role globalization plays or may play in the development of our country, there is an absolute unanimity as

---

[1] Prof. Artemov was invited as the keynote speaker of the Conference on Glocalization 2009, held by College of General Studies of Yuan Ze University. This paper was provided for the Conference.

to the agreement it is an objective process started when people managed to reach far away lands. In this sense the two events we may consider as the opening of the era of globalization. First, Chingishan's bridging the East and the West. Second, the geographical discoveries of the great fleet under the command of admiral Zheng He. Columbus and Magellan sailed by the Chinese charts. And I have the honour to congratulate you as the descendants of the pioneers of globalization.

Since that time numerous processes and forces have been underway to create a system of international relations that include actually the whole of the planet of Earth. To understand the present day situation as it presents itself for us in Russia, one have to look back at the events of the past century.

Politically, the past 100 years can be divided into three periods. The first period began with World War One, the Russian Revolution and the unfair Treaty of Versailles; then it continued with the first Cold War and ended with Stalinism, Fascism and World War Two. The next period began with the construction of a two-bloc confrontation, the classical Cold War and, simultaneously, the creation of the United Nations and the system of governance over the global economy and finance, which was dominated by the U.S. and the West. This system should have been rebuilt after the defeat of Communism and the breakup of the Soviet Union, which marked the beginning of the third period in the history of the last century. However, the international system was never rebuilt to meet the new challenges and opportunities. The West and the U.S., ecstatic over their new status as winners, decided to leave everything intact. A confused and weakened Russia had nothing to offer. Developing countries were still on the periphery of the world economy and politics. The following decade saw the establishment of a unipolar world based on old institutions.

The West decided to preserve NATO – which had lost its main goal – and began to expand the alliance; however, as time went on, NATO became the main source of tensions in Europe, at least in relations with Russia, and predictably began to restore Cold War stereotypes. The UN kept losing its influence and effectiveness. Ecstatic over their victory, the winners overlooked the beginning of nuclear proliferation to such countries as India and Pakistan and failed to solve a single problem in the Middle East. Having missed the beginning of the Yugoslav war, they launched an attack on Yugoslavia. The arms control system shattered. The system of governance over international relations and security, established over the previous 50 years, was gradually disintegrating.

We have to admit much more. Actually, the end of the Cold War marked the end of a longer stage in global development, which lasted for 400 to 500 years and when the world was dominated by European civilization. This domination was consistently led by the historical West . The tone in the global economy was set by the International Monetary Fund, the World Bank and the Washington Consensus, whose authors argued that the whole world could only develop according to the super-liberal Anglo-Saxon model.

Broadly speaking, in modern international relations it is difficult to find a more fundamental issue than the definition of the current stage in global development. This is important for any country in order to correlate a development strategy and a foreign policy with the vision of the world we live in. It seems that a consensus is already being formed on this score, albeit at the level of the expert community both in Russia and abroad. And the major point most experts come to agree upon is that individual problems of world politics cannot be solved without understanding the "big issues" of global development and without reaching a common vision of them in the international community.

THE END OF THE COLD WAR: SUMMING UP

As regards the content of the new stage in humankind's development, there are two basic approaches to it among countries. The first one holds that the world must gradually become a Greater West through the adoption of Western values. It is a kind of "the end of history." The other approach – advocated by Russia – holds that competition is becoming truly global and acquiring a civilizational dimension; that is, the subject of competition now includes values and development models.

The new stage is sometimes defined as "post-American." But, of course, this is incorrect, this is not "a world after the United States," the more so without the U.S. It is a world where – due to the growth of other global centers of power and influence – the relative importance of the U.S. role has been decreasing, as it has already happened in recent decades in the global economy and trade. Leadership is another matter, above all a matter of reaching agreement among partners and a matter of ability to be the first – but among equals.

Various terms have been proposed to define the content of the emerging world order, among them multi-polar, polycentric and nonpolar. The latter characteristic is given, in particular, by Richard Haass. It is difficult not to agree with him that power and influence are now becoming diffused. But even the former director of policy planning for the U.S. State Department admits that ensuring the governability of global development in the new conditions requires establishing a core group of leading nations. That is, in any case the matter at hand is the need for collective leadership, which Russia has been consistently advocating. Of course, the diversity of the world requires that such collective leadership be truly representative both geographically and civilizationally.

We do not share the apprehensions that the ongoing reconfiguration in the world will inevitably bring about "chaos and anarchy." It is a natural process of forming a new international architecture – both political and financial-economic – that would meet the new realities and stipulate progress throughout the world.

One such reality is the return of Russia to global politics, the global economy and finance as an active, full-fledged actor. This refers to our place on the world energy and grain markets; to our leadership in the field of nuclear energy and space exploration; to our capabilities in the sphere of land, air and sea transit; and to the role of the ruble as one of the most reliable world currencies.

Unfortunately, the Cold War experience has distorted the consciousness of several generations of people, above all political elites, making them think that any global policy must be ideologized. And now, when Russia is guided in international affairs by understandable, pragmatic interests, void of any ideological motives whatsoever, not everyone is able to adequately take it. Some people say we have some "grievances," "hidden agendas," "neo-imperial aspirations" and all that stuff. This situation will hardly change soon, as the matter at issue is psychological factors – after all, at least two generations of political leaders were brought up in a certain ideological system of coordinates, and sometimes they are simply unable to think in categories beyond those frameworks. Other factors include quite specific, understandably interested motives pertaining to privileges that the existing global financial-economic architecture gives to individual countries.

THE FINANCIAL UPHEAVAL

The world's increasingly rapid economic growth from the mid-1980s throughout the next 20 years was generally interpreted as the result of applying the Washington Consensus prescriptions, although now it is obvious that this growth was not so much due to them as to the huge expansion of the sphere of world capitalism. The markets of several dozen countries and a new cheap labor force made up of over two billion people in East, Southeast and South Asia, Central and Eastern Europe, and the former Soviet Union joined the world capitalist economy. Another factor that contributed to the growth was a technological revolution – this time with an emphasis on information technologies which ensured an unprecedented mobility of finance.

The new growth of the world economy, although uneven, was beneficial almost to all, especially to the Old West at the initial stage. The new financial class of the West grew fabulously rich through ever new financial instruments, whose essence many of their creators had already ceased to understand. The U.S. continued to get rich, as well, as it used a U.S.-oriented financial and monetary system which let the new financiers and the country at large live beyond their means.

No one cared to invent a new system for managing the rapidly growing economy. Countries continued to rely on the old, seemingly effective instruments and on the domination of the U.S. dollar. Only Europeans created a local and more or less new system and switched to the euro.

The patently unstable political unipolar world could have been rebuilt after the September 11, 2001 terrorist attacks against the U.S. There was a chance to set up a global coalition led – but not dominated – by the United States. Instead there followed a second wave of NATO enlargement and an attempt to extend American political and economic model to the Middle East using force.

At the same time, one more powerful process emerged. By the end of the 1990s, the globalization and the increasing openness of the world economy, which initially gave benefits mainly to the Old West, became more advantageous to young capitalist countries. A new industrial revolution began, based on the cheap and relatively educated labor force in China, India, and Southeast Asian countries. Global industrial production began to shift to new centers. The old economic winners suddenly began to lose the competition. Resource flows moved to the younger ones.

The U.S. and the West, carried away by the establishment of the world domination of their political system, overlooked one more revolutionary change – the redistribution, within a surprisingly short period of time, of control over resources, above all oil, from Western companies to national states and their companies.

The increased consumption of raw materials due to the economic growth of young capitalist states triggered a worldwide increase in their prices, particularly oil and gas prices. This factor caused a new large-scale redistribution of finance – trillions of dollars within several years – to extracting countries and their companies. Energy-rich Russia was among the countries that gained from this second wave of resource redistribution. Huge financial bubbles emerged in the U.S. and other countries. An enormous surplus of money appeared in the world due to the vast savings of Asian citizens who had started earning money but who did not have social security systems, and due to a money surplus in oil-producing countries, which amounted to trillions of dollars.

At the moment it is clearly seen and understood that the main troubles formed in the United States.

All these basically new phenomena occurred under the old system of regulating global finance. The system almost did not work, but the wealth, which "rained down from heaven," stopped the mouths of those, both in the US and outside, who warned of the system's inadequacy and of its inevitable breakdown.

Oil-producing states and countries of the young non-resource capitalism, which had freed themselves from the oppression of the bipolar world, felt increasingly independent. Apart from investing in U.S. government securities, thus financing debts and unbridled consumption, they started buying up Western companies and banks, dumbfounding the Old West and arousing fear in it that their new economic might would inevitably be followed by a redistribution of forces in world politics.

POLITICAL SHIFTS

The United States were not the only loser. Western Europe was also intoxicated with victory in the Cold War. Europe, wishing to consolidate the results of victory and having lost strategic benchmarks for its development, launched a recklessly rapid expansion of the European Union. This caused Europe to focus still more on itself and further complicated and delayed the possibility of conducting a common foreign policy. Europe continued to lose its foreign-policy influence, although, unlike the United States of George W. Bush, its soft power – the attractiveness of its development model and the appeal of its lifestyle – was not weakened.

At the same time, it turned out that the Old West's model of a mature liberal-democratic capitalism, which seemed to have won for good, was no longer the only ideological benchmark for the rest of the world. States of the new capitalism – naturally more authoritarian, in line with their stage of economic and social development – offered a much more attractive and attainable political development model for lagging countries. Moreover, they did not impose their models in their foreign expansion, but built roads, mines and plants to provide their industrial complexes and markets with raw materials and semi-finished goods.

In many ways, energy-rich Russia, which had dramatically increased its political clout, became the symbol of all those changes, disadvantageous to the West. In addition, unlike more cautious emerging Asian giants, it assumed a contemptuous and arrogant attitude toward the Cold War "winners" which had recently humiliated it and which had started to lose.

The former "winners" tried to regroup. As if from a horn of plenty, numerous projects emerged for a "union of democracies" – a tragicomic stillborn association of liberal-democratic "elders" against the authoritarian "younger" ones. At the same time the West stepped up its efforts to curb the rapidly growing influence of an ever mightier and more independent Russia and some other emerging giants.

Georgia attacked South Ossetia in August 2008, after which an attempt was made to organize a new Cold War against Russia. The incursion in South Ossetia, Russia's harsh reaction, and the attempt to start a confrontation after that, mainly using NATO, have shown the dangerous non-reconstruction of the European security system, which failed to prevent the conflict. Moreover, the de facto division of Europe into two security zones and the rivalry between them in many ways generated this conflict.

Russia not only retaliated, stopping the killing of its citizens and peacekeepers, but also said "no" to NATO's further expansion and to the inertia that suited the Old West. Now, even those who did not want to listen can see that the present Cold War-style system of European security, which has been artificially maintained for over a decade and a half, can no longer exist and that it only leads to the escalation of conflicts and ultimately to war.

CRISIS: OUT OF THE BLUE SKIES

Back in late August it seemed that the political semi-farcical Cold War would be the main political trend for the next two to three years. But then the global financial crisis broke out, which is now being followed by a global economic crisis.

Many experts believe, and quite rightly, that world financial and economic crisis will give birth to new challenges and threats. Specifically, it will affect socio-economic sphere.

It is easy to foresee speedy augmentation of streams of illegitimate migrants seeking jobs in more prosperous countries, specially from Africa due to the prospect of cancelling of the humanitarian programs of food and medical aid to hunger plagued lands and victims of regional conflicts. Rise in illegal migration is always accompanied by growth of trade in people.

The crisis is going to contribute considerably to aggravation of territorial, ethnical and religious clashes in the regions regularly experiencing acute sweet water and food shortage.

Inevitable is a striking rise of crime in the countries of European Union, USA and former republics of the USSR. Obviously, a part of the people having got used to a certain level of comfort during the economic boom, will try to make up for the material losses they suffered due to the crisis   and will   indulge in   unlawful machinations.

All these and the like problems are of an international dimension. Their solution demands working out and introducing new "critical technologies" in politics, economics and law.   That is the reason we, in Russia, see one of the ways out in restructuring of the global   financial architecture, reconsidering the role the present day international institutions play and establishing new, including an adequate legal regulation on the basis of well balanced system of international and national standards of behaviour and activities of the participants of the financial markets.

Here I would like to stress an issue of special importance at this juncture, which is so often is overlooked or ignored in the context of our numerous hot discussions of the problems of globalization. This is the role the law has played and is to play in the processes of globalization.

From economist's point of view, the world crisis is, first of all, a result of violation of the laws of economics. At the same time, the crisis testifies to a deformation of the principles of law both in the legislation that regulates economy and in the law application practice in financial and economical sphere. It is absolutely obvious that the lawgivers have failed to timely provide proper law forms (measures of responsibility, inclusive) intended to meet such a crisis. On the other hand, politicians, economists and lawyers haven't demonstrated due professionalism having failed to timely anticipate and take necessary steps to prevent this worldwide crisis.

The acute crisis has forced countries to start correcting the entire system of global economic governance. The United States and its ideas of the superiority of liberal capitalism and the limited role of the state in the economy have been dealt a hard blow. Faced with a possible severe depression, comparable to the crisis of the late 1920s-1930s, Washington has decided to nationalize failed system-forming financial companies and banks and to invest hundreds of billions of dollars in the economy. This policy is directly opposite to the Washington Consensus ideology, which was so confidently imposed in recent decades on other countries, including Russia. True liberals should have let bankrupt enterprises and the bankrupt policy fail completely and should have made room for the sprouts of a new economy. The U.S. has been followed by other countries in resorting to "socialist" methods to save failed companies and banks.

Reasonable apprehensions have already been expressed that the retreat from the former ideology of super-liberalism may go too far toward an increased state interference and may make the Western economy even less competitive. (I wish these warnings were first heeded by Russia, which is successfully destroying its competitiveness by quasi-socialist and reckless increases of labor costs and by the massive interference of corrupt state capitalism.)

THE RESUME: WHAT IS AFTER THE CRISIS

It is clear that the global crisis is only beginning and will affect everyone. But it is not clear how and when all countries will jointly start overcoming it.

But we should already sum up the preliminary results of the recent developments.

The period from August to October 2008 will likely go down in history as the start of the fourth stage in the world's development over the past century, which began – really, not according to the calendar – in August 1914, closing the door on the splendid 19th century and ushering in the savage and revolutionary 20th century. Actually, the 21st century is beginning right now.

This crisis and this new period in world history threaten to inflict inevitable hardships on billions of people, including Russians. Coupled with the aforementioned rapid geopolitical changes, with the collapse of the former system of international law and security systems, and with attempts by the weakening "elders" to stop the redistribution of forces not in their favor, this period may bring a dramatic destabilization of the international situation and an increased risk of conflicts. I would have dared to describe it as a pre-war situation and compare it with August 1914, but for one factor: huge arsenals of nuclear weapons remain, along with their deterrent factor, which makes politicians more civilized. Yet one must keep in mind the objective growth of military danger anyway.

The world economic crisis will fix the new redistribution of forces. But it can also change its speed. Quite possibly, the crisis will inflict even more economic damage on new industrial giants, especially at first. External markets, on which their growth largely depends, are shrinking. The super-fat years have come to an end for oil producing countries, as well, including Russia, which has proved reluctant or unable to switch to a new economy and renovate its infrastructure.

The matter at hand is not just a deep financial and economic crisis. This is an overall crisis of the entire system of global governance; a crisis of ideas on which global development was based; and a crisis of international institutions.

I do not think anybody will disagree that this new global crisis could be named " crisis of confidence", and many dimensional at that. It is a crisis of confidence in the present financial, banking and economic systems. It is a crisis of confidence in Western economy. And it is a crisis of confidence in the liberal doctrine of free market. As President Sarcozi put it, "noninterference is over". One has but to say just the same about the general attitude towards globalization itself. It cannot be that simple and one dimensional as we have been assuming until quite recently. If globalization is to continue, and it cannot but continue, constitutional and national laws are going to develop as a synthesis with universal human law.

There must be a new model of globalization. Not unified, but complex, rich in content, many dimensional, able to bring back true confidence to all the spheres of human life. To politics and culture, to religion and philosophy, to finances and law. As I see it, the only alternative scenario is an eventual prevalence of the dictate of the strong in the form of the world government with an ensuing collapse of the collective institutions and international law as a guardian of everybody's rights and interests.

That is why we are absolutely in disagreement with the idea to drop the UNO with its ideas of democracy and human rights on the claims it is an ostensibly archaic institution and to reorganize the global structure along the lines of the principles of Vienna Congress with the rule of a few over the rest of the world.

So, overcoming this overall crisis will require a new round of reforms, the construction of international institutions and systems for governing the world economy and finance, and a new philosophy for global development.

This crisis will clear out what has been artificially preserved or not reformed since the end of the Cold War. A new global governance system will have to be built on the ruins of the old one.

When this overall crisis is over, its relative beneficiaries will include not only countries that will have been less affected by it, but also those that will have seized the initiative in building a new world order and new institutions. They will have to correspond to the emerging balance of forces and effectively respond to new challenges.

One must be morally and politically ready for that period of creation, and already now, despite the crisis, one must start building up one's intellectual potential so that in a year or several years one could be ready to put forward one's own, well-grounded proposals for rebuilding the international governance system on a more just and stable basis.

As far as Russia is concerned, it has so far proposed a very modest plan for rebuilding the European security system and supported, at last, the idea to establish a new Concert of Nations as an association of not seven to eight old countries, but 14 to 20 of the most powerful and responsible states capable of assuming responsibility for global governance.

We need to go further and start thinking about the future already now – however difficult this might be during a crisis.

In Russia there has been going a dispute on the future trends in globalization. The major constructive principles proposed for building the future system could be somehow summarized as follows:

– Not boundless and irresponsible liberalism, but support for free trade and a liberal economic order coupled with basically stricter international regulation.

– The goal of development must be progress, rise of productivity and quality of life. Only having achieved progress one may speak about democracy. Democracy comes as a consequence and an instrument of progress.

– Joint elaboration and coordination of policies by the most powerful and responsible countries able to invest in the overall world progress rather than attempts to establish hegemony by one country, or a struggle of all against all.

Collective efforts to fill the security vacuum, rather than create new dividing lines and sources of conflict.

Joint solution of energy problems, rather than artificial politicization of the energy security problem.

– Russia and the European Union must strive not for a strategic partnership in their relations, but for a strategic alliance.

Surely, many of the proposed principles will be objected to and rejected. But the habitual politically correct clichés will not help to improve the situation and build a new world. Meanwhile, the time is coming for creation.

後記

　　今年 3 月 19 日，元智大學通識教學部舉辦了「2009 全球在地文化國際學術研討會」，在王立文主任的主持和邀請下，來自兩岸三地和俄羅斯的學者齊聚一堂，發表論文探討了這項議題。我在俄羅斯留學期間的指導教授阿爾丘莫夫教授應邀來台，專程為大會發表了主題演講，題為「全球化問題：俄羅斯的前景」(THE PROBLEM OF GLOBALIZATION: THE RUSSIAN PERSPECTIVE)。我自己則發表的論文是「全球化時代俄美中三國新聞輿論戰發展特點與對外政策的變化」，這次也都收錄在本書當中。我導師此行的參訪對台灣留下了美好深刻的印象，對此，我先生吳非無怨無悔地付出辛勞，對我指導教授在台全程的導覽功不可沒。我導師盛讚他是真正的記者：眼光敏銳，下筆快速且筆耕不輟，廣學多聞且見解獨到而透徹，擅於剖析與發現問題，因此我導師多次告訴我非常欣賞他的才華。

　　我最要感謝的是本部的大家長王立文教授，王老師是一位極富學養的學者，是本校公認極具智慧的管理者，並且學貫中西，涉獵的領域包括機械工程、熱對流研究、流體藝術、孫子兵法、佛學、信息磁場、通識教育、陽明學說、全球在地文化等等，並且都發表了相關的文章和出版了專著。自從我跟著王老師創辦本部雙月刊物——《元智全球在地文化報》以來，耳濡目染其豐富的思想，也很受他的啟發，他的各種理念都在《元智全球在地文化報》的頭版專

欄「大聯結」當中體現出來。我也每期發表文章，至今未曾有過懈怠！此次承蒙王老師的信任，我的俄國導師才有如此殊勝的因緣，在一輩子的外交官生涯中，足跡遍及了全世界 72 個國家之後，才第一次光榮地踏上了台灣的土地。

由衷感謝元智大學給我一個進入全球在地文化研究領域的工作機會，感謝彭宗平校長、國際交流處余念一處長、孫一明研發長，感謝通識教學部孫長祥教授、謝登旺教授、尤克強教授、呂佳思小姐以及人社院長劉阿榮教授等前輩師長的支持。感謝廈門大學陳培愛教授和廣州暨南大學林如鵬教授、蔡銘澤教授、劉家林教授。感謝文化大學楊爾瑛教授、明驥教授、曾垂典教授、畢英賢教授、歐茵西教授、李細梅教授、陳兆麟教授、楊景珊教授、王愛末教授過去對我的教導和栽培。感謝政大的李瞻教授、香港城市大學的李金銓教授、復旦大學李良榮教授與童兵教授、《China Media Research》的總編輯 Z. J. Edmondson、《Intercultural Communication Studies》主編陳國明教授近幾年來對我發表論文的鼓勵和肯定。感謝交大教授、玄奘資傳院長郭良文教授以及政大馮建三教授、台大林麗雲教授幾位先進對我回國任教的推薦和鼓勵！要感謝的人很多，筆者在此無法一一列舉，但是要感謝的對象將永遠令我銘感在心。感謝教育部留學公費的支持！

最後筆者還要感謝秀威出版社多年來的出版支持，尤其是總經理宋政坤先生、出版部經理林世玲小姐以及執行編輯藍志成先生。雖然每次出書之前總感覺研究尚不夠充分，但是我仍慣於對每一個階段性的研究工作做出一個總結，周而復始放空之後，該做的工作繼續做，該寫的文章努力寫，如此日復一日耕耘也是一種使命和樂趣！

胡逢瑛

2009 年 6 月 3 日

國家圖書館出版品預行編目

俄羅斯傳媒新戰略：從普京到梅普共治的時代
／胡逢瑛著. -- 一版. -- 臺北市：秀威資訊
科技, 2009.07
　　面；　　公分. -- (社會科學類；AF0114)
BOD 版
部分內容為英文
含參考書目
ISBN 978-986-221-258-5 (平裝)

1.大眾傳播　2.新聞媒體　3.俄國

541.83　　　　　　　　　　　98011333

社會科學類　AF0114

俄羅斯傳媒新戰略
——從普京到梅普共治的時代

作　　者／胡逢瑛
發 行 人／宋政坤
執行編輯／藍志成
圖文排版／黃莉珊
封面設計／蕭玉蘋
數位轉譯／徐真玉　沈裕閔
圖書銷售／林怡君
法律顧問／毛國樑　律師
出版印製／秀威資訊科技股份有限公司
　　　　　台北市內湖區瑞光路 583 巷 25 號 1 樓
　　　　　電話：02-2657-9211　　　傳真：02-2657-9106
　　　　　E-mail：service@showwe.com.tw
經 銷 商／紅螞蟻圖書有限公司
　　　　　台北市內湖區舊宗路二段 121 巷 28、32 號 4 樓
　　　　　電話：02-2795-3656　　　傳真：02-2795-4100
　　　　　http://www.e-redant.com

2009 年 7 月 BOD 一版
定價：260 元

讀　者　回　函　卡

感謝您購買本書，為提升服務品質，煩請填寫以下問卷，收到您的寶貴意見後，我們會仔細收藏記錄並回贈紀念品，謝謝！

1. 您購買的書名：＿＿＿＿＿＿＿＿＿＿＿＿＿＿＿＿

2. 您從何得知本書的消息？

　　□網路書店　　□部落格　　□資料庫搜尋　　□書訊　□電子報　□書店

　　□平面媒體　□　朋友推薦　□網站推薦　□其他＿＿＿＿＿＿

3. 您對本書的評價：(請填代號　1.非常滿意 2.滿意 3.尚可 4.再改進)

　　封面設計＿＿　版面編排＿＿　內容＿＿　文/譯筆＿＿　價格＿＿

4. 讀完書後您覺得：

　　□很有收獲　　□有收獲　　□收獲不多　　□沒收獲

5. 您會推薦本書給朋友嗎？

　　□會　□不會，為什麼？＿＿＿＿＿＿＿＿＿＿＿＿＿＿＿＿

6. 其他寶貴的意見：＿＿＿＿＿＿＿＿＿＿＿＿＿＿＿＿＿＿

＿＿＿＿＿＿＿＿＿＿＿＿＿＿＿＿＿＿＿＿＿＿＿＿＿＿＿＿

＿＿＿＿＿＿＿＿＿＿＿＿＿＿＿＿＿＿＿＿＿＿＿＿＿＿＿＿

＿＿＿＿＿＿＿＿＿＿＿＿＿＿＿＿＿＿＿＿＿＿＿＿＿＿＿＿

讀者基本資料

姓名：＿＿＿＿＿＿＿＿＿　年齡：＿＿＿＿　性別：□女 □男

聯絡電話：＿＿＿＿＿＿＿＿　E-mail：＿＿＿＿＿＿＿＿＿

地址：＿＿＿＿＿＿＿＿＿＿＿＿＿＿＿＿＿＿＿＿＿＿＿＿

學歷：□高中(含)以下　　□高中　　□專科學校　　□大學

　　　□研究所(含)以上 □其他＿＿＿＿＿＿＿

職業：□製造業 □金融業 □資訊業 □軍警 □傳播業 □自由業

　　　□服務業 □公務員 □教職　□學生 □其他＿＿＿＿＿